LOTUS 18

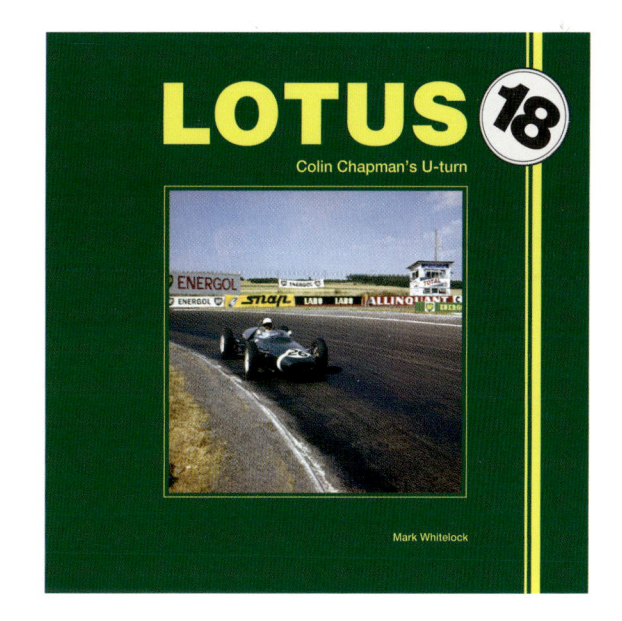

Colin Chapman's U-turn

Mark Whitelock

Those Were The Days ... Series

Alpine Trials & Rallies 1910-1973 (Pfundner)
American 'Independent' Automakers – AMC to Willys 1945 to 1960 (Mort)
American Station Wagons – The Golden Era 1950-1975 (Mort)
American Trucks of the 1950s (Mort)
American Trucks of the 1960s (Mort)
American Woodies 1928-1953 (Mort)
Anglo-American Cars from the 1930s to the 1970s (Mort)
Austerity Motoring (Bobbitt)
Austins, the last real (Peck)
Brighton National Speed Trials (Gardiner)
British and European Trucks of the 1970s (Peck)
British Drag Racing – The early years (Pettitt)
British Lorries of the 1950s (Bobbitt)
British Lorries of the 1960s (Bobbitt)
British Touring Car Racing (Collins)
British Police Cars (Walker)
British Woodies (Peck)
Café Racer Phenomenon, The (Walker)
Don Hayter's MGB Story – The birth of the MGB in MG's Abingdon Design & Development Office (Hayter)
Drag Bike Racing in Britain – From the mid '60s to the mid '80s (Lee)
Dune Buggy Phenomenon, The (Hale)
Dune Buggy Phenomenon Volume 2, The (Hale)
Endurance Racing at Silverstone in the 1970s & 1980s (Parker)
Hot Rod & Stock Car Racing in Britain in the 1980s (Neil)
Last Real Austins 1946-1959, The (Peck)
Mercedes-Benz Trucks (Peck)
MG's Abingdon Factory (Moylan)
Motor Racing at Brands Hatch in the Seventies (Parker)
Motor Racing at Brands Hatch in the Eighties (Parker)
Motor Racing at Crystal Palace (Collins)
Motor Racing at Goodwood in the Sixties (Gardiner)
Motor Racing at Nassau in the 1950s & 1960s (O'Neil)
Motor Racing at Oulton Park in the 1960s (McFadyen)
Motor Racing at Oulton Park in the 1970s (McFadyen)
Motor Racing at Thruxton in the 1970s (Grant-Braham)
Motor Racing at Thruxton in the 1980s (Grant-Braham)
Superprix – The Story of Birmingham Motor Race (Page & Collins)
Three Wheelers (Bobbitt)

Biographies

A Chequered Life – Graham Warner and the Chequered Flag (Hesletine)
Amédée Gordini ... a true racing legend (Smith)
André Lefebvre, and the cars he created at Voisin and Citroën (Beck)
Chris Carter at Large – Stories from a lifetime in motorcycle racing (Carter & Skelton)
Cliff Allison, The Official Biography of – From the Fells to Ferrari (Gauld)
Edward Turner – The Man Behind the Motorcycles (Clew)
Driven by Desire – The Desiré Wilson Story
First Principles – The Official Biography of Keith Duckworth (Burr)
Inspired to Design – F1 cars, Indycars & racing tyres: the autobiography of Nigel Bennett (Bennett)
Jack Sears, The Official Biography of – Gentleman Jack (Gauld)
Jim Redman – 6 Times World Motorcycle Champion: The Autobiography (Redman)
John Chatham – 'Mr Big Healey' – The Official Biography (Burr)
The Lee Noble Story (Wilkins)
Mason's Motoring Mayhem – Tony Mason's hectic life in motorsport and television (Mason)
Raymond Mays' Magnificent Obsession (Apps)
Pat Moss Carlsson Story, The – Harnessing Horsepower (Turner)
Tony Robinson – The biography of a race mechanic (Wagstaff)
Virgil Exner – Visioneer: The Official Biography of Virgil M Exner Designer Extraordinaire (Grist)

General

1½-litre GP Racing 1961-1965 (Whitelock)
AC Two-litre Saloons & Buckland Sportscars (Archibald)
Alfa Romeo 155/156/147 Competition Touring Cars (Collins)
Alfa Romeo Giulia Coupé GT & GTA (Tipler)
Alfa Romeo Montreal – The dream car that came true (Taylor)
Alfa Romeo Montreal – The Essential Companion (Classic Reprint of 500 copies) (Taylor)
Alfa Tipo 33 (McDonough & Collins)
Alpine & Renault – The Development of the Revolutionary Turbo F1 Car 1968 to 1979 (Smith)
Alpine & Renault – The Sports Prototypes 1963 to 1969 (Smith)
Alpine & Renault – The Sports Prototypes 1973 to 1978 (Smith)
Anatomy of the Works Minis (Moylan)
Armstrong-Siddeley (Smith)
Art Deco and British Car Design (Down)
Autodrome (Collins & Ireland)
Autodrome 2 (Collins & Ireland)
Automotive A-Z, Lane's Dictionary of Automotive Terms (Lane)
Automotive Mascots (Kay & Springate)
Bahamas Speed Weeks, The (O'Neil)
Bentley Continental, Corniche and Azure (Bennett)
Bentley MkVI, Rolls-Royce Silver Wraith, Dawn & Cloud/Bentley R & S-Series (Nutland)
Bluebird CN7 (Stevens)
BMC Competitions Department Secrets (Turner, Chambers & Browning)
BMW 5-Series (Cranswick)
BMW Z-Cars (Taylor)
BMW Boxer Twins 1970-1995 Bible, The (Falloon)
BMW Cafe Racers (Cloesen)
BMW Custom Motorcycles – Choppers, Cruisers, Bobbers, Trikes & Quads (Cloesen)
BMW – The Power of M (Vivian)
Bonjour – Is this Italy? (Turner)
British 250cc Racing Motorcycles (Pereira)
British at Indianapolis, The (Wagstaff)
British Cars, The Complete Catalogue of, 1895-1975 (Culshaw & Horrobin)
British Custom Motorcycles – The Brit Chop – choppers, cruisers, bobbers & trikes (Cloesen)
BRM – A Mechanic's Tale (Salmon)
BRM V16 (Ludvigsen)
BSA Bantam Bible, The (Henshaw)
BSA Motorcycles – the final evolution (Jones)
Bugatti Type 40 (Price)
Bugatti 46/50 Updated Edition (Price & Arbey)
Bugatti T44 & T49 (Price & Arbey)
Bugatti 57 2nd Edition (Price)
Bugatti Type 57 Grand Prix – A Celebration (Tomlinson)
Caravan, Improve & Modify Your (Porter)
Caravans, The Illustrated History 1919-1959 (Jenkinson)
Caravans, The Illustrated History from 1960 (Jenkinson)
Carrera Panamericana, La (Tipler)
Chrysler 300 – America's Most Powerful Car 2nd Edition (Ackerson)

Chrysler PT Cruiser (Ackerson)
Citroën DS (Bobbitt)
Classic British Car Electrical Systems (Astley)
Cobra – The Real Thing! (Legate)
Competition Car Aerodynamics 3rd Edition (McBeath)
Concept Cars, How to illustrate and design (Dewey)
Cortina – Ford's Bestseller (Robson)
Coventry Climax Racing Engines (Hammill)
Daily Mirror 1970 World Cup Rally 40, The (Robson)
Daimler SP250 New Edition (Long)
Datsun Fairlady Roadster to 280ZX – The Z-Car Story (Long)
Dino – The V6 Ferrari (Long)
Dodge Challenger & Plymouth Barracuda (Grist)
Dodge Charger – Enduring Thunder (Ackerson)
Dodge Dynamite! (Grist)
Dorset from the Sea – The Jurassic Coast from Lyme Regis to Old Harry Rocks photographed from its best viewpoint (Belasco)
Dorset from the Sea – The Jurassic Coast from Lyme Regis to Old Harry Rocks photographed from its best viewpoint (souvenir edition) (Belasco)
Draw & Paint Cars – How to (Gardiner)
Drive on the Wild Side, A – 20 Extreme Driving Adventures From Around the World (Weaver)
Ducati 750 Bible, The (Falloon)
Ducati 750 SS 'round-case' 1974, The Book of the (Falloon)
Ducati 860, 900 and Mille Bible, The (Falloon)
Ducati Monster Bible (New Updated & Revised Edition), The (Falloon)
Dune Buggy, Building A – The Essential Manual (Shakespeare)
Dune Buggy Files (Hale)
Dune Buggy Handbook (Hale)
East German Motor Vehicles in Pictures (Suhr/Weinreich)
Fast Ladies – Female Racing Drivers 1888 to 1970 (Bouzanquet)
Fate of the Sleeping Beauties, The (op de Weegh/Hottendorff/op de Weegh)
Ferrari 288 GTO, The Book of the (Sackey)
Ferrari 333 SP (O'Neil)
Fiat & Abarth 124 Spider & Coupé (Tipler)
Fiat & Abarth 500 & 600 – 2nd Edition (Bobbitt)
Fiats, Great Small (Ward)
Fine Art of the Motorcycle Engine, The (Peirce)
Ford Cleveland 335-Series V8 engine 1970 to 1982 – The Essential Source Book (Hammill)
Ford F100/F150 Pick-up 1948-1996 (Ackerson)
Ford F150 Pick-up 1997-2005 (Ackerson)
Ford GT – Then, and Now (Streather)
Ford GT40 (Legate)
Ford Model Y (Roberts)
Ford Small Block V8 Racing Engines 1962-1970 – The Essential Source Book (Hammill)
Ford Thunderbird From 1954, The Book of the (Long)
Formula 5000 Motor Racing, Back then ... and back now (Lawson)
Forza Minardi! (Vigar)
France: the essential guide for car enthusiasts – 200 things for the car enthusiast to see and do (Parish)
From Crystal Palace to Red Square – A Hapless Biker's Road to Russia (Turner)
Funky Mopeds (Skelton)
Grand Prix Ferrari – The Years of Enzo Ferrari's Power, 1948-1980 (Pritchard)
Grand Prix Ford – DFV-powered Formula 1 Cars (Pritchard)
GT – The World's Best GT Cars 1953-73 (Dawson)
Hillclimbing & Sprinting – The Essential Manual (Short & Wilkinson)
Honda NSX (Long)
Inside the Rolls-Royce & Bentley Styling Department – 1971 to 2001 (Hull)
Intermeccanica – The Story of the Prancing Bull (McCredie & Reisner)
Italian Cafe Racers (Cloesen)
Italian Custom Motorcycles (Cloesen)
Jaguar, The Rise of (Price)
Jaguar XJ 220 – The Inside Story (Moreton)
Jaguar XJ-S, The Book of the (Long)
Jeep CJ (Ackerson)
Jeep Wrangler (Ackerson)
Karmann-Ghia Coupé & Convertible (Bobbitt)
Kawasaki Triples Bible, The (Walker)
Kawasaki Z1 Story, The (Sheehan)
Kris Meeke – Intercontinental Rally Challenge Champion (McBride)
Lamborghini Miura Bible, The (Sackey)
Lamborghini Urraco, The Book of the (Landsem)
Lambretta Bible, The (Davies)
Lancia 037 (Collins)
Lancia Delta HF Integrale (Blaettel & Wagner)
Land Rover Series III Reborn (Porter)
Land Rover, The Half-ton Military (Cook)
Laverda Twins & Triples Bible 1968-1986 (Falloon)
Lea-Francis Story, The (Price)
Le Mans Panoramic (Ireland)
Lexus Story, The (Long)
Little book of microcars, the (Quellin)
Little book of smart, the – New Edition (Jackson)
Little book of trikes, the (Quellin)
Lola – The Illustrated History (1957-1977) (Starkey)
Lola – All the Sports Racing & Single-seater Racing Cars 1978-1997 (Starkey)
Lola T70 – The Racing History & Individual Chassis Record – 4th Edition (Starkey)
Lotus 49 (Oliver)
Marketingmobiles, The Wonderful Wacky World of (Hale)
Maserati 250F In Focus (Pritchard)
Mazda MX-5/Miata 1.6 Enthusiast's Workshop Manual (Grainger & Shoemark)
Mazda MX-5/Miata 1.8 Enthusiast's Workshop Manual (Grainger & Shoemark)
The book of the Mazda MX-5 Miata – The 'Mk1' NA-series 1988 to 1997 (Long)
Mazda MX-5 Miata Roadster (Long)
Maximum Mini (Booij)
Meet the English (Bowie)
Mercedes-Benz SL – R230 series 2001 to 2011 (Long)
Mercedes-Benz SL – W113-series 1963-1971 (Long)
Mercedes-Benz SL & SLC – 107-series 1971-1989 (Long)
Mercedes-Benz SLK – R170 series 1996-2004 (Long)
Mercedes-Benz SLK – R171 series 2004-2011 (Long)
Mercedes-Benz W123-series – All models 1976 to 1986 (Long)
MGA (Price Williams)
MGB & MGB GT– Expert Guide (Auto-doc Series) (Williams)
MGB Electrical Systems Updated & Revised Edition (Astley)
Micro Caravans (Jenkinson)
Micro Trucks (Mort)
Microcars at Large! (Quellin)
Mini Cooper – The Real Thing! (Tipler)
Mini Minor to Asia Minor (West)
Mitsubishi Lancer Evo, The Road Car & WRC Story (Long)

Montlhéry, The Story of the Paris Autodrome (Boddy)
Morgan Maverick (Lawrence)
Morgan 3 Wheeler – back to the future!, The (Dron)
Morris Minor, 60 Years on the Road (Newell)
Moto Guzzi Sport & Le Mans Bible, The (Falloon)
Motor Movies – The Posters! (Veysey)
Motor Racing – Reflections of a Lost Era (Carter)
Motor Racing – The Pursuit of Victory 1930-1962 (Carter)
Motor Racing – The Pursuit of Victory 1963-1972 (Wyatt/Sears)
Motor Racing Heroes – The Stories of 100 Greats (Newman)
Motorcycle Apprentice (Cakebread)
Motorcycle GP Racing in the 1960s (Pereira)
Motorcycle Road & Racing Chassis Designs (Noakes)
Motorhomes, The Illustrated History (Jenkinson)
Motorsport In colour, 1950s (Wainwright)
MV Agusta Fours, The book of the classic (Falloon)
N.A.R.T. – A concise history of the North American Racing Team 1957 to 1983 (O'Neil)
Nissan 300ZX & 350Z – The Z-Car Story (Long)
Nissan GT-R Supercar: Born to race (Gorodji)
Northeast American Sports Car Races 1950-1959 (O'Neil)
Nothing Runs – Misadventures in the Classic, Collectable & Exotic Car Biz (Slutsky)
Off-Road Giants! (Volume 1) – Heroes of 1960s Motorcycle Sport (Westlake)
Off-Road Giants! (Volume 2) – Heroes of 1960s Motorcycle Sport (Westlake)
Off-Road Giants! (volume 3) – Heroes of 1960s Motorcycle Sport (Westlake)
Pass the Theory and Practical Driving Tests (Gibson & Hoole)
Peking to Paris 2007 (Young)
Pontiac Firebird (Cranswick)
Porsche Boxster (Long)
Porsche 356 (2nd Edition) (Long)
Porsche 908 (Födisch, Neßhöver, Roßbach, Schwarz & Roßbach)
Porsche 911 Carrera – The Last of the Evolution (Corlett)
Porsche 911R, RS & RSR, 4th Edition (Starkey)
Porsche 911, The Book of the (Long)
Porsche 911SC 'Super Carrera' – The Essential Companion (Streather)
Porsche 914 & 914-6: The Definitive History of the Road & Competition Cars (Long)
Porsche 924 (Long)
The Porsche 924 Carreras – evolution to excellence (Smith)
Porsche 928 (Long)
Porsche 944 (Long)
Porsche 964, 993 & 996 Data Plate Code Breaker (Streather)
Porsche 993 'King Of Porsche' – The Essential Companion (Streather)
Porsche 996 'Supreme Porsche' – The Essential Companion (Streather)
Porsche Racing Cars – 1953 to 1975 (Long)
Porsche Racing Cars – 1976 to 2005 (Long)
Porsche – The Rally Story (Meredith)
Porsche: Three Generations of Genius (Meredith)
Preston Tucker & Others (Linde)
RAC Rally Action! (Gardiner)
RACING COLOURS – MOTOR RACING COMPOSITIONS 1908-2009 (Newman)
Racing Line – British motorcycle racing in the golden age of the big single (Guntrip)
Rallye Sport Fords: The Inside Story (Moreton)
Renewable Energy Home Handbook, The (Porter)
Roads with a View – England's greatest views and how to find them by road (Corfield)
Rolls-Royce Silver Shadow/Bentley T Series Corniche & Camargue – Revised & Enlarged Edition (Bobbitt)
Rolls-Royce Silver Spirit, Silver Spur & Bentley Mulsanne 2nd Edition (Bobbitt)
Runways & Racers (O'Neil)
Russian Motor Vehicles – Soviet Limousines 1930-2003 (Kelly)
Russian Motor Vehicles – The Czarist Period 1784 to 1917 (Kelly)
RX-7 – Mazda's Rotary Engine Sportscar (Updated & Revised New Edition) (Long)
Scooters & Microcars, The A-Z of Popular (Dan)
Scooter Lifestyle (Grainger)
SCOOTER MANIA! – Recollections of the Isle of Man International Scooter Rally (Jackson)
Singer Story: Cars, Commercial Vehicles, Bicycles & Motorcycle (Atkinson)
Sleeping Beauties USA – abandoned classic cars & trucks (Marek)
SM – Citroën's Maserati-engined Supercar (Long & Claverol)
Speedway – Auto racing's ghost tracks (Collins & Ireland)
Sprite Caravans, The Story of (Jenkinson)
Standard Motor Company, The Book of the
Subaru Impreza: The Road Car And WRC Story (Long)
Supercar, How to Build your own (Thompson)
Tales from the Toolbox (Oliver)
Tatra – The Legacy of Hans Ledwinka, Updated & Enlarged Collector's Edition of 1500 copies (Margolius & Henry)
Taxi! The Story of the 'London' Taxicab (Bobbitt)
Toleman Story, The (Hilton)
Toyota Celica & Supra, The Book of Toyota's Sports Coupés (Long)
Toyota MR2 Coupés & Spyders (Long)
Triumph Bonneville Bible (59-83) (Henshaw)
Triumph Bonneville, Save the – The inside story of the Meriden Workers' Co-op (Rosamond)
Triumph Motorcycles & the Meriden Factory (Hancox)
Triumph Speed Twin & Thunderbird Bible (Woolridge)
Triumph Tiger Cub Bible (Estall)
Triumph Trophy Bible (Woolridge)
Triumph TR6 (Kimberley)
TT Talking – The TT's most exciting era – As seen by Manx Radio TT's lead commentator 2004-2012 (Lambert)
Two Summers – The Mercedes-Benz W196R Racing Car (Ackerson)
TWR Story, The – Group A (Hughes & Scott)
Unraced (Collins)
Velocette Motorcycles – MSS to Thruxton – New Third Edition (Burris)
Vespa – The Story of a Cult Classic in Pictures (Uhlig)
Volkswagen Bus Book, The (Bobbitt)
Volkswagen Bus or Van to Camper, How to Convert (Porter)
Volkswagens of the World (Glen)
VW Beetle Cabriolet – The full story of the convertible Beetle (Bobbitt)
VW Beetle – The Car of the 20th Century (Copping)
VW Bus – 40 Years of Splitties, Bays & Wedges (Copping)
VW Bus Book, The (Bobbitt)
VW Golf: Five Generations of Fun (Copping & Cservenka)
VW – The Air-cooled Era (Copping)
VW T5 Camper Conversion Manual (Porter)
VW Campers (Copping)
You & Your Jaguar XK8/XKR – Buying, Enjoying, Maintaining, Modifying – New Edition (Thorley)
Which Oil? – Choosing the right oils & greases for your antique, vintage, veteran, classic or collector car (Michell)
Works Minis, The Last (Purves & Brenchley)
Works Rally Mechanic (Moylan)

www.veloce.co.uk

For post publication news, updates and amendments relating to this book, please visit http://www.veloce.co.uk/books/V4520

First published in May 2016 by Veloce Publishing Limited, Veloce House, Parkway Farm Business Park, Middle Farm Way, Poundbury, Dorchester DT1 3AR, England. Fax 01305 268864 / e-mail info@veloce.co.uk / web www.veloce.co.uk or www.velocebooks.com.

ISBN: 978-1-845845-20-9 UPC: 6-36847-04520-3 © 2016 Mark Whitelock and Veloce Publishing. All rights reserved. With the exception of quoting brief passages for the purpose of review, no part of this publication may be recorded, reproduced or transmitted by any means, including photocopying, without the written permission of Veloce Publishing Ltd. Throughout this book logos, model names and designations, etc, have been used for the purposes of identification, illustration and decoration. Such names are the property of the trademark holder as this is not an official publication. Readers with ideas for automotive books, or books on other transport or related hobby subjects, are invited to write to the editorial director of Veloce Publishing at the above address. British Library Cataloguing in Publication Data – A catalogue record for this book is available from the British Library. Typesetting, design and page make-up all by Veloce Publishing Ltd on Apple Mac. Printed in India by Replika Press.

LOTUS 18

Colin Chapman's U-turn

Veloce Publishing
THE PUBLISHER OF FINE AUTOMOTIVE BOOKS

CONTENTS

Introduction & Acknowledgements 5
List of Abbreviations. 7

1 Background 8
2 Colin Chapman's U-turn 15
3 High Torque Racer – the Coventry Climax
   FPF Racing Engine 29
4 1960 Formula 1 Season – Great
   Expectations 35
5 1960 Formula 2 Season – Promise Unfulfilled .. 67
6 1961 Formula 1 Season – Against the Odds.. .. 77
7 1961 Inter-Continental Formula
   Season – a Damp Squib 116
8 1962 Formula 1 Season – Second Division 120
9 1963–66 Formula 1 Seasons – the End
   of the Road ... and Beyond 137
10 Analysis and Statistics 149
11 Variations on a Theme 1960-65 152

Appendices:
I Summary of Individual Chassis
   Histories 161
II Lotus 18 Race Record – Chassis by Chassis . . . 171
III Drivers who Raced the Lotus 18 180
IV Entrants of the Lotus 18 185

Bibliography 186
Index 191

4 | Lotus 18

INTRODUCTION AND ACKNOWLEDGEMENTS

INTRODUCTION

On Easter Monday, 18 April 1960, sitting in the Chicane Grandstand at Goodwood alongside my dad, I witnessed Innes Ireland beat Stirling Moss in both the Formula 1 and 2 races held that afternoon. This was a pretty sensational performance, as Stirling was rarely beaten, let alone twice in the same afternoon. The deciding factor in both races was the first rear-engined single-seater from the pen of Colin Chapman: the Lotus 18. From that day on, I was a dedicated fan of both Innes and the Lotus 18.

Colin Chapman's previous attempts to produce a race winning single-seater had been pretty disappointing. The Lotus 16 – possibly the technically most advanced front-engined Formula 1 car – had failed to deliver. Clearly something drastic had to be done. In the event, this would involve making a U-turn and adopting the rear-engined layout pioneered by arch-rival Cooper. This was not an easy decision to make, not least in facing the inevitable taunts of those who accused Chapman of copying Cooper. As it was, his first attempt at designing a rear-engined single-seater was one of his greatest creations, and one that would set new performance standards from the outset.

Visually unremarkable, the Lotus 18 turned Lotus from an also-ran in Grand Prix racing into a force to be reckoned with, and was the first of a wave of innovative designs over succeeding years. It was a milestone in the history of the Grand Prix car, and a trendsetter, not least in the design of its rear suspension which became much copied. It may not have achieved ultimate greatness in itself, for the reasons discussed in the text, yet there is little doubt that it had greatness thrust upon it by Stirling Moss in defeating the Ferrari team at both Monaco and the Nürburgring in 1961, against all the odds, when it was a year old and, to all intents and purposes, obsolete.

More than 56 years have elapsed since that memorable day at Goodwood, and newer generations of motorsport enthusiasts may not be aware of the significance of the Lotus 18. This book may not be the definitive history of the Lotus 18 but does provide a competition history of Formula 1, Formula 2 and the Inter-Continental Formula versions of the 28 Lotus 18 chassis raced over the seasons from 1960 to 1966. In period, the car was known both as the 'Eighteen' and the '18,' but for the purposes of this

The author's admission ticket for Goodwood, Easter Monday 1960.

book I have adopted the latter. The Formula Junior Lotus 18 was a separate entity and does not fall within my remit. Nevertheless, I have summarised its dominance in that category in Chapter 11, together with a brief description and summary of the career of the sports racing Lotus 18, the charismatic Lotus 19.

Little thought was given in period to the preservation of racing cars, each generation looking to next year's newer, faster model rather than preserving the past to be admired and enjoyed by future generations. Now ever-increasing numbers of enthusiasts are interested in historic motorsport, perhaps as a response to the inaccessibility and lack of charisma of the current Formula 1. The importance of historic racing cars has grown, as has their value, and with it the responsibility to preserve the examples that remain of motorsport history. The Lotus 18 has survived well. Of the 28 examples manufactured, three were written-off in period and the remaining 25 survive, in one form or another, in museums or private collections. A good half-dozen continue to enjoy an extended career in historic racing. The history of each Lotus 18 chassis post-front line competition can be complicated and confusing. Rather than become embroiled in this subject, I have chosen to terminate the history of the Lotus 18s at their last recorded front line competition appearance and have not pursued enquiries as to their current whereabouts.

ACKNOWLEDGEMENTS

I am grateful to all those to whom I have spoken about the Lotus 18 and who have helped in the preparation of this book, and especially to Rod Grainger of Veloce Publishing for once again taking a gamble.

In writing any book about Lotus, it would be negligent not to consult Clive Chapman, Colin's son. Clive and his mother Hazel are directors of Classic Team Lotus, established in 1992 to restore and maintain its own and customers' Team Lotus Formula 1 cars at its base in Hethel. I am grateful to Clive for allowing me access to the Team Lotus archives, although unfortunately they contained little information on the Lotus 18. I was, however, able to rummage through the collection of original Lotus 18 drawings that I found particularly informative and interesting. I should like to thank him for permission to reproduce the general arrangement drawing of the 18 included in the text.

Sadly the passage of time has robbed us of the first hand reminiscences of many of the key players in the Lotus 18 story, including Colin Chapman himself, Innes Ireland, Alan Stacey and Jim Clark. Nevertheless, I have been able to talk with a number of other people, including Dan Gurney, and former Team Lotus chief mechanic Bob Dance when I visited Hethel.

As a regular subscriber to *Autosport* from 1959 through into the mid-1990s, I always looked forward to its up to the minute reporting every Friday. I was not a fan of the monthly *Motor Sport* until much later, when I came to appreciate the detail of Denis Jenkinson's reporting. These two magazines have been an important source for this book, along with *A Record of Grand Prix and Voiturette Racing* compiled by Paul Sheldon with Duncan Rabagliati. The history of the Lotus 18 is covered in Volumes 7 and 8, and is the source of race results and the data used to compile the chassis histories, updated where applicable to reflect new information.

Haynes Publishing was kind enough to allow me to quote the words of Stirling Moss in describing the strengths and weaknesses of the Lotus 18 from *Stirling Moss: My Cars, My Career* by Stirling Moss with Doug Nye (Patrick Stephens 1992/Haynes Publishing 1999).

Illustrations come from four main sources. The majority are from the archives of LAT Photographic, custodians of the archives of *Motor Sport*, *The Autocar*, *Motor* and *Autosport*. Kevin Wood was most helpful in allowing me to trawl through those archives, and in accommodating my requirements. I should also like to thank David Pearson of motoprint.co.za in South Africa, who supplied some rarer images of the Lotus 18 in that country from his archive. Likewise, I am grateful to Ted Walker of Ferret Fotographics and Annie Lydon at Sutton-Images for their assistance. Other illustrations are from my own archive, including donations from Roger Nixon – who also provided amusing company at various Goodwood Revivals.

I am particularly indebted to Paul Cooper for his willingness to read appropriate parts of the text relating to Coventry Climax Engines and provide advice, comments and corrections, as appropriate. During his holidays from university between 1958 and 1961 he worked in the development shop at Coventry Climax, giving him a unique insight into the goings-on of the company.

Finally, my everlasting thanks to Anne for her love, support and encouragement, without which none of what follows would have been possible.

Mark Whitelock
East Sussex

ABBREVIATIONS USED THROUGHOUT THE TEXT

ACF	Automobile Club de France
BARC	British Automobile Racing Club
BRDC	British Racing Drivers' Club
CSI	Commission Sportive International
DNF	Did not finish
DNPQ	Did not pre-qualify
DNQ	Did not qualify
DNS	Did not start
DSQ	Disqualified
FIA	Fédération International de l'Automobile
FL	Fastest Lap
F2	Formula 2 (1960)
I/C	Inter-Continental Formula (1961)
N/A	Not available
NC	Not classified
NT	No time
PP	Pole position
Q	Qualifying grid position

International abbreviations

B	Belgium
CDN	Canada
CH	Switzerland
D	Germany
F	France
GB	Great Britain
I	Italy
NZ	New Zealand
RSR	Southern Rhodesia
S	Sweden
USA	United States of America
ZA	South Africa

1 BACKGROUND

EARLY YEARS – THE LOTUS SPORTS CARS

Anthony Colin Bruce (Colin) Chapman's first Lotus cars were Austin 7-based specials. A Mk III version performed so well on track that it generated a demand for replicas, prompting Chapman to form the Lotus Engineering Co, on 1 January 1952, in small outbuildings behind his father's Railway Hotel in Tottenham Lane, Hornsey, North London. The Lotus Mk VI featured the first Chapman-designed space frame chassis and was sold in component form to avoid purchase tax. This enabled the enthusiast to build a competition sports car to his own specification, supplying his own engine and transmission, etc. The car proved highly competitive in various classes of racing, around 110 examples being sold between 1952 and 1955. On 25 September 1952, Lotus Engineering became a limited company, despite having only one full-time employee at the time – the workforce made up of enthusiasts helping out in their spare time, including Chapman, who worked after hours from his day job with the British Aluminium Co. The Mk VIII was the first Lotus with a fully enveloping and efficient aerodynamic bodyshell, devised by Frank Costin, the brother of Mike Costin, Chapman's engine and chassis maintenance engineer. Frank was an aircraft design engineer with the de Havilland Aircraft Company who joined the ranks of enthusiasts working with Chapman in their spare time.

Lotus quickly established itself as a successful specialist sports car manufacturer with numerous competition successes, many achieved by Chapman himself. Come 1955, Chapman resigned from British Aluminium to work full time for Lotus Engineering, and the premises behind the Railway Hotel were extended to provide a large assembly area to cater for greater volume production. Initially, a range of proprietary engines powered the cars, including Ford, British Motor Corporation (BMC), Bristol and MG. In late 1954, the Coventry Climax 1100cc, 4-cylinder, single overhead camshaft FWA racing engine became available, and the 'Eleven' introduced in 1956 was designed specifically around this, or its larger 1500cc FWB brother. The Lotus Eleven became the single most successful Lotus, both in terms of sales and competition successes, 270 examples selling between 1956 and 1959. Whilst Chapman's contemporary rival, Cooper, was building strong, but relatively crude, chassis, the Lotus Eleven was designed

Colin Chapman poses at a remarkably tidy and uncluttered desk. (LAT Photographic)

1: Background

scientifically for performance, through chassis and suspension excellence, low weight and aerodynamic efficiency.

Chapman applied his qualifications in structural engineering and stress analysis to his Lotus designs, and his expertise in chassis and suspension technology became widely acknowledged in British motor racing circles. At the end of the 1955 Formula 1 season, Tony Vandervell approached him for his views on the ill-handling Vanwall chassis. Chapman jumped at the opportunity of an involvement in Grand Prix racing, and agreed to design a new space frame chassis and rework the rear suspension for the Vanwall, with Frank Costin devising the legendary teardrop-style bodywork. In May 1957, Peter Berthon, Chief Engineer of BRM, sought Chapman's input to resolve inadequacies in the Type 25 Grand Prix car's handling. Although his recommendations were implemented, the BRM had other problems that hindered its performance. Meanwhile, Chapman's input played a significant role in the successes achieved by Vanwall, from its first win in the 1957 British Grand Prix, through to victory in the 1958 World Manufacturers' Championship.

TEAM LOTUS

Formed at the beginning of 1954 to separate out the production side of Lotus Engineering from the development and proving of new cars, this 'works' racing team would also be staffed by an enthusiastic little band of volunteers, giving up their evenings and weekends to work at Hornsey far into the night prior to an event.

Cliff Allison rounds the Mulsanne Corner at Le Mans, in 1956, in the 1100cc Lotus Eleven he shared with Keith Hall. (LAT Photographic)

Team would be managed by Colin's father, Stanley, with Colin himself as the mainstay of the driving force, joined by many other enthusiastic Lotus drivers, including Graham Hill, Cliff Allison, Alan Stacey and Innes Ireland, all of whom feature in the story of the Lotus 18.

FIRST SINGLE-SEATER – THE LOTUS TYPE 12

The Fédération International de l'Automobile (FIA) announced a new single-seater, 1½-litre Formula 2 category for 1957 to act as a stepping-stone for drivers and constructors alike between the contemporary 500cc Formula 3 and Formula 1. The British Racing Drivers' Club (BRDC) decided to organise a Formula 2 support race for the 1956 British Grand Prix at Silverstone, as a foretaste of the new formula. The winning rear-engined Cooper of Roy Salvadori was the only single-seater in the race, ahead of a field of stripped down 1500cc sports cars, headed by the Lotus Eleven of Colin Chapman who set the fastest lap. This promising new category offered Lotus the opportunity for increased exposure and customer sales potential, although this would stretch its resources – at that point fully employed in sports car racing. Nevertheless, Chapman sat down and sketched out his design for the first single-seater Lotus.

The Lotus Type 12 followed the layout of the successful Eleven, in that it was front-engined, and incorporated all the experience gained over preceding years on lightweight space frame construction and superior roadholding through advanced suspension technology. The prototype was unveiled to the press in early October 1956, before being exhibited on the Lotus stand at the Earls Court Motor Show in London. The chassis comprised a fully-triangulated tubular space frame with front suspension by unequal length fabricated wishbones (a new departure for Lotus) with combined coil spring/damper units. Initially, a de Dion layout was adopted for the rear suspension, similar to that used on the Lotus Eleven; until Chapman came up with an essentially simple innovation to distribute loadings more widely throughout the chassis. The de Dion tube was replaced by the 'Chapman strut' in which each wheel was located by a tall coil spring/damper unit rigidly aligned with the hub, a fabricated radius arm and fixed length half-shafts providing lateral location. The layout combined precise geometry with light weight, through the use of the minimum number of components to perform all the necessary tasks.

The 12 was powered by the new 1½-litre 4-cylinder, twin overhead camshaft Coventry Climax FPF engine, rigidly mounted and raked downwards in the chassis about its front end, towards a new Lotus-designed 5-speed transmission and final drive unit. Having previously used proprietary gearboxes in his sports racing cars and experienced all the problems associated with adapting them to a racing environment, Chapman decided that the time had come to design and produce a pure Lotus racing gearbox. He had regular contact with Harry Mundy, the highly-experienced engineer who had previously worked on the BRM V16 project and at Coventry Climax, before becoming the Technical Editor for *The Autocar* magazine. Mundy introduced Chapman to gifted engineer, Richard Ansdale and, between them, they schemed a 5-speed gearbox incorporating a Volvo ring-gear and pinion final drive. The input shaft centre was spaced 5in below the output shaft so as to lower the line of the propeller shaft beneath the driver's seat.

As most drivers changed gear sequentially, both up and down through each gear in order, it was reasoned that a motorcycle-type progressive gear change mechanism would be adequate for the purpose. This positive stop gear change was not progressed, however, as the designers were wary of its complications and decided on a gearlever operating in a straight quadrant, with the gate arranged in a series of 'Z's, a gear being engaged in the bottom right corner of each 'Z.' In original form the unit was extremely compact with a length of only 3¼in over the gears, and a weight of just 49lb.

Transmission components and gears were supplied by the German ZF (Zahnradfabrik Friedrichshafen AG) transmission manufacturer along with its limited-slip differential. This transmission unit would consume a great deal of time and effort to make it function reliably; the two main problems being inefficient lubrication of the crown wheel and pinion, and the slimness of the gears. When new, it worked perfectly, but the slightest wear on the teeth allowed the gears to jump out of engagement. During 1957, a London University graduate named Keith Duckworth joined Lotus, first to work on gearbox preparation, and then, as gearbox development engineer. He solved the lubrication problem and recommended a 0.1in increase in gear width, so that wear would be less critical. Cost considerations prevented the manufacture of new gears at that time, however, as there was an existing stock of gears to be utilised. In 1959, Duckworth would join forces with fellow Lotus employee, Mike Costin, to form Cosworth Engineering to produce the highly successful line of racing engines bearing that name.

The chassis was finished with close-fitting alloy body panels, designed by Frank Costin to minimise frontal area. New for Lotus were cast magnesium alloy disc wheels of a 'wobbly-web' pattern, their six bolt attachment saving considerable weight over centre lock wire wheels. The complete car weighed barely 700lb in race trim, some 50lb lighter than its direct rival, the Cooper T43. The Type 12 ran a restricted Formula 2 programme in 1957, due to sports racing car priorities, making little impression on the all-conquering rear-engined Coopers.

FIRST STEPS INTO FORMULA 1

The 1958 Formula 2 season began more encouragingly, before Team Lotus redirected its efforts towards Formula 1. During 1957, Cooper had made tentative steps into Grand Prix racing with an adapted Formula 2 car powered by a Coventry Climax FPF engine enlarged to 1960cc. Driving Rob Walker's Cooper, Stirling Moss utilised this engine to score a sensational win in the 1958 Argentine Grand Prix, thanks to the car's superior roadholding and his ability to conserve tyres. Lotus was in the market for this 1960cc version of the FPF, it being a relatively easy exercise to replace the Formula 2 1475cc FPF of the Type 12 with the larger capacity engine, and go Grand Prix racing. Chapman maintained that he did not want to become involved in Formula 1 at this stage, as he was only interested in getting the ground-breaking glass-fibre-hulled Lotus Elite GT car into production, beyond Formula 2 and sports car racing activities. Nevertheless, Lotus made its Formula 1 debut in the non-Championship International Trophy at Silverstone, when Graham Hill finished eighth with a 1960cc engine, albeit two places and 20sec behind Cliff Allison's Formula 2 version.

Moss' success in Argentina encouraged Coventry Climax to further enlarge the FPF engine to 2203cc to improve its competitiveness against its full 2½-litre rivals, and Chapman ordered a pair for Team Lotus. A Lotus made its Grand Prix debut at Monaco on 18 May 1958, Allison and Hill both driving 1960cc Climax-engined cars – but not without problems. Allison had a

Lotus 12: Cliff Allison finished an impressive fourth in the 1958 Belgian Grand Prix at Spa. (LAT Photographic)

2203cc Climax engine for the Dutch Grand Prix, where he finished a creditable sixth behind Mike Hawthorn's Ferrari. In the Belgian Grand Prix, Allison finished in an outstanding fourth place, the first car home in a healthy state: had the race lasted a further lap, the Lotus could well have run out the winner. In practice for the British Grand Prix at Silverstone, Allison qualified a remarkable fifth, equalling Hawthorn's Ferrari time, but his engine failed before one third distance when in 10th place. Thereafter, emphasis switched to the new Type 16.

Lotus 18 | 11

Lotus 18 – Colin Chapman's U-turn

LOTUS TYPE 16 – FRONT-ENGINED FAILURE

In early January 1958, even before the Type 12 had made its Grand Prix debut, Colin Chapman was working on a much more advanced and sophisticated successor. He was intent on achieving lightweight and minimal frontal area for the new car, by carefully integrating the mechanicals and chassis within an aerodynamic bodyshell. As with the Type 12, the 16 was designed as a Formula 2 car, but was easily adaptable to Formula 1 via a change of engine.

The chassis was similar to the Type 12, yet broader, to improve torsional capacity. Minimal frontal area was achieved by sitting the driver low in the chassis alongside the drive-line, and laying the Climax engine on its side, a feature successfully adopted for the Offenhauser engine at Indianapolis, and by Mercedes-Benz for its 1954 W196 Grand Prix car. Wally Hassan of Coventry Climax did not approve, and had told Chapman that serious problems would be encountered with cooling, lubrication and induction if the engine were installed on its side. Nevertheless, Chapman pressed on to lay the engine over at 62° to the right. It was also angled across the frame at 5½° to the chassis centre line to run the propeller shaft across to the left of the driver's seat. This installation required modifications to the Lotus 'queerbox,' as the transmission unit was popularly known around the works. It was turned on its side and, with modifications to the internals, a total left offset of 8in from the centre line was achieved. Incorporated with the revisions was a positive-stop gear selection mechanism successfully devised by Keith Duckworth to supersede the quadrant change, the casing for which dwarfed the actual gearbox. Even with improvements the 'queerbox' remained fragile, and susceptible to jumping out of gear or selecting neutral of its own accord.

Frank Costin created an elliptical bodyshell on the lines of his successful work for Vanwall, but in a far more compact form. A minimal radiator aperture in the nose blended into a closely fitting engine cover, narrow cockpit opening and a high tail section, all formed in 22-gauge aluminium alloy. The overall effect was of the lowest, most compact and slippery looking front-engined Grand Prix car ever devised.

Early season experience of the 'lay-down' engine in the Lotus Fifteen sports racer soon showed up the problems predicted by Wally Hassan. Despite the 'lay-down' angle, the carburettors remained horizontal, sacrificing the straight portion of the inlet manifold that generated ram effect for the fuel/air mixture into the combustion chamber. This robbed power by circa 20bhp. High oil temperatures indicated circulation and scavenge problems, despite modifications to the scavenge and pressure pumps. In desperation an engine was re-mounted in a chassis at a more modest 17° inclination to the left reinstating the straight inlet pipes, and suddenly performance was regained.

Two Type 16s were entered for the French Grand Prix meeting at Reims on 7 July 1958, the prototype contesting the Formula 2 Coupe de Vitesse with the 17° inclined engine, angled across the frame at 6½° from right to left to pass the propeller shaft under the driver's left leg. The gearbox was aligned at 4° away from the transverse, creating some awkward angles in the drive shafts and generating further power losses. Shortage of preparation time ensured that the Formula 1 version of the Type 16 made its debut with the 'lay-down' engine. Reims is an area of France well known for its blistering summer temperatures and 1958 was no exception. Overheating of the engine, and power losses generated by both the engine installation and the complex drive-line, restricted performance before the engine ultimately failed. Aerodynamic theory suggesting that hot air would be drawn away from the engine and cockpit, proved to be mistaken, and Graham Hill was suitably 'cooked' in the closely-cowled cockpit.

Following the British Grand Prix, the 'lay-down' chassis was adapted to take a 17° engine inclination, angled across the frame at 10½° with a central universal joint in the propeller shaft to bring the transmission into alignment with the rear axle line. This marked the abandonment of the 'lay-down' engine concept. In the German Grand Prix at the Nürburgring, Cliff Allison worked this 16 up from the back of the grid to run in fourth place for eight of the 15 race laps, before his radiator split and lost its water. Over the 1958 season, the Type 16 made seven Grand Prix starts without recording a single finish.

A full 2½-litre version of the Coventry Climax FPF engine became available for 1959, the increase in available power and torque of which would push the 16 chassis beyond the limits of its durability. A revised chassis was produced over the winter of 1958/59, stiffened around the scuttle area by an elliptical 'perforated hoop'-type bulkhead fabricated from two tubular hoops, one within the other, linked by perforated sheet steel. Engine installation was standardised at 17° to the left, angled across the frame by 10½° from right to left to run the propeller shaft at a compound angle of 12°, rather high for a normal Hooke-type joint. Chapman strut-type rear suspension was retained, with a new three-element lower wishbone to increase rigidity and prevent toe-in variation. The drivers were still required to sit astride the driveline, with their legs spread apart to the clutch pedal on its left, and the brake and accelerator to its right.

1: Background

Lotus 16: Graham Hill being hassled by Carroll Shelby's Aston Martin DBR4, during the 1959 British Grand Prix at Aintree. (LAT Photographic)

Lotus 18 – Colin Chapman's U-turn

The strength of the ultra-light chassis proved marginal for the reacting torque and power of the full 2½-litre Coventry Climax engine at the front and the transmission loads at the rear. It was prone to cracking and fracturing, and was constantly being re-welded both before, during and after every running. Inspection of the chassis for cracks became a routine matter, with the welding torch an essential item of the tool kit. The thin aluminium bodyshell was also prone to cracking and splitting, due to vibration – its lightness more than offset by the number of repairs necessary to counter its fragility. Such was Colin Chapman's obsession with lightness, heavier gauge materials were never contemplated.

Highlights of the 1959 season were fourth and fifth place finishes in the Dutch and United States Grands Prix respectively, whilst numerous non-finishes were accounted for by a string of transmission and chassis failures. Meanwhile Lotus' erstwhile rival Cooper, powered by the same Coventry Climax engine, had dominated the 1959 Grand Prix season with five wins, to take the Constructors' World Championship title. Lotus' advanced technology had been defeated by Cooper's relatively unsophisticated yet effective rear-engined chassis.

Graham Hill had started at Lotus Engineering as storeman and a mechanic working on the 'queerbox,' before proving himself as a driver and eventually becoming number one for Team Lotus. By the end of 1959, he had had enough of Lotus fragility, recounting in his autobiography *Graham*, in 1976, that after two seasons of Grand Prix racing "I had finished once … So I told Colin Chapman I was brassed-off and that I was going to join BRM for 1960 and I told him why." Even when Chapman revealed the plans for what would become the Lotus 18, Graham would not be dissuaded.

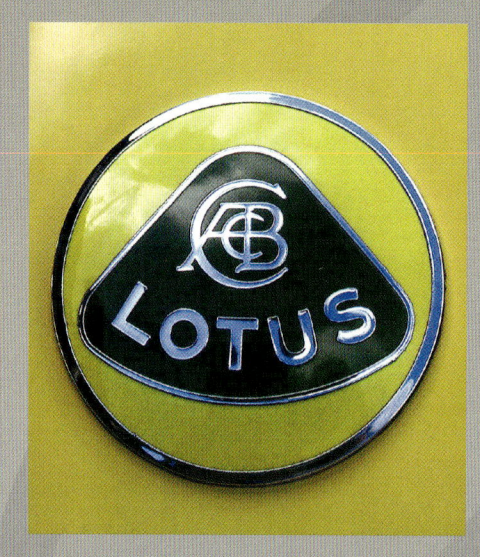

The Lotus logo, incorporating Colin Chapman's initials. (Author)

NEW PREMISES

By 1957, space at Tottenham Lane was no longer adequate for the expanding Lotus business, and Colin acquired a site at Delamare Road in Cheshunt on which to erect a purpose-built factory. On 14 October 1959 the new factory was officially opened with a ceremony attended by some 200 guests, including many motorsport dignitaries, prominent racing drivers and motoring journalists.

The premises comprised two buildings, one fronting on to Delamare Road housing the Elite production line, the sales office with a modest car showroom (Lotus Cars Ltd) and administrative offices above. To the rear, a separate building accommodated customer race car production (Lotus Components Ltd), Team Lotus racing operations, race car design and development, the drawing office and experimental department.

At last Lotus had the necessary space for both its current needs, plus space behind the factory buildings for future expansion.

The new Lotus premises at Delamare Road, Cheshunt. (LAT Photographic)

COLIN CHAPMAN'S U-TURN 2

The Lotus 16 had been a complete disappointment and, as such, was impacting on the company's reputation. Technically the most advanced front-engined Formula 1 car ever constructed, it was small, extremely light, aerodynamically efficient and endowed with generally good handling. Yet it had failed to meet expectations due to the inefficiency of its multi-angled drive-line, which absorbed too much power, and the extreme weight-saving theories applied to the chassis that made it insufficiently substantial to absorb the loadings to which it was subjected.

Looking back from a distance of more than 55 years, it is difficult to understand why Colin Chapman, with all his technical foresight, did not design a rear-engined single-seater sooner. He had always been convinced that the engine had to be in the front, however, and had been preoccupied with both getting the Elite GT car into production and relocating the Lotus factory to new, larger premises at Cheshunt. With these distractions out of the way by October 1959, Chapman had time to think seriously about Formula 1. The failure of the Type 16 had concentrated his mind, especially considering that arch-rival Cooper was winning Grands Prix and scooping the 1959 Constructors' Championship, using identical Coventry Climax power units to his Lotus. Chapman had always been dismissive of Cooper's engineering abilities, and the almost cavalier attitude to chassis technology of its ruggedly-built rear-engined cars. He would not have been impressed, either, when BRM showed a hurriedly-completed rear-engined prototype at Monza, tested extensively before and after the 1959 Italian Grand Prix. Nevertheless, Chapman decided to bite the bullet and start out with a clean sheet of paper, to assess the basic requirements for the contemporary 2½-litre Formula 1 car and identify the most straightforward and uncomplicated way of achieving them. That the answer lay in locating the engine behind the driver came as no surprise.

Chapman could not deny that such a layout made the car much easier to build and to maintain. It offered the ability to react loads between the engine and transmission directly in a single package. Deletion of the troublesome drive-line minimised power losses compared to the 16, and reduced frontal area to little more than the cross-sectional area of the seated driver – who was relieved of heat problems emanating from the mechanicals. In fact the front-engined single-seater did everything wrong – the mass of the engine was at the front, the driver in the middle and the fuel in the tail. As the fuel load reduced, it generated tremendous variations in weight distribution that made it virtually impossible to balance the car on either full or empty tanks, whilst the rear-engined car placed the fuel close to the centre of gravity. The only apparent disadvantage Chapman noted was of a low polar moment of inertia, yet designers and drivers were coming to appreciate the rapid response advantages available from such characteristics.

It was not always thus. Various attempts had been made to adopt a rear-engined layout over the years, but only the spectacular V16 Auto Unions of 1934-37 had met with any success, despite being flawed by their handling eccentricities. The popular misconception was that placing the driver ahead of the engine denied him the ability to sense incipient tail slide until it was too late to correct, making the car difficult to control. The Auto Unions oversteered, as did most early rear-engined cars, because they all relied on swing axle rear suspension, and a myth grew up that all rear-engined cars oversteered. The real issue, not appreciated at the time, was that swing axle rear suspension and spindly 7in tread tyres were never really going to be able to cope with transmitting over 500bhp to the road. Even though the de Dion suspension of the subsequent Auto Union typ D of 1938-39 rectified the problems, the rear-engine concept had been almost completely discredited. Cooper had happened upon the rear-engined concept more by chance than by design during the 1950s, yet had established its credibility once and for all.

Lotus 18 – Colin Chapman's U-turn

Close fitting, slab-sided body panels and minimal frontal area – the Lotus 18. Jim Clark at Reims in 1960 with '373.' (Ferret Fotographics)

Having made the ultimate decision, Chapman had to overcome the inevitable taunts of those accusing him of copying his rival constructor. Though the new Lotus might follow the general Cooper layout, he could rest in the knowledge that it would be designed and constructed to Lotus standards of expertise and technology.

Chapman always held the view that both the Lotus 12 and Lotus 16 were really Formula 2 cars subsequently upgraded for Formula 1 racing. The first true Formula 1 Lotus would be the Type 18 – and yet it was actually designed as an all-purpose chassis for both Formula 1 and Formula 2, with a simpler variant for the new Formula Junior category.

LOTUS 18 – DESIGN AND CONSTRUCTION

Developments in tyre technology had increased cornering forces dramatically since the mid-1950s, and it was important to realise these improved levels of grip through a scientific approach to suspension design. Colin Chapman was one of the few to appreciate that, to work effectively and maintain their geometrical accuracy under conditions of acceleration, braking and cornering, it was crucial that the suspension mounting points were firmly anchored in relationship to one another. This could only be achieved through a torsionally stiff chassis.

By the late 1950s, the multi-tubular frame had become universal. The most efficient type was the space frame, in which relatively small diameter steel tubing was utilised in a fully triangulated structure, carefully calculated to provide both adequate levels of torsional rigidity and rigidity in bending. Chapman had been instrumental in the wider use of the space frame in race car construction, and it came as no surprise that the chassis of his first rear-engined single-seater should continue this philosophy.

Chapman sketched out the overall scheme for his new single-seater at home, as he always did, specifying the wheelbase, track, suspension geometries, engine, gearbox and driver location,

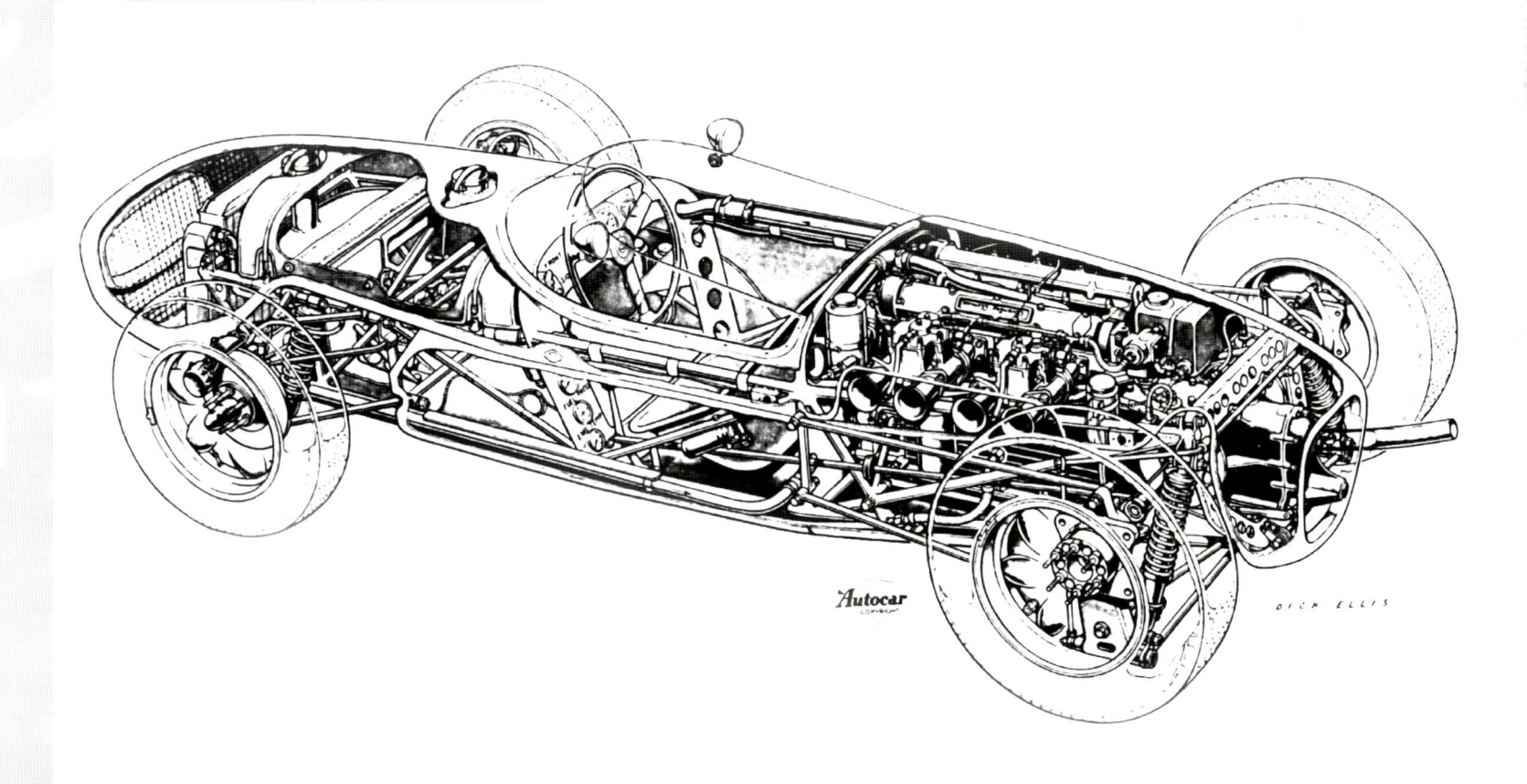

A fine Dick Ellis cutaway from The Autocar of 8 April 1960, depicting the Lotus 18 in 2½-litre Formula 1 form. (Author)

together with a few relevant cryptic notes. After a short briefing, he then passed the project on to his team of draughtsmen, headed by Alan Styman, assisted by Ian Jones, Bill Wells, Mike Wardle, David Shuttle and Paul Wright. They filled in the details between them, the first chassis layout drawing being dated as late as 6 January 1960, well after build had commenced.

The chassis was a masterpiece of geometrical refinement and mechanical simplicity. In the absence of the extreme weight-saving measures of the past, the fully triangulated space frame was constructed in mainly robust 18- with some 16-gauge mild steel tubing of 1in and ¾in diameters, compared to a considerable amount of 20-gauge material in the Type 16. The four main tubular members were of 1in diameter and formed a rectangle in section, spaced 2ft 2in apart horizontally, to enhance frame stiffness with a depth of 1ft 3¼in at the cockpit to minimise the frontal area.

The structure consisted of three bays. The forward bay incorporated a fully triangulated front suspension bay that formed a complete structure in itself. This provided mounting points for the rack and pinion steering, brake and clutch master cylinders and their respective foot pedals, together with the front suspension pick-up points. The forward chassis bay itself was fully braced, the floor section by a stressed sheet aluminium undertray running the length of the cockpit area. This bay extended rearwards to a 'perforated hoop'-type bulkhead at the scuttle fabricated from two tubular hoops, one within the other, linked by perforated sheet steel. Devised by Len Terry, who had joined Lotus in 1958 for his first stint as designer/draughtsman, it was designed to eliminate the need for diagonal bracing in a bulkhead through which the driver's legs protruded whilst providing mountings for his seat, the steering column, instruments and switches.

The central bay between the scuttle and engine bulkhead was braced on only five sides to allow entry and exit for the driver. It only became torsionally stiff as part of the complete chassis structure by drawing rigidity from the adjoining bays. In the engine bay the upper and lower main tubular members terminated in a second perforated hoop forming the rear bulkhead. The upper tubes met this bulkhead just above the pick-up points for the rear coil spring/damper units whilst the lower tubes converged to meet at the lower rear suspension pick-up points almost on the chassis centre line. A detachable Y-shaped member combined with the top section of the rear bulkhead braced the top of the engine bay and could be unbolted to allow for engine removal/installation. Diagonals running from the bottom of the engine bulkhead to the top of the rear bulkhead were braced by tubes running down from the top of the engine bulkhead and meeting at the forward engine mounting points, positioning the latter at the junction of three tubes. Although the rear bulkhead was effectively triangular in section, its shape was influenced by the need to accommodate

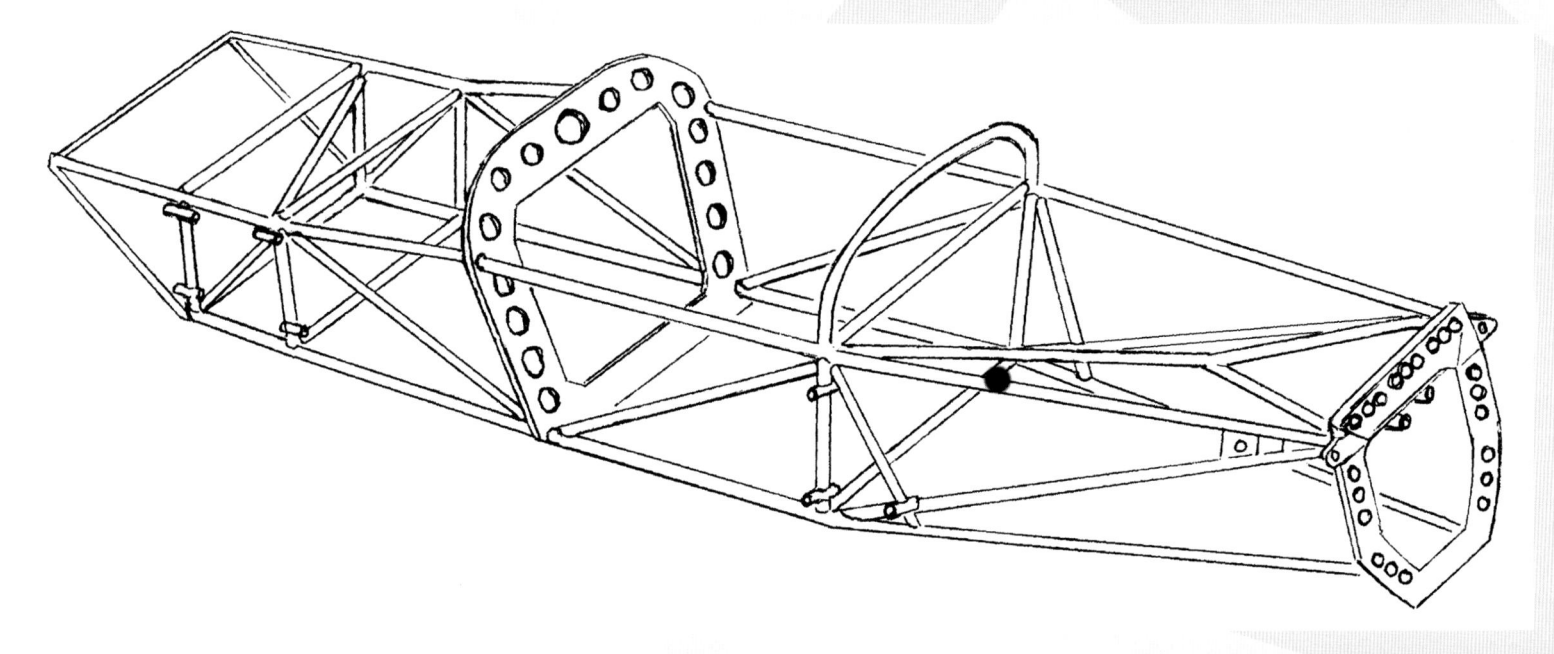

Lotus 18 space frame chassis. (Author)

inboard rear brakes. The top member of this bulkhead acted as a beam, with suspension loadings feeding into it at either end, plus engine and transmission loadings via twin rubber bushed central mounting points. Complete with all brackets, the frame weighed approximately 70lb with a torsional stiffness of circa 1400lb-ft per degree of deflection. This compared with a stiffness of just 365lb-ft/degree for the 1958 Cooper T45.

The suspension design saw Chapman adopt unequal length non-parallel wishbones at the front, first seen on the Type 16 at the 1959 United States Grand Prix. For the rear, he devised a new 'double-transverse link' rear suspension layout to overcome the lack of height for the 'Chapman-strut' of the Type 16. Front suspension wishbones were fabricated from ⅞in diameter 14swg steel tubing, the upper wishbone including a threaded, ball-jointed outer end allowing adjustment to camber angles. The coil springs were combined with adjustable Armstrong damper units. An anti-roll bar was located on the chassis beneath the rear mount of the top wishbone, connected to the wishbone through spherical bearings beneath the ball joint. Proprietary Standard-Triumph uprights were utilised with machined steel hubs. Steering was by Alford & Adler rack and pinion gear in a lightweight casing mounted just ahead

Double wishbone front suspension with the anti-roll bar mounting beneath the ball joint. (Author)

SPECIFICATION: LOTUS 18 (1960)

Engine:	Rear-mounted Coventry Climax FPF 4-cylinder in line 2495cc, 243bhp at 6750rpm (F1) or 1475cc, 143bhp at 7250rpm (F2).
Chassis:	Fully triangulated multi-tubular space frame constructed in 1in and ¾in diameter 18- and 16-gauge steel tubing. Fabricated perforated hoop-type bulkheads at scuttle and rear. Engine bay braced by Y-shaped detachable frame. Front subframe supporting combined oil/coolant radiator and 9-gallon oil tank.
Transmission:	Lotus 5-speed in unit with final drive and ZF differential. Sequential gear change.
Fuel tanks:	Fabricated aluminium tanks, 22 gallons above driver's legs, 9½ gallons behind seat.
Suspension:	Front: fabricated unequal length, non-parallel tubular wishbones with combined coil spring/damper unit and anti-roll bar. Standard-Triumph upright.
	Rear: long, low mounted reversed tubular wishbones with fixed length driveshafts doubling as upper suspension links. Longitudinal location by twin parallel radius arms picking up from seatback bulkhead. Combined coil spring/damper unit and anti-roll bar. Cast alloy hub carrier.
Brakes:	Girling discs, 10½in diameter front, 9½in diameter rear. Front outboard, rear inboard on either side of the transmission.
Wheels:	Lotus 'wobbly web' cast magnesium alloy, bolt on, 15in diameter. Rim width 4½in or 5in front, 6½in rear. Tyre sizes 5.00 front, 6.50 rear.
Dimensions:	Wheelbase 7ft 6in (2.286m); track 4ft 4in (1.320m) front, 4ft 5¼in (1.352m) rear.
Start line weight:	1316lbs (597kg) (approximately) – distribution 44% front, 56% rear.

Lotus 18 – Colin Chapman's U-turn

Rear suspension detailing the reversed wishbone, alloy hub carrier, location points of the anti-roll bar and twin parallel radius arms and, on this example, outboard disc brakes. Note the diminutive casing for the 'queerbox.' (Author)

2: Colin Chapman's U-turn

of the wheel centre line with a straight steering column, a luxury not enjoyed on the Lotus 16.

The design of the rear suspension would be a trend setter, taken up by most other constructors over subsequent years. Basically of the wishbone type, widely-spaced angled pivots achieved a controlled degree of toe-in at full bump. The convergence of the main lower chassis tubes of the engine bay with the rear bulkhead, provided pivot points for long reversed tubular wishbones. These were threaded at the inner ends to allow for camber change, and at the outer ends for adjustment to toe-in. Fixed length drive shafts doubled as upper links, very little tensile or compressive load being taken through them ensured they were not heavily loaded. Cast alloy hub carriers extended down to within 3in of the road surface where they picked up the reversed wishbones and the lower end of the combined coil spring/damper unit. Twin parallel radius arms, anchored to the engine bulkhead uprights on either side, provided longitudinal location, the upper arm picking up from the hub carrier just above the driveshaft, the lower at its foot. An anti-roll bar, attached to the rear bulkhead via the upper coil spring mounts, was connected to the lower wishbones by drop links.

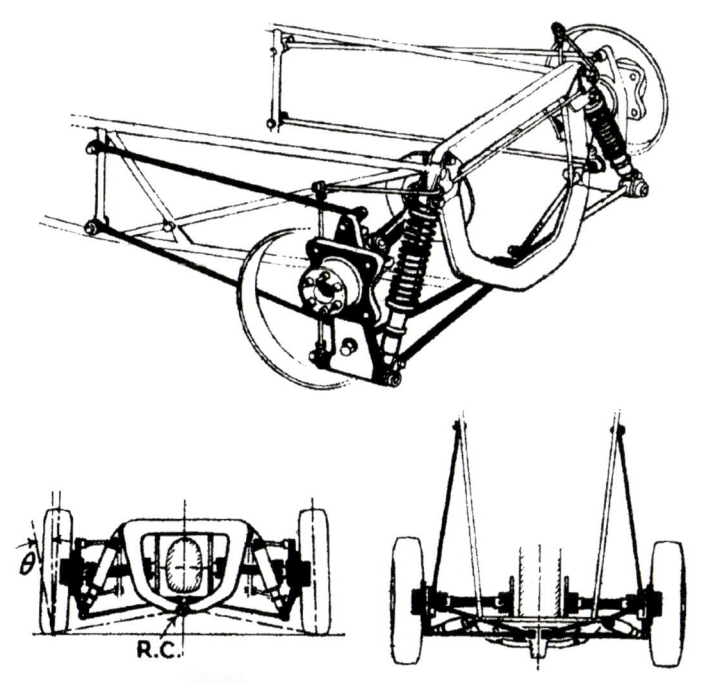

Rear suspension detail and geometry. (Author)

The 22-gallon fabricated aluminium fuel tank located above the driver's legs. (Author)

Lotus 18 – Colin Chapman's U-turn

Side view of the main fuel tank. (Author)

Triple section radiator, twin oil coolers flanking the main coolant section – the fire extinguisher is a modern addition. (Author)

The rigidity of the chassis allowed for fine-tuning of the handling, the availability of adjustment to camber angles, toe-in, spring rates, dampers and anti-roll bars, etc, making it possible to match the chassis to the different characters of each Grand Prix circuit in order to realise the full potential offered from tyre, engine and chassis performance. Unequal length, non-parallel wishbones in the suspension made it possible for the outside wheel to remain virtually upright under all conditions of body roll. Suspension geometry located the roll centres within 4in of the ground, front and rear, with 1° negative wheel camber at the front, and 2° at the rear, generating pronounced negative camber on bump to maintain the outer tyre's contact area with the road – even under conditions of extreme roll. Weight transfer from inner to outer wheel during cornering was dramatically reduced; only a small percentage sacrificed by the addition of the anti-roll bars to trim the car and provide a hint of oversteer, giving the essentially neutral handling characteristics Chapman had hoped to achieve, and the driver-feel necessary for the car to be taken to its true limits of cornering power.

2: Colin Chapman's U-turn

the engine to the radiator ran along the upper right side of the chassis, returning along the lower left. Other pipework and cabling, including oil pressure and temperature lines, water temperature, fuel and fuel pressure gauge piping, brake and clutch hydraulic lines and the accelerator cable, passed through the cockpit area.

Girling disc brakes at the rear were normally mounted on either side of the transmission, although provision was made to relocate them outboard, should overheating problems be encountered. Brake callipers could be either ahead of, or behind, the axle line. Lotus cast magnesium alloy wheels incorporating six stiffening 'wobbly-webs' were of 15in diameter, retained by six studs, and modified in rim section to complement the suspension design and

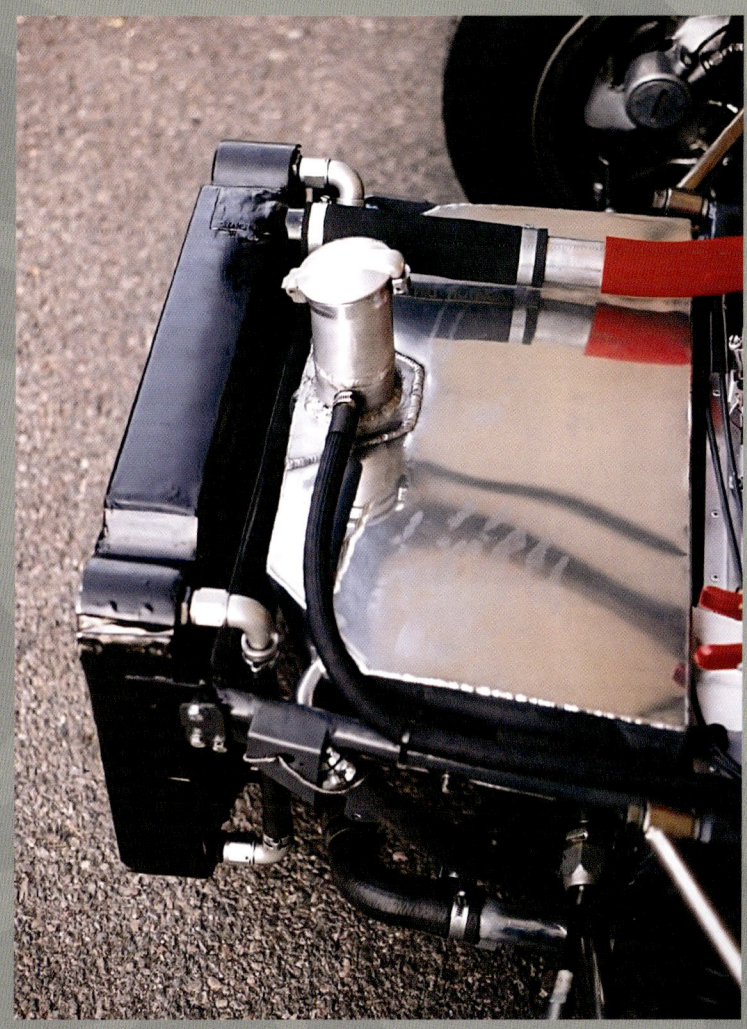

6-gallon oil tank immediately behind the radiator. A triangular shaped lower section helps duct hot air out of the sides of the car. (Author)

Fuel was concentrated within the wheelbase to minimise its effect on handling. Rather than contain it within pannier tanks on either side of the chassis, where it would necessarily increase the frontal area of the car, Chapman located a huge 22-gallon fabricated aluminium tank above the driver's legs, with a further 9½-gallon tank behind and to the right of his seat. A large, triple section radiator comprised a central coolant section flanked by twin oil coolers, and was carried on a light subframe attached to the front of the chassis. A 6-gallon oil tank (4½ gallons of oil, 1½ of air), mounted immediately behind the radiator, incorporated a triangular shaped lower section to help duct hot air out of the sides of the car, away from the driver. The oil and coolant pipes from

Front Girling 10½in disc brake and suspension detail. (Author)

Lotus 18 | 23

Lotus 18 – Colin Chapman's U-turn

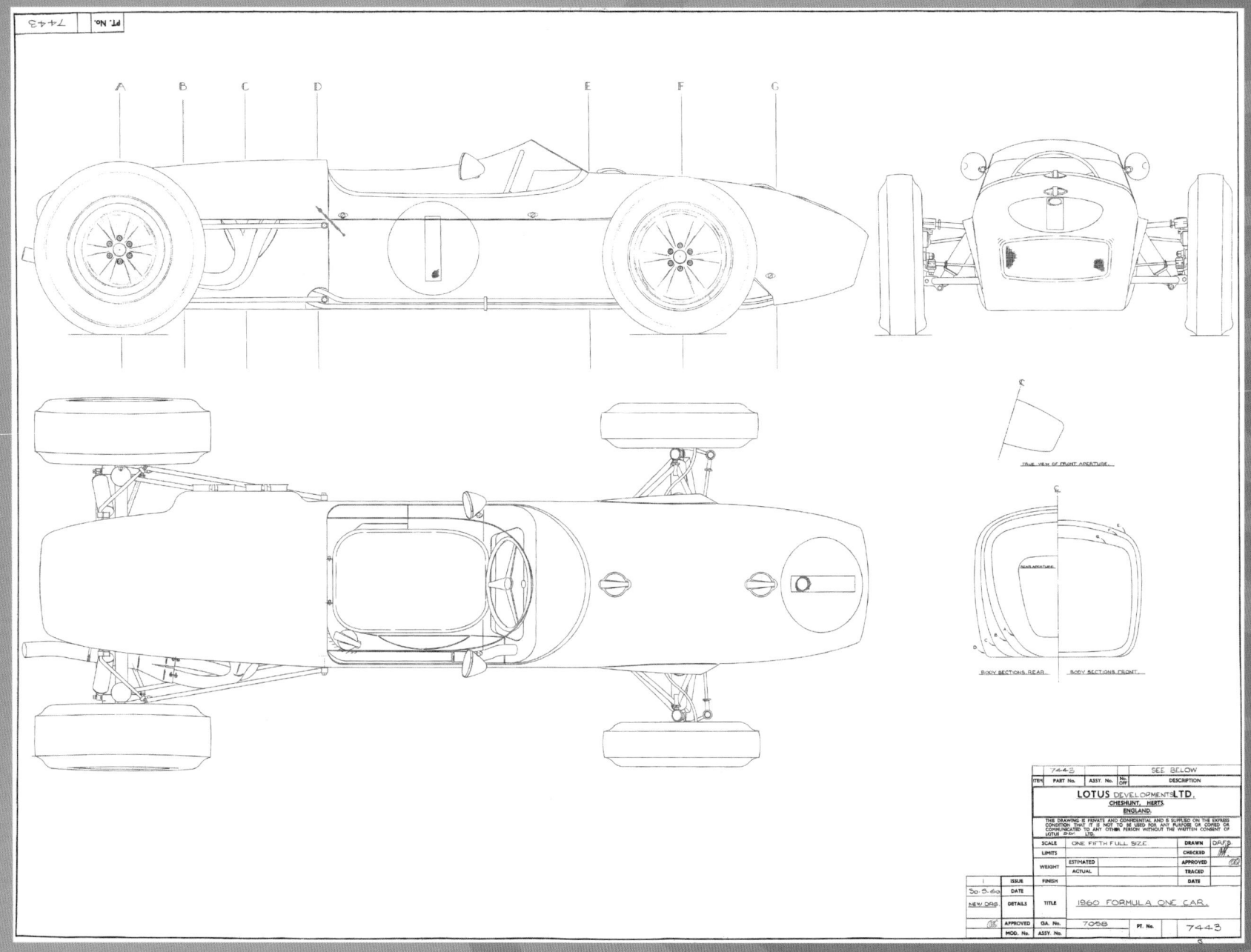

'1960 Formula 1 car' general layout drawing. (Courtesy Classic Team Lotus)

2: Colin Chapman's U-turn

the Dunlop D9 versions of the R5 tyre. Dry weight at approximately 770lb, with a start line weight of 1316lb, was some 85lb lighter than rival Cooper.

Gone was the elliptical styling of the Type 16, replaced by close-fitting panels moulded in glass-fibre by Williams & Pritchard from an aluminium prototype, giving the 18 a more-functional-than-attractive 'brick' shape. Body panels comprised a nose cone integrated into the cockpit surround with perspex wrap-around windscreen, engine cover and side panels, all secured by Dzus fasteners, and easily removable. A large aperture in the rear of the engine cover (another trendsetter) was designed to allow air to enter to cool the transmission, rear brakes, clutch and engine, before exiting through a slot in the undertray located in a low pressure area. The styling would earn various descriptions, ranging from 'biscuit tin' to 'coffin bodied.'

Above: The Lotus 15in diameter cast magnesium alloy 'wobbly-web' style wheel. (Author)

Below: Left-hand gearchange and tubular linkage for the 5-speed 'queerbox.' (Author)

Lotus 18 | 25

Lotus 18 – Colin Chapman's U-turn

Cockpit layout, this example with a right-hand gearchange for a Colotti transmission. (Author)

The power unit for this, and all previous Lotus single-seaters, was the 4-cylinder Coventry Climax FPF engine in either 2½-litre capacity for Formula 1 or 1½-litre for Formula 2. A detailed description of these engines can be found in the following chapter. Unlike the convoluted angles adopted for the Type 16, the Climax engine was mounted squarely and centrally in the chassis, and was mated via a twin-plate Borg & Beck clutch to a third generation Lotus 5-speed 'queerbox' with its positive-stop selection mechanism.

This version of the gearbox first ran in a sports racing 15 at Le Mans in 1959, and reverted to the vertical layout of the Lotus 12, but with the gear cluster overhung behind the rear axle. From the clutch, the primary drive passed beneath the differential, where the positive stop mechanism was located, to the first motion shaft on which there were five free-running forward gears. These were selected progressively in turn by a sliding dog coupling, engaging with internal splines in each gear. Drive passed up to the mating gears splined directly on to the second motion shaft, thence to the bevel pinion of the final drive and ZF limited-slip differential on its forward end. Lubrication was provided by a dedicated system circulated by individual pressure and scavenge pumps driven off the input shaft. The outstanding advantage of this version of the transmission was the ease with which ratios could be changed: simply by removing the end cover of the casing and sliding the gear sets in and out.

Gears were selected by a left-hand lever operating a long, tubular linkage rod running along the left side of the driver and engine to the transmission. The positive stop mechanism required the driver to push the lever forward to select a lower gear, or pull backwards for a higher one. Originally the lever always sprang back to the central position. Now that a migratory lever was utilised, positive selection was ensured by a series of stops on a pair of racks, one controlling up-changes, the other down-changes.

BEHIND THE WHEEL

The cockpit of the 18 was relatively roomy for its time, though regarded as tight by those familiar with contemporary front-engined Grand Prix cars. Climbing aboard was easy, first stepping onto the bucket seat, then sliding down into it, taking care not to put any weight on the flimsy glass-fibre body panels. Once installed, the slightly-reclining seat was comfortable and relaxed with arms outstretched to the 14in diameter, red leather-bound alloy steering wheel. Elbow room was generous, and the selector lever for the 'queerbox' within easy reach down to the left. Set into the upper section of the red, leatherette-faced scuttle bulkhead, were dials for the major instruments – water temperature, tachometer and oil pressure, reading from left to right. Down to the left of the bulkhead, and out of the line of sight, were engine oil temperature, fuel pressure and gearbox oil temperature gauges. To the right of the cockpit, a well-lagged water pipe ran at elbow height between the engine and front-mounted radiator.

Seated on the floor, a mere 6in above the track surface, the driver's shoulders were on a level with the tops of the rear wheels; only his head and the top of the windscreen standing higher than 28in above the ground. Ahead, the front wheels appeared beyond the wrap-around windscreen that did its best to provide protection from the buffeting of the slipstream swirling through the cockpit. The Coventry Climax engine produced a flat bark from the exhaust somewhere over the right shoulder, complemented by the sucking of air into the twin-choke Weber carburettor bell mouths over to the left, and the clatter of the valve gear. Vibration from the big engine was substantial as it reverberated through the chassis, blurring the images in the mirrors and agitating the needles on the instruments.

Although the 'queerbox' only allowed selection of the gears in sequence via the stubby lever, in theory it avoided potential disaster to both engine and transmission from wrong selection. It took some getting used to, and yet the overriding feeling of frailty and uncertainty remained as to whether an actual gear or neutral had been engaged. It required deliberate, positive unrushed movements, yet with practice could be made to work well.

The sophistication of the Lotus 18 chassis kept both front wheels in contact with the road on turning in hard to a corner, something not enjoyed by a Cooper driver. This was a crucial advantage that offered the driver the opportunity to brake deep into the apex of a corner and get back on to the throttle quicker – the shorter the time on the brakes and the longer on the throttle, the quicker the lap time. Given equality of power, it could out-corner any of its rivals on the track. The Lotus responded easily to its ultra-sensitive controls, the steering moving the car across the road in direct proportion to the slightest tweak of the wheel. The small inherent degree of built-in oversteer could be increased at will, by judicious control over the throttle or a touch of extra lock, either one being all-too-easy to over compensate.

The Lotus was never as easy to drive as a Cooper, demanding a precision to keep it operating within tight limits that rewarded the skilled driver with superior braking, cornering power and traction.

Lotus 18 – Colin Chapman's U-turn

Cockpit of the 1960 Goodwood Glover Trophy-winning chassis 371. (Ferret Fotographics)

HIGH TORQUE RACER – THE COVENTRY CLIMAX FPF RACING ENGINE 3

For the majority of the period between 1954 and 1958, under the 2½-litre Formula 1 Regulations, Grand Prix racing was dominated by established manufacturers, such as BRM, Ferrari, Maserati, Mercedes-Benz and Vanwall, that designed and constructed the complete car, inclusive of chassis, transmission and, particularly, the engine. By 1959, the balance of power had swung away from these manufacturers, of whom only BRM and Ferrari remained, towards a new breed of specialist British racing car constructors represented by Cooper and Lotus. These smaller, closely-knit constructors operated from modest premises with only a handful of employees to design and build their own chassis whilst sourcing other components from proprietary suppliers. The most important component was the engine; it was only the availability of off-the-shelf engines from Coventry Climax that made their participation in Grand Prix racing possible.

Coventry Climax Engines Ltd was set up in Coventry, in 1919, by H Pelham Lee as a proprietary engine manufacturing business. These engines powered a number of both known and lesser-known makes of automobile, until the Depression of the 1920s sent their manufacturers to the wall. In 1938, Coventry Climax won a contract to supply transportable fire-pump engines to the Fire Service that became standard equipment throughout World War II. By 1950, Leonard Lee, the son of the founder, was running the company and he assembled a highly experienced design team around him. Walter Hassan was Technical Director – his experience embraced the Bentley racing department during its Le Mans winning heyday, a number of Brooklands-orientated racing teams and projects, and time with Jaguar on the design of the legendary XK engine. He had recruited his old friend Harry Mundy from the BRM V16 project to work alongside him as Chief Designer.

In 1950, the Home Office issued a specification for a brand new, lightweight fire-pump engine capable of producing 35bhp at 3500 rpm. Lee's team won the contract with an all-aluminium, single overhead camshaft 4-cylinder petrol engine of just over 1-litre capacity. The requirements for a fire-pump engine of good power-to-weight ratio, high efficiency and reliability matched those of a racing engine, and, with the designers' motorsport backgrounds, the engine soon generated interest from British racing car constructors. Lee foresaw a potential additional market for his FW (feather weight) engine and gave the go-ahead to upgrade it for competition work. Designated FWA, the engine produced an output of 90bhp at 7300 rpm and dominated the 1100cc sports racing class from 1954 through into the 1960s.

Even before production had commenced on the FWA, Coventry Climax was to become involved in a far more ambitious project. The company's talented design duo of Hassan and Mundy began working on a V8 engine in their spare time for the new 2½-litre Grand Prix formula, due to come into force from 1 January 1954. This was very much a low-key project, yet received the backing of Leonard Lee. When completed, the FPE, or 'Godiva' as it was known, produced 264bhp at 7900 rpm. Compared to the outputs claimed by continental manufacturers, this figure was considered insufficient and, despite pressure from the British constructors, the engine was never released for racing. In the event, the power output would have been sufficient to be competitive and, with continuous development, would no doubt have remained so throughout the seven year life of the 2½-litre formula.

Rather than be wasted, the time and experience gained on the V8 was applied to a new 4-cylinder engine, the FPF, to suit both the 1500cc sports car class and the new 1½-litre Formula 2 category due to come into force from 1957. It was apparent that there was a much larger market for such an engine – constructors Cooper and Lotus, in particular, keen to see such a power unit whilst they were not at that time interested in the V8. A popular myth arose that the FPF was developed from a fire pump unit. Whilst this was true of the earlier FPA racing engines, the twin overhead camshaft engine was designed for racing from the outset.

COVENTRY CLIMAX FPF – FORMULA 2 ENGINE – 1957-60

Harry Mundy had left Coventry Climax in 1955 to become an outstanding Technical Editor of *The Autocar* magazine, and the FPF was developed by Hassan with Peter Windsor-Smith. Investigations revealed that, with small alterations to water passages and ports, the cylinder head assembly of the V8 could be utilised for the 4-cylinder engine. Increasing capacity of four cylinders of the V8 from 1.25 to 1.50 litres was achieved by enlarging the bore by 0.2in to 3.20in (81.2mm) and the stroke by just 0.125in to 2.80in (71.1mm), the latter driven by the desirability of utilising V8 connecting rods.

At a glance:	Coventry Climax FPF 1½-litre Formula 2
Bore	81.2mm
Stroke	71.1mm
Capacity	1475cc
Stroke/bore ratio	0.88:1
Compression ratio	10.0:1
Piston area	207.22cm²
Valves per cylinder	2
Valve sizes:	
• Inlet	1.75in
• Exhaust	1.60in
Carburetion	2 t/c Weber 40DCO
Max bhp/rpm	143 @ 7250
Max torque lb/ft	108.5 @ 6500
Bhp/litre	96.9
Fuel	100oct petrol
Dry Weight	255lb

The cylinder head and combined cylinder block and crankcase were cast in LM7 aluminium alloy. The crankcase extended down well below the crankshaft centre line, was barrel-shaped for stiffness and completed by a shallow sump casting. Wet cylinder liners were spigotted at the top and sealed by a pair of toroidal rubber rings at the bottom. The crankshaft was an EN24 nickel-chromium steel forging with integral counter weights running in five 2.5in diameter main bearings. Twin overhead camshafts driven by a train of spur gears operated the valves through inverted tappets with closure by double helical springs. The inlet valve was positioned at 32° and the exhaust at 34° from the vertical, both slightly offset from the geometrical centre point of the hemispherical combustion chamber to permit larger valve areas. Valve sizes were 1.75in for the inlet and 1.60in for the exhaust. Slightly-domed pistons with cutouts on the crowns, featured twin Dykes compression rings and an oil control ring. The connecting rods were of angled (45°) split-type construction for the convenience of withdrawing them up the cylinder bore.

Dry sump lubrication was provided by three oil pumps of equal capacity placed low in the shallow sump in line with the crankshaft, immediately below the main bearings. Driven in tandem by a jackshaft off the auxiliary timing gear, scavenge pumps were located at each end of the sump with a single pressure pump between them. The water pump was driven from the exhaust camshaft gear train on the front of the engine. Ignition was by a single sparkplug per cylinder powered by a vertical Lucas racing magneto driven by skew gears from a forward extension of the oil pump jackshaft.

Initially the engine was supplied with a pair of new SU HD6 twin choke carburettors with 1¾in diameter bores, although work proceeded on twin choke Weber 40DCO carburettors and these would become the standard caburettors. Maximum power was 142.8bhp at 7250rpm on a 10:1 compression ratio and 100 octane petrol. Between 1957 and 1959, the FPF dominated Formula 2, with only spasmodic interruptions from Ferrari, Porsche or, in 1959, the technically advanced four valve per cylinder, fuel-injected German Borgward engine.

Progressive Enlargement

Hardly had the new Formula 2 FPF been fitted in a chassis, than Rob Walker and John Cooper made a request for a 2-litre version, to enable them to compete in the 1957 Monaco Grand Prix. Walter Hassan was not keen on enlarging the FPF, but did not prevent it from proceeding, especially as it was being financed by Walker. The bore and stroke were increased by 5.2mm and 12.7mm respectively to 86.4mm and 83.8mm for a capacity of 1960cc. The power output increased to 176bhp at 6500rpm and torque to 162ft.lb at 5000rpm on twin choke Weber 42DCO carburettors. In 1958, Stirling Moss used the engine to win the Argentine Grand Prix, the first Grand Prix win for a Coventry Climax engine. This success encouraged Leonard Lee to sanction a further enlargement of the FPF to 2203cc to increase its competitiveness. Both the bore and stroke were increased to 88.9mm, necessitating the fitting of a packing plate between the cylinder head and block to provide the additional height to accommodate the increased stroke. The angled split-type connecting rods had not proved sufficiently rigid and the convenience of withdrawing them up the cylinder bore was forgone in favour of a stiffer horizontal split design with an increased bolt diameter. This engine produced 194bhp at 6250rpm on an 11:1 compression ratio, but it never ran smoothly, vibrated and proved very frail if over-revved. The longer stroke severely weakened the crankcase and the crankshaft counterbalance

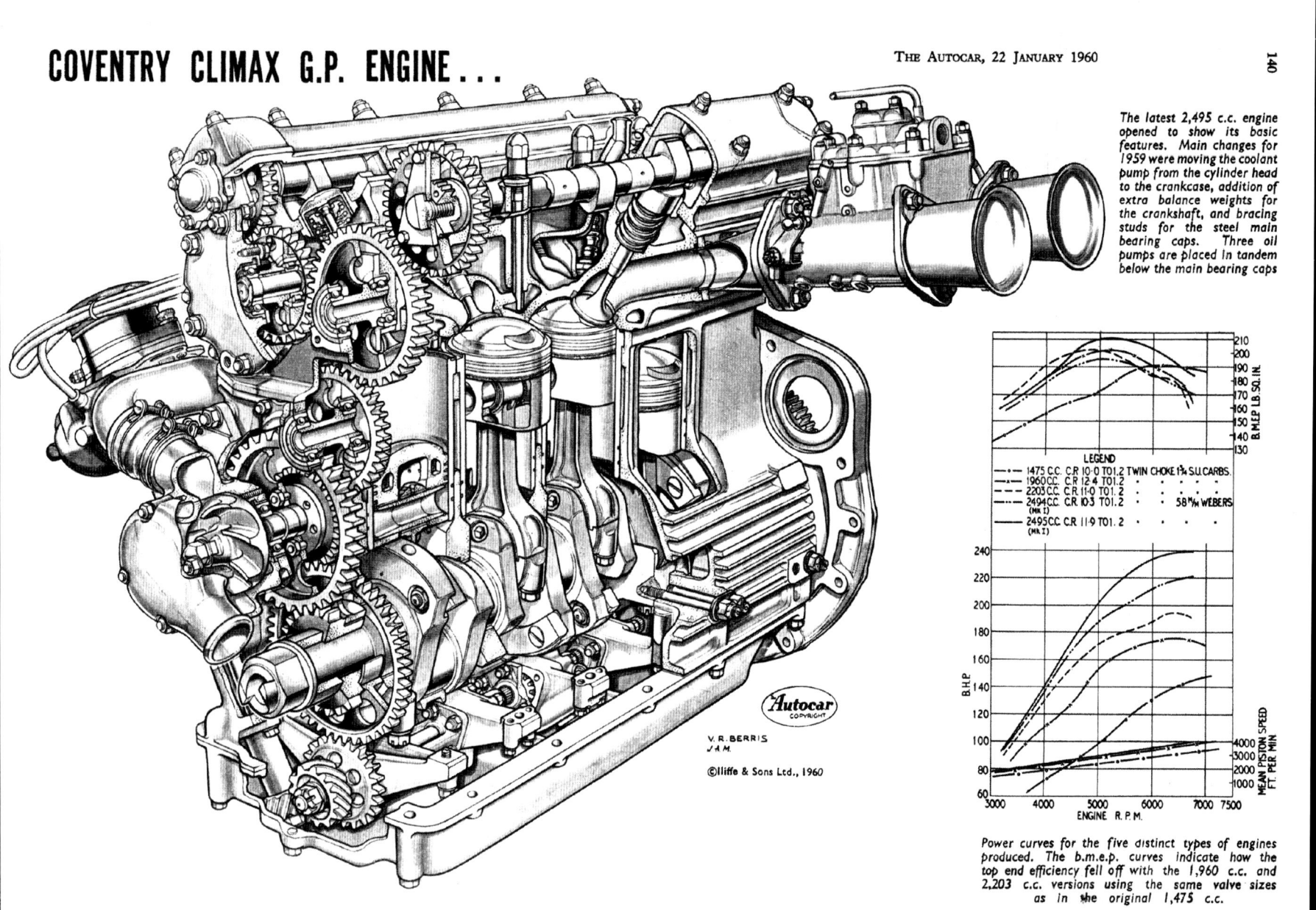

3: High Torque Racer – the Coventry Climax FPF Racing Engine

COVENTRY CLIMAX G.P. ENGINE...

THE AUTOCAR, 22 JANUARY 1960

The latest 2,495 c.c. engine opened to show its basic features. Main changes for 1959 were moving the coolant pump from the cylinder head to the crankcase, addition of extra balance weights for the crankshaft, and bracing studs for the steel main bearing caps. Three oil pumps are placed in tandem below the main bearing caps

LEGEND
- - - 1475 C.C. C.R 10·0 TO 1.2 TWIN CHOKE 1¾ S.U. CARBS.
— — 1960 C.C. C.R 12·4 TO 1.2   "
- — - 2203 C.C. C.R 11·0 TO 1.2   "
— · — 2494 C.C. C.R 10·3 TO 1.2 58 M/M WEBERS
(MK I)
——— 2495 C.C. C.R 11·9 TO 1.2   "
(MK II)

Power curves for the five distinct types of engines produced. The b.m.e.p. curves indicate how the top end efficiency fell off with the 1,960 c.c. and 2,203 c.c. versions using the same valve sizes as in the original 1,475 c.c.

More Autocar artistry: the 2½-litre Coventry Climax FPF engine as originally drawn by Vic Berris, updated by John Marsden. (LAT Photographic)

weights became less effective. The centre main bearing support webs would crack after a few races and it was possible for the complete centre main bearing panel to be punched out of the crankcase. Temporary stiffening of the crankcase was achieved by running a steel plate attached to the sides of the crankcase under the centre main bearing cap nuts.

Coventry Climax FPF – 2½-litre Formula 1 Engine

Under considerable pressure from Jack Brabham and John Cooper (Lotus was not yet a major player in Formula 1) to provide a full size, competitive 2½-litre engine, Leonard Lee gave Wally Hassan the go-ahead to proceed, and the necessary re-design work commenced on 1 December 1958.

At a glance:	Coventry Climax FPF 2½-litre Mk 2
Bore	94.0mm
Stroke	89.9mm
Capacity	2495cc
Stroke/bore ratio	0.96:1
Compression ratio	11.9:1
Piston area	277.7cm^2
Valves per cylinder	2
Valve sizes:	
• Inlet	2.062in
• Exhaust	1.687in
Carburetion	2 t/c Weber 58DCO3
Max bhp/rpm	243 @ 6750
Max torque lb/ft	212 @ 5300
Bhp/litre	97.4
Fuel	130oct AvGas
Dry weight	290lb

The requirements of the re-design had to be balanced against the necessity of retaining the ability to machine the major components on existing jigging. This dictated the retention of the existing cylinder centres and main bearing stud centres, with only a very small variation in cylinder head stud centres.

Birmal cast a brand new cylinder block in RR50 aluminium alloy to overcome the weakening that the progressive enlargement had created. The height of the top of the block was increased by 0.25in to replace the packing plate introduced on the 2203cc engine in 1958. Successive lengthening of the stroke of the original FPF had seen casting webs linking the cylinder walls almost completely cut away, apparently without incurring any serious distortion problems. Nevertheless, the crankcase extended down 3½in below the crankshaft centre line and retained its barrel form, heavily ribbed externally to enhance lower half stiffness. Bore and stroke were increased to 94.0mm by 89.9mm, larger by 12.8mm and 18.8mm respectively than the original 1½-litre FPF, to give a capacity of 2495cc.

The basic layout remained unchanged, with gear-driven overhead camshafts and a five-bearing crankshaft running in 2.5in diameter and 1.0in width main bearings. To counter the balance problems incurred in the successive enlargements, arcuate weights of GEC 'heavy metal' were recessed in, and bolted to, the existing crankshaft balance weights to increase their mass. The entire bottom end was robustly cross-braced to improve rigidity, each main bearing cap braced by two 0.3125in diameter transverse studs into the crankcase casting on each side, effectively tying the crankcase and the bearing caps together in the horizontal plane.

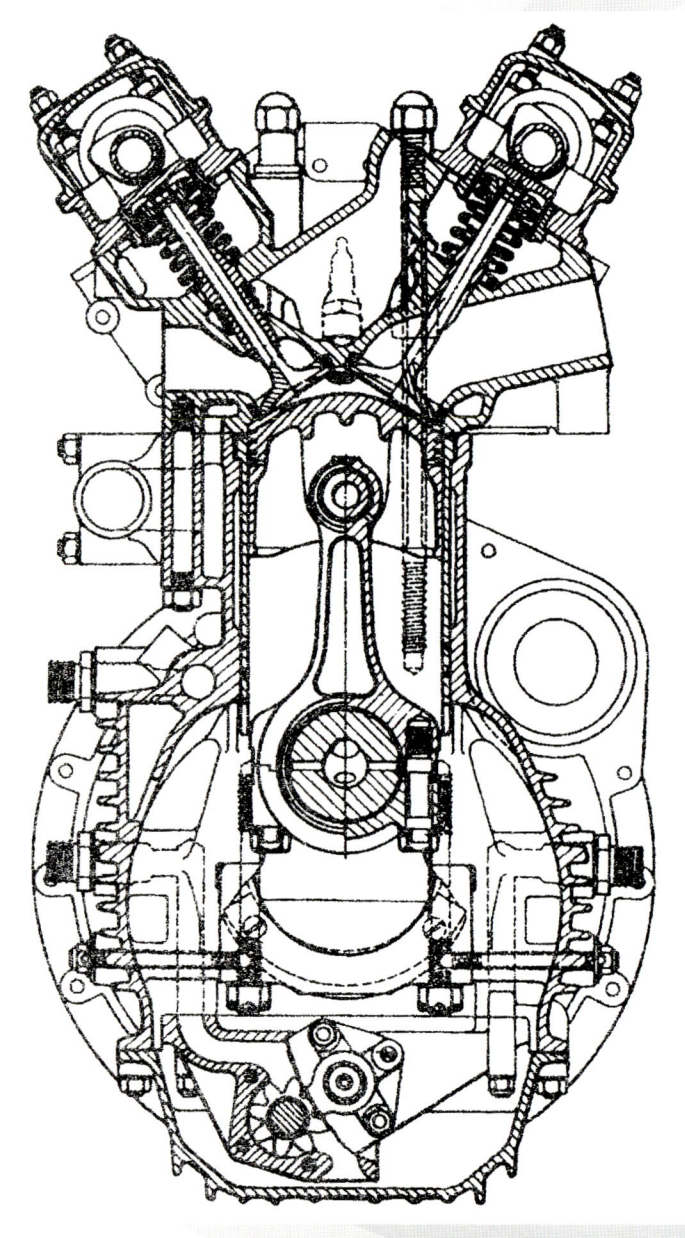

Cross-section of the Coventry Climax FPF engine, detailing the compact form of the combustion chamber. (Author)

3: High Torque Racer – the Coventry Climax FPF Racing Engine

Coventry Climax FPF, left side view. (Author)

Coventry Climax FPF, right side view. (Author)

Lotus 18 | 33

Connecting rod and big-end bolt diameters were increased to 0.5in. The big end bearings were of 2.125in diameter and 0.875in wide, the centre distance between them and the little ends 5.1in. Difficulties with combustion chamber sealing on the 1960cc and 2203cc engines were resolved by a laminated metal fire ring recessed into the top of each liner. Although the steady enlargement of the cylinder bores had reduced the water spaces between them, there had been no reduction in cooling efficiency, as the volume of water in circulation remained as before. The water pump was relocated from the cylinder head to lower down on the crankcase, to relieve chassis installation problems, and was driven off one of the camshaft drive intermediate gears. The existing lubrication was retained, with the two scavenge outlets on the right side of the block and the inlet to the pressure pump on the left.

An outstanding feature of all FPF engines was the narrow inlet port size compared to competitor engines. Gas velocities were relatively high, to produce power by speeding up the velocity of the incoming charge in a long port ahead of the inlet valve, so that the mixture was piled up at the time of opening. The advice of gas flow specialist Harry Weslake was taken on porting – the inlet ports slightly curved to promote swirl and improve combustion. A single 14mm sparkplug was angled at 25° to suit the swirl pattern and optimise combustion. An included angle of 66° between the valves was as for the previous versions of the FPF, 32° for the inlet and 34° for the exhaust, allowing a shallow hemispherical recess to the combustion chamber. Solid valves devoid of internal cooling were deliberately under-sized at 1.937in for the inlet and 1.687in exhaust, to restrict the power output in case the new crankcase proved to be insufficiently sturdy. Brico fully-skirted, slightly-domed aluminium pistons carried two Dykes compression rings with a single oil ring.

An output of 230bhp was obtained early in development on twin choke Weber 58DC03 carburettors, and the first two engines were delivered on this basis without further testing to the Cooper Car Co and to Rob Walker for Stirling Moss. They made their debut at Goodwood on Easter Monday, 30 March 1959, where they finished first and second in the 100-mile Glover Trophy race – just three months after commencement of the redesign work.

Race-winning combination. (Author)

Team Lotus received its first engine in time for the Silverstone International Trophy in May, and fielded two front-engined type 16s so equipped over the season with little success, as already recorded. Meanwhile, the engine scored its first Grand Prix victory at Monaco and went on to win a further four Grands Prix over the course of the season, providing the motive power for Cooper's success in winning the 1959 Constructors' Championship.

The more robust bottom end enabled the engine to rev up to 7000rpm without problem and, with the initial concerns alleviated, a Mk II cylinder head was produced in July 1959, with the inlet valve size increased to 2.062in diameter, but with no change to the exhaust size. The spacing between the front and rear pairs of inlet ports was increased from 3in to 4.125in to line up with the twin chokes of the carburettors. This involved reversing the direction of swirl in cylinders one and four and the slight offset of the spark plugs from the combustion chamber centres. The compression ratio was raised to 11.9:1 and power went up to 243bhp at 6750rpm. The secret of the engine's success would be its immense mid-range torque, the product of careful development that included pioneering work on exhaust pulse tuning. Torque peaked at 212lb/ft at 5000rpm with an ability to pull powerfully from as low as 4000rpm.

Cooper was recipient of the first Mk II engine, used to win the British Grand Prix, and, whilst both works Coopers, together with Stirling Moss' Walker Cooper, were equipped with them by the United States Grand Prix at the end of the season, there were none for Team Lotus. Colin Chapman never enjoyed a close rapport with Coventry Climax (as did Jack Brabham and Cooper) and it showed.

Overall, the new engine was incredibly reliable, with only two engine-related failures in 50 starts (4%) over the 1959 Grand Prix season. Five wins plus 15 other top five finishes were supplemented by five pole positions and five fastest laps.

Having initially focused supply solely on Cooper and Rob Walker, Lotus became a recipient of the Mk II engine for Formula 1 use in 1960. The engine also became available over the counter for purchase by other teams/entrants at a cost of £2250 per unit. A total of 48 examples of the 2½-litre FPF were eventually sold that would appear in both single-seater and sports car applications.

1960 FORMULA 1 SEASON – GREAT EXPECTATIONS 4

The first public appearance of a Lotus 18 was the prototype Formula Junior chassis at the 1959 Boxing Day Brands Hatch meeting – see Chapter 11. Meanwhile, the prototype alloy-bodied Formula 1 Type 18 (chassis 369) was under construction at Cheshunt. Glitzy new car launches were unknown in the 1960s, even had time allowed – the new 18 was hurriedly completed over several all-night sessions. Following a 100yd test run outside the factory to ensure that all the systems were working and the wheels were pointing in the right directions, it was broken down into component form just in time to be air-freighted out to Buenos Aires for the opening round of the 1960 World Championships.

Gran Premio de la Republica Argentina, Buenos Aires, 6 February 1960

On arrival at the Buenos Aires circuit, the new Lotus was assembled in the paddock garages where its low frontal area and slab-sided bodywork generated some interest. Innes Ireland took the car out for some practice laps and began lapping spectacularly fast straight out of the 'crate.' This Cooper-challenging performance immediately attracted the attention of rival teams, journalists and spectators alike, that beseiged the Lotus pit for more information. Following adjustments to the braking and handling, the Lotus went faster and faster, Ireland setting a 1min 38.5sec lap in the final practice session, second only to Stirling Moss who was on pole 1.6sec quicker. Lotus had never previously been anywhere near the front of the grid in Formula 1 yet suddenly had become the sensation of practice by challenging for pole position.

Despite having never attempted any standing starts with the new car, Ireland leapt ahead from the start of the Grand Prix, pulling out a 2sec lead over the first two laps. Alas, he spun off halfway around the third lap, when a gear jumped out of

INNES IRELAND ON DRIVING THE LOTUS 18

Writing in an article entitled 'Down South America Way' in *Autosport* on 29 April 1960, Innes gave his first impressions of the Lotus 18:

"I soon found out that a completely different technique was required to drive it, compared with our 1959 cars, but after a few slow laps I began to get the 'feel' of the car. Generally the car was very good considering that this was the first time it had ever been in one complete piece.

"We didn't do any startling times with the new Lotus as we were still being careful about getting it to handle better and get the brakes sorted out. Also we had trouble with the carburettors. [The next day] my car was now going much better, the brakes were to my liking and the handling was improved – although I was still not getting the best out of the car due to my lack of experience of rear-engined cars. My time was in the region of 1min 41sec.

"Saturday was the final day of practice when official times were taken for grid positions. I was first out and after doing a few warming-up laps I put in a time of 1min 39sec and then the car was put away to have a minor adjustment made. Soon all the cars were on the track and by the way the drivers were trying it appeared that they didn't like the idea of a Lotus going so quickly. Bonnier (BRM) turned in a time of 1min 38.8sec ... I then took out the Lotus again and after a few laps did 1min 38.5sec. This seemed to stir things up a bit and soon the BRMs were out again trying like mad but unable to improve. Moss (Cooper) was on pole position with 1min 36.9sec.

"I must say that it was a pleasant change for the opposition to be taking the Lotus seriously and it served as a great morale booster to our whole team to be on the front row of the grid with second best time. As this was the very first outing for this car we were all very well pleased with it, as it had shown tremendous potential."

engagement. This dropped him to sixth behind the front-engined BRMs of Jo Bonnier and Graham Hill, the Coopers of Moss and Jack Brabham and Phil Hill's Ferrari. He quickly disposed of the Ferrari, then closed on Brabham, whom he shadowed for a number of laps, closely studying the Australian's style with a rear-engined car. Passing the Cooper on lap 14, he caught and passed Hill's BRM for third four laps later, before inheriting second on lap 41 when Moss had a rear suspension wishbone fail. The Lotus continued to jump out of gear, so Ireland played safe by remaining in top gear.

Less than 20 laps from the finish and in a secure second place, Ireland spun wildly on some recently-deposited oil, banging a curb and breaking the nearside steering arm bolt. Regaining the track in fourth place, parts of the nearside front hub and brake disc flew off half a lap later and the front wheel began flapping around uncontrollably. He managed to maintain some control over the car, but, unable to defend his position over the final laps, dropped back to sixth to score at least a single Championship point. Nevertheless, Colin Chapman could be well satisfied with the sheer pace of his new single-seater.

Whilst in Argentina, the teams were expected to compete in a second race a week later, the Formule Libre Buenos Aires Grand Prix at Cordoba, 500 miles away to the north-west. The circuit came as a shock to the drivers: laid out around the city park, it was rough, bumpy, lined with trees, stone walls, straw bales and traffic furniture. Innes Ireland was sixth fastest in 369 during practice, but on race day, with temperatures standing at 100°F, his transmission failed at the start and the car was pushed away into the shade.

Even though a Cooper (driven by Bruce McLaren) had won the Argentine Grand Prix, John Cooper and Jack Brabham realised that they needed to improve their chassis or be left for dead. On the flight home from South America, Cooper and Brabham began planning a new car, and, once back in Surbiton in mid-March, had a little over two months before the Monaco Grand Prix in May in which to counter the threat posed by the Lotus 18. A great deal of detail work was undertaken on reducing frontal area and generally refining their car. Had Colin Chapman committed the tactical error of showing his hand early and allowing his rival time in which to respond?

Team Lotus' driver line-up for 1960 had evolved into Innes Ireland as No 1, ably backed up by Alan Stacey, both faithful Lotus drivers for some years. Nevertheless, Chapman was never one to pass up the chance of recruiting a 'star driver' and approached Tony Brooks. The Grand Prix winner for Vanwall and Ferrari had virtually decided on a sabbatical in 1960 to pursue his garage business interests whilst being retained by Vanwall in a test and development role. He had declined a similar offer in early 1959, and did so once again, feeling uncertain as to the build-strength of the Lotus, despite his admiration for Chapman as a designer.

On 369's return from South America, there was just time to convert it to Formula 2 specification, in which form Innes Ireland further demonstrated its potential, both at Syracuse, and in winning the Formula 2 Oulton Park Trophy on 2 April (see Chapter 5). Clearly, test and development was likely to be a luxury limited to race weekends. Two weeks earlier, Jim Clark had driven a Formula Junior version to its first victory in a BARC club event at Goodwood. Remarkably, this was the first ever single-seater victory for a Lotus in three years of trying. Meanwhile, Team Lotus had been busy building new chassis for the season ahead, two of which (371 and 373) were built with 2½-litre Climax FPF engines and would debut in the non-Championship events at Goodwood and Silverstone respectively.

Innes Ireland and the Lotus 18 made everyone sit up and take notice at Goodwood on Easter Monday, when they beat none other than Stirling Moss in both the non-Championship Formula 1 Glover Trophy and the Formula 2 Lavant Cup. This was a sensational performance by any standards, as you would hardly expect Stirling to be beaten at all, let alone twice in one afternoon. Moss had

All smiles at Team Lotus: from the left, Colin Chapman, Innes Ireland, Jim Clark and Alan Stacey (Sutton Images)

4: 1960 Formula 1 Season – Great Expectations

Innes' Big Day – Easter Monday 18 April 1960. Ireland and the Lotus 18 lead Moss (Cooper) into the Goodwood Chicane to a sensational win in the Glover Trophy. Sitting in the Grandstand behind them is the author and his father. (LAT Photographic)

taken an initial lead in the Glover Trophy before Ireland (371) slipped past on lap 4, leaving the acknowledged 'maestro' to snap at his heals for 37 laps. Moss would close up under braking at the end of the Lavant Straight, yet "the Lotus demonstrated a high-speed stability and poise through the long corners at Goodwood that my Walker-team Cooper simply could not match," he recalled. Innes remained calm and consistent under the intense pressure to win by a margin of 2.8sec. To add to his tally that day, Innes was awarded the 'Goodwood Ton,' a specially-commissioned solid silver trophy cast in the shape of a 'ton weight,' in recognition of lapping the Goodwood circuit at 100mph.

Goodwood proved significant in that it was the first ever Formula 1 win for Lotus, and that Cooper – the instigator of the modern rear-engined race car – had been beaten at its own game by the marque that would come to supersede it as trendsetter within a couple of years.

Easter Monday had provided BRM Chief Engineer Peter Berthon with his first opportunity to examine the 18 at close quarters in the paddock. He was highly amused by the suspension, chortling: "How stupid! There must be something dreadfully wrong with it, it's got a roll bar each end!" His reaction when the Lotus easily outperformed the new rear-engined BRM P48s is not recorded. Suffice to say, Berthon

A delighted Innes receives the Glover Trophy at Goodwood. (LAT Photographic)

4: 1960 Formula 1 Season – Great Expectations

did not appreciate the finer points of contemporary suspension technology in the use of a roll bar to trim the handling, an art mastered by both Colin Chapman and Jack Brabham/John Cooper.

Having witnessed the superiority of the Lotus 18 at Goodwood, it came as no surprise to learn that Rob Walker had ordered an example for his man Moss. This purchase was a straight-forward customer deal with no special concessions, yet it was quite a coup for Colin Chapman to have the best driver in the world in one of his cars.

The Silverstone International Trophy offered the season's first real opportunity to assess the competitiveness of all the major marques against the apparent supremacy being demonstrated by the Lotus 18. 1960 marked the final season of the seven year run under

GOODWOOD MOTOR CIRCUIT

World War II left Britain devoid of any racing circuits, both Brooklands and Donington Park having been requisitioned by the military. There was, however, a surfeit of former RAF aerodromes around the country, including Westhampnett, a satellite to the more well-known Tangmere and part of the Goodwood Estate owned by former racing driver the Duke of Richmond and Gordon. The airfield perimeter road would make an excellent circuit and the Duke overcame formidable bureaucratic difficulties for Goodwood circuit to organise its first motor race meeting on 18 September 1948.

The 2.4-mile circuit gently undulated around the former airbase through an interesting set of corners widely different in character. Paddock Bend, or the Chicane, was introduced in 1952 to slow cars passing the pits but also provided the opportunity for some spectacular overtaking moves, not all successful. Set at the foot of the South Downs, the circuit possessed unique charm and charisma with its expansive grassy infield. Over the years, the circuit played host to all categories of motor racing, and British drivers including Moss, Hawthorn, Brooks, Hill, Surtees and Clark, to name a few, learned their craft there. One of the most important meetings was on Easter Monday, with the feature Glover Trophy (first run in 1953) that established itself as the Formula 1 season opener.

Goodwood will be remembered as the circuit on which Innes Ireland and the Lotus 18 sensationally beat Stirling Moss twice in the same afternoon and established themselves as new forces in Formula 1.

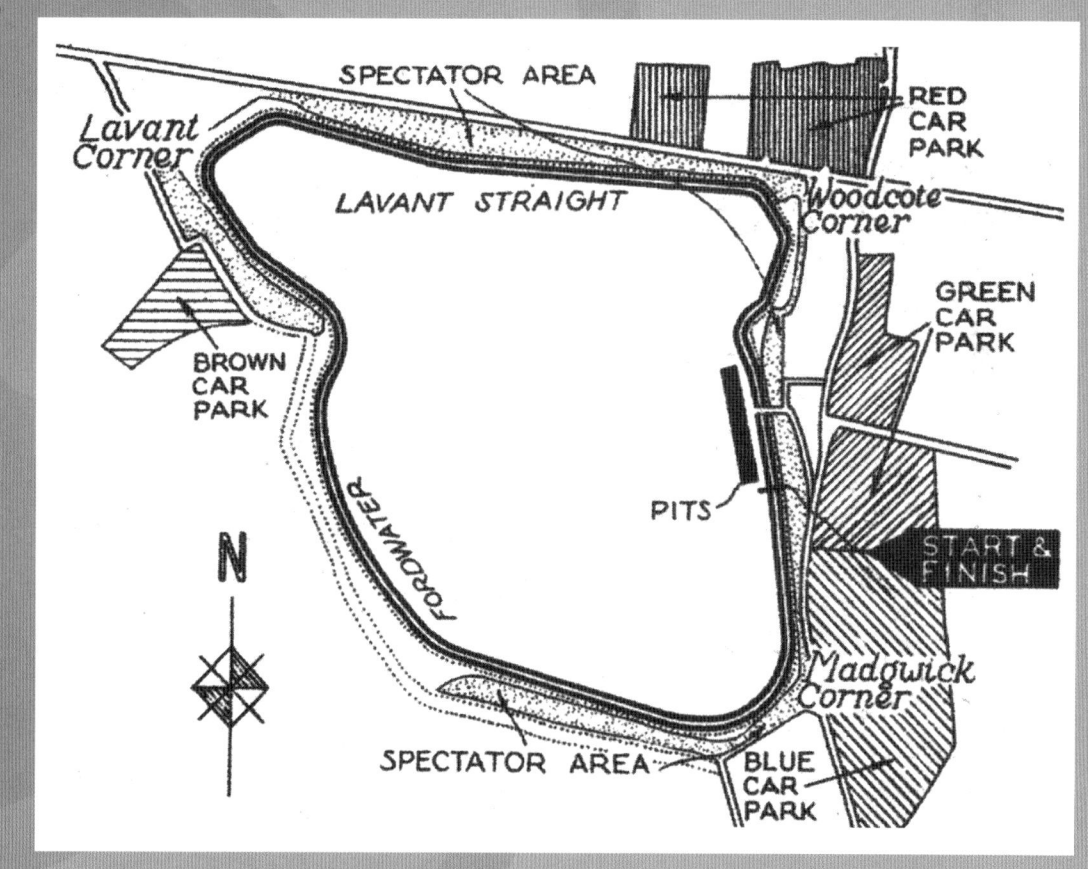

Lotus 18 – Colin Chapman's U-turn

the 2½-litre Formula 1 Regulations and, in such circumstances, you would not necessarily expect to find any completely new designs on the grid. Nevertheless, aside from the Lotus 18, there was a new rear-engined car from BRM and the first appearance of the new 'lowline' Cooper T53 – the latter built as a response to the Lotus. The BRM had undergone extensive testing over the winter, yet remained relatively uncompetitive and rather bulky compared to the brand new Cooper which had lapped Silverstone 5.6sec quicker than the lap record on its first airing. Meanwhile, Ferrari remained faithful to the classic front-engined layout, but had made considerable changes to weight distribution in an attempt to promote a lower polar moment of inertia and make it handle more like a rear-engined chassis.

The performance of the Lotus 18 at Goodwood had captured the imagination of enthusiasts, not only for its speed and roadholding, but also its compact, low-slung, refreshingly different lines compared to the contemporary Cooper. Team Lotus was now at full strength with three 18s on the grid: for Innes Ireland in the Goodwood winning chassis (371), his regular No 2 Alan Stacey (370) and new signing John Surtees (373). Surtees was embarking on a four-wheeled career, having originally signed to drive for Tony Vandervell. With a new Vanwall unlikely to materialise, Colin Chapman was quick to offer a Lotus drive, even though he had a full complement of drivers. The multi-World Motorcycle Champion proved fastest of the Team trio in an impressive sixth on the grid, whilst Stacey in ninth was two places ahead of Ireland, who had gone off the road during practice and damaged the front of his car. Innes was now sporting a double black and white chequered band around his helmet in celebration of his victories at Easter.

A fourth Lotus 18 present was the original, well-used alloy-bodied prototype (369) last driven by Alan Stacey in the Glover Trophy at Goodwood, from which he had retired with engine problems. This chassis had since been acquired from Team Lotus by keen amateur Michael Taylor, financially supported by his father's London-based motor dealership, Taylor & Crawley. The car was scheduled to appear in a number of Grands Prix, prepared by Mike Hawthorn's former mechanic Britt Pearce assisted by Peter Bryant.

From the start Ireland, not fully recovered from a recent tonsillectomy, quickly had his Lotus up from his lowly grid position into second behind Moss. Gradually closing on the Rob Walker Cooper, he set a new lap record on lap 19, before taking the lead

Stirling Moss struggled to stay ahead of Innes Ireland during the International Trophy. The Cooper's wheels adopt odd angles under cornering, whilst the Lotus maintains its own virtually upright. (LAT Photographic)

4: 1960 Formula 1 Season – Great Expectations

Innes Ireland damaged '371' during practice at Silverstone. He stands to the left, cigarette in hand, his helmet newly adorned with a double black and white chequered band. (LAT Photographic)

Lotus 18 | 41

on lap 25. Moss fought back to regain the lead five laps later, cornering the Cooper on three wheels in his determination to stay ahead. By contrast Ireland seemed in complete control, the Lotus 18 seemingly glued to the road. On lap 34, an offside front wishbone failed on the Cooper, putting Ireland in a comfortable lead. Brabham, now second, upped his pace in the closing stages, but found the handling of the new Cooper not yet to his liking, a little alarmed that it was not as quick as the Lotus. Ireland was equal to the situation and, despite a misfire, won his second Formula 1 race of the season by 1.9sec to a tremendous reception from the 80,000-strong crowd for whom he was the new 'golden boy.' Stacey was fourth, Surtees had stopped early on with an oil leak and Taylor had been troubled by a misfire, completing only 32 of the 50 laps.

Harry Mundy, reviewing the technical aspects of the cars at Silverstone for *The Autocar*, commented on the outstanding level of cornering power and traction demonstrated by the Lotus 18. He put this down to the layout and geometry of its rear suspension and the use of very low bottom wishbones linked to the rear hub carrier to generate a roll centre around 4in above ground level. The very close proximity of the 18's lower wishbones to the track surface came in for some criticism, however, particularly from a foreign member of the Commission Sportive International (CSI – the rule-formulating section of the FIA). Questions were raised as

RRC WALKER RACING TEAM

Great-great-grandson of Johnny Walker of whisky fame, Rob Walker had raced a variety of cars himself before World War II. Following their marriage, he promised his new wife he would no longer compete, and in 1953 he turned his attention to entering cars for others to drive, including Tony Brooks and Jack Brabham. The team was based at his Pippbrook garage premises in Dorking, Surrey where his cars were immaculately prepared in dark blue with white nosebands by his chief mechanic, the legendary Polish born 'Alf Francis' (Alphons Kovaleski). Francis was a gifted engineer who had maintained cars for Stirling Moss from 1953 before joining the Walker team in 1957. Moss won his first Grand Prix for Walker in 1958, followed by a further two in 1959 when he began driving the Walker Coopers full time. Significantly Moss never had a contract with Walker, it being a gentleman's agreement sealed with a handshake and evidence of the friendly atmosphere he enjoyed within the team, a direct comparison to the politics of a works team.

Stirling now looked forward to driving a Lotus 18 for the team, despite remaining slightly dubious of the Lotus reputation for frailty. Rob Walker had been purchasing Coopers since 1956 and Charles Cooper, who had no time for Colin Chapman or his products, saw his defection to Lotus as an act of treachery.

Gentleman entrant – Rob Walker. (LAT Photographic)

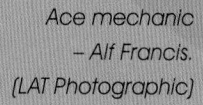

Ace mechanic – Alf Francis. (LAT Photographic)

4: 1960 Formula 1 Season – Great Expectations

to its safety in the event of a puncture. In fact, Ireland had suffered such a puncture during the BARC 200 Formula 2 race at Aintree two weeks earlier without the wishbone making contact with the road or the deflated tyre rubbing against it.

The exceptional cornering power of the Lotus 18 undoubtedly enabled it to realise the performance advantages of the new D9 version of the R5 racing tyre, phased in by Dunlop during 1960. Constructed in a higher grip compound, the elimination of both the rubber layer between the carcase and tube, and the separate sidewall rubber saved 2lb in weight per tyre. Rear tread width was in excess of 4in and the extra grip generated by the D9 would be immediately evident from improved lap times over the season, with a reduction of circa 2sec per lap on a circuit such as Monte Carlo.

Grand Prix de Monaco, Monte Carlo, 29 May 1960

The Lotus 18 was rapidly establishing itself as the revelation of the season, as memories of the frailties and unreliability of the Lotus 16 rapidly faded into the past. Would it dominate the Monaco Grand Prix in the same way as it had the non-Championship races? The situation looked promising when a Lotus proved easily fastest during practice. Rather than Team Lotus, however, it was Stirling Moss, in his first drive in the new Rob Walker Lotus 18 (chassis 376),

INNES IRELAND
(b 12 June 1930, d 22 October 1993)

Destined to live with the tag of having been born ten years too late, Innes Ireland's fun-loving, carefree attitude to life put him in the same category as his illustrious predecessors Mike Hawthorn and Peter Collins. As it was, this Scotsman with an Irish name arrived in Grand Prix racing at a time of change, when drivers were becoming more 'professional' and spending less time at the bar.

A long time Lotus sports car driver, his performances impressed Colin Chapman enough to invite him to join Team Lotus. In 1959, a vacancy arose in the Grand Prix team to drive the unreliable 16. Nevertheless, he managed to finish in the points twice, the only Team driver to do so. In 1960, he was promoted to Team leader following the departure of Graham Hill to BRM, a move that coincided with the introduction of the Lotus 18.

Innes shot into prominence courtesy of the Lotus 18 on Easter Monday 1960, when he beat Stirling Moss in both the Formula 1 and 2 events at Goodwood. That Moss was rarely beaten, let alone twice in the same afternoon, demonstrates the impact of this achievement. He continued to set the pace with the 18 until Moss assumed the role in the Rob Walker car (despite it being a private entry). Innes knew that, on the right day, as at Goodwood, he was capable of competing seriously against Moss, yet was realistic enough to acknowledge that Stirling would always be the superior driver. The Team Lotus 18s never demonstrated the necessary pace or reliability to challenge Jack Brabham's domination of the 1960 Grand Prix season, always more effective in sprint type races.

At the end of a successful 1961 season, Chapman made plans for Team Lotus that excluded Innes, unforgivably failing to tell him so until cornered. Innes felt justifiably hard done by, as he had always been intensely loyal to Lotus and had recently scored the first Grand Prix win for Team Lotus. He took up the offer of a drive for the BRP-run UDT-Laystall Racing Team, but it proved not to be a successful move and sadly Innes would never again drive for a top team. Retiring at the end of 1966, he continued to be associated with the sport in both organisational and journalistic capacities until his death from cancer in 1993.

Innes Ireland 'crosses up' at the Monte Carlo Station Hairpin. (LAT Photographic)

Lotus 18 – Colin Chapman's U-turn

who dominated. Typically taking little time in which to adjust to his new car, he took a full 4sec off the lap record to claim pole position 1sec quicker than Jack Brabham. Walker had only taken delivery of the car in the preceding week, leaving insufficient time to adapt the chassis to take his preferred Colotti transmission – that would have necessitated relocating the rear brakes outboard. In anticipation of this modification, the car had been fitted with larger section rear suspension radius rods. Moss just had time for a quick shakedown run at Goodwood, where, despite blustery conditions, he recorded a lap time 0.3sec quicker than he had managed in his Cooper on Easter Monday.

Team Lotus and Innes Ireland, by comparison, were struggling. In a demonstration of 1960s camaraderie, Stirling sportingly offered to lead Ireland (371) around the track in the Saturday afternoon session, pointing out the correct lines and braking points etc. Innes proved a quick learner, clocking up a 1min 38.2sec time for seventh on the grid. Stacey (370) was 0.7sec slower in 13th with Surtees (373), on his Grand Prix debut, a further 0.1sec back in 15th after gear selection problems.

At the start on an untypically dull Monte Carlo afternoon, Jo Bonnier's BRM shot through from the second row to lead the pack into the Gasworks hairpin and complete the lap closely followed by Brabham and Moss. These three drivers would dominate the first half of the race, with Moss taking second on lap 5 – content to sit on Bonnier's tail and allow him to set the pace despite the Swede's attempts to wave him through. With pressure from Brabham et al

Stirling Moss rounds the Gasworks Hairpin, on his way to his first Grand Prix win with the brand new Rob Walker Lotus (376). (LAT Photographic)

4: 1960 Formula 1 Season – Great Expectations

Chris Bristow (Yeoman Credit Cooper) and Graham Hill (BRM) follow Innes Ireland down the hill from the Station Hairpin. (LAT Photographic)

Lotus 18 – Colin Chapman's U-turn

29 May 1960: Moss acknowledges the chequered flag to win the 1960 Monaco Grand Prix. To the right is Innes Ireland's abandoned (371). (Sutton Images)

building up behind him, Moss finally nipped past Bonnier on lap 17 and began pulling away. By lap 20, he had a 2.7sec lead over Brabham, who had also passed Bonnier. At this point, Ireland was down in eighth, whilst Surtees had retired with a jammed gear selector. Stacey was shortly to clout a kerb when his front engine mountings failed, allowing the engine to tilt forward and jam the throttle open.

Around lap 28, it began to rain, making the circuit extremely slippery and persuading Moss to ease his pace with a 6sec margin over Brabham. Brabham judged it was safe to close and relieve Moss of the lead on lap 34, although it was now raining quite hard. Around lap 38, the sun re-appeared, but the road remained slippery, catching out Brabham who ended his race against the wall at Ste Devote with a bent Cooper chassis. The rain

4: 1960 Formula 1 Season – Great Expectations

Colin Chapman was one of the first to congratulate Stirling on scoring the first Grand Prix victory for the Lotus marque. Yet it had not been achieved by Team Lotus, but courtesy of private entrant Rob Walker, providing Chapman with food for thought. None of the Team entries had lasted the distance, displaying a degree of unreliability reminiscent of previous years. Even Moss had handled his Lotus aware of its potential fragility, coaxing the Lotus 'queerbox' to hold together over this punishing 100-lap, multiple gear-changing race. Post-race examination revealed that the front engine mountings had failed during the afternoon, leaving the engine held in place only by a water pipe and the rear suspension radius arms. It would have been quite possible for the car to fall apart.

Grote Prijs van Nederland, Zandvoort, 6 June 1960

There were only five short days before the first practice session at Zandvoort on Whit Monday, most teams opting to travel direct to Holland. Team Lotus remained in Monaco to rebuild Surtees' gearbox, install new engine mounts on Stacey's car and straighten out Ireland's chassis from the after effects of clouting a curb. Once again, four Lotus 18s were entered: the Walker car plus three from Team Lotus. John Surtees was not present due to motorcycling commitments on the Isle of Man, a young Scotsman by the name of Clark taking his place in chassis 373.

Jim Clark had shown considerable talent in a range of cars of various engine capacities in British club racing, but had no experience in single-seaters. Nevertheless, that talent earned him test sessions with both Aston Martin and Team Lotus. Clark found the front-engined Aston big and clumsy compared to the small and exquisitely balanced Formula Junior Lotus 18 that held the road so tenaciously that it seemed to be 'glued to the road,' a phrase often used by drivers experiencing the Lotus 18 for the first time. With only the offer of a retainer from Astons, he chose a place in Colin Chapman's Formula Junior team, a category he quickly came to dominate. Chapman lost no time in lining him up for promotion to the Formula 2 team, whilst his debut with the Grand Prix team had been delayed only by the unexpected availability of John Surtees.

Stirling Moss predictably set the pace, the Walker Lotus 18 continuing to display its impressive form, 0.9sec faster than Jack Brabham's Cooper around the sand dune-lined circuit. On Sunday, Moss and Brabham swapped fastest times until the Lotus clinched pole position with a 1min 33.2sec lap, a comfortable

Colin Chapman was one of the first to congratulate Stirling on scoring the first Grand Prix victory for the Lotus marque. (Sutton Images)

finally stopped on lap 46 and, by lap 50, Moss had a comfortable 13.6sec lead over Bonnier. Ireland had been suffering a persistent misfire, and his engine suddenly expired completely on the hill up to the Casino. Unaware that his magneto earthing wire had worn through and was shorting on the rev counter drive, he chose to push the car all the way around the circuit back to the pits. He eventually crossed the finish line totally exhausted, yet to no avail, as he was unclassified having completed only 56 laps.

On lap 60, Moss' Climax engine suddenly went onto three cylinders – was this the end of another superlative drive? He swept into the pits, where a sparkplug lead was quickly found to have come adrift, and he rejoined in second place, his 20sec lead now a 10sec deficit. He quickly caught Bonnier and regained the lead on lap 67, the BRM suffering a split rear suspension upright a few laps later. Moss continued on his way, completing the remaining 33 laps without further incident to record an immaculate win by a margin of 52sec over Bruce McLaren's Cooper.

Lotus 18 | 47

Ferodo dominated the Formula 1 brake pad market. (Author)

Jim Clark (373) tries the outside line around Tony Brooks (Yeoman Credit Cooper) during the early laps at Zandvoort. Maurice Trintignant (Cooper) and Wolfgang von Trips (Ferrari) follow. (LAT Photographic)

0.2sec quicker than the Australian. Team Lotus performed more in keeping with its performances at Goodwood and Silverstone, Ireland joining the front row 0.7sec slower than Moss, with Stacey 2.4sec down in seventh, and Clark a further 0.9sec away in eleventh.

Brabham took the initiative from the fall of the flag, closely followed by Moss, Ireland and Stacey, the latter making a superlative start from the third row. Moss had decided to bide his time and remain in second, confident that he could find a way past Brabham when he was ready. Everything suddenly changed on lap 17, when the Cooper's rear wheel dislodged a piece of granite curbing and pitched it at the Lotus, damaging the offside front wheel rim and deflating the tyre. Moss limped back to the pits where he was stationary for 2min 51sec as the Walker mechanics struggled with the six wheel nuts, having first had to borrow a spare wheel from Team Lotus. He finally rejoined in 12th, more than a lap and a half in arrears. Brabham was now 25sec ahead of the two works Lotuses of Ireland and Stacey, who were engaged in their own private duel. Jim Clark had worked up the order to fifth, giving Graham Hill's BRM a hard time before the Lotus' final drive failed on lap 42.

Moss settled into one of the come-back drives he relished, charging up the order to reach eighth place by lap 41, consistently lowering the lap record on his way. Stacey retired on lap 58 with another Lotus final drive failure, by which time Moss was fourth, 46sec behind Hill's BRM. All attention now focused on Moss' efforts to reduce the deficit, lap by lap. In the process, he caught and passed leader Brabham to unlap himself, but failed to catch the BRM by just 1.1sec, having established yet another new circuit record on the final lap. Brabham cruised, unchallenged, to his first Grand Prix victory of the year, 24sec ahead of Ireland. The race had morally belonged to Moss, who had, once again, underlined the performance potential of the Lotus 18.

4: 1960 Formula 1 Season – Great Expectations

Innes Ireland (371) leads Alan Stacey (370) during their private duel at Zandvoort. (LAT Photographic)

Grand Prix de Belgique, Spa-Francorchamps, 19 June 1960

Less than two weeks later, the Team 18s were loaded up to head for Spa. Many teams used converted coaches as transporters – not so Team Lotus: it built its own, based on a Ford 1500cwt van and known as 'PMT' after its registration number '903 PMT.' Powered by a Ford Zephyr engine with an Alvis gearbox, the chassis had been stretched by 5ft to provide a platform to carry a single car (Stacey's on this occasion), with storage below for spares. The cabin took the driver and three passengers. The 18s of Clark and Ireland were towed on a double-deck four-wheel trailer, a combination that proved somewhat unreliable, under-powered and over-loaded – especially when faced with ascending any inclines en route. A secondary transporter, when necessary, comprised a Thames Trader flatbed truck, incorporating a tubular steel superstructure converting it into a two-tier three car transporter.

The World Championship was returning to the super-fast, demanding Spa circuit for the first time since 1958, when Mike Hawthorn had set the fastest lap in 3min 57.1sec (132.3mph). Two years' developments in tyre technology, roadholding and engine performance was expected to reduce this time significantly – but not by the 7sec achieved by Jack Brabham during the first practice session on Friday afternoon. Stirling Moss was third fastest at the end of the day 2.6sec slower, his Lotus sporting trunking along the left side of the bodywork to duct cool air from the nose to the carburettors. Ireland did a lap 5.4sec slower than Brabham, despite not getting maximum revs on the straight, and before clutch slip intervened, whilst Stacey had a bolt shear in the steering. Jim Clark was driving the third Team Lotus entry once again.

Saturday afternoon was so hot that the road surface began to melt at La Source hairpin. With the session less than an hour old, the circuit fell silent as news began to filter through that Stirling Moss had crashed heavily. On the exit from Burnenville corner, taken at around 140mph in one long sweeping 150° curve, the left rear stub axle on the Lotus 18 had broken and shed the wheel. The car spun, hit the bank on the outside of the corner, threw Moss out and bounced across the road, coming to rest on the opposite verge. Moss was taken to hospital in Malmédy where he was found to have crushed three spinal vertebrae, broken both legs and his nose.

Whilst Moss was being recovered, it was realised that Michael Taylor, having his second outing in the Taylor & Crawley 18, had gone missing. His Lotus had plunged off the circuit out of sight into trees on the uphill return leg of the circuit at La Carrière after a steering failure. He was lucky to get away with a broken collar bone, ribs and a neck injury. He would recover fully, but not race again, successfully suing Lotus for undisclosed damages, as the accident had been caused by the failure of a faulty weld in the steering column.

It was over an hour and a quarter before practice resumed, Team Lotus taking no further part in proceedings, the three cars wheeled away to have their rear hubs examined. Ireland remembered that: "The results were just terrifying … one of Stacey's was cracked halfway round the hub and mine was all but sheared off!" Chapman put the problem down to a manufacturing fault, and replacement components were flown out from England and fitted to all three cars that evening. The strength of the hubs was always going to be tested to the limit by Moss simply because he drove so much faster than anyone else, thereby putting much more loading through them.

This failure re-opened the debate as to whether Colin Chapman sacrificed strength and safety in the relentless pursuit of lightness – if a component broke it was deemed to be too light, if it did not

Lotus 18 – Colin Chapman's U-turn

Alan Stacey (370) crests the hill above Eau Rouge during the tragic Belgian Grand Prix at Spa. (LAT Photographic)

it was too heavy. The cars were obviously built down to a specific weight, but as a result needed a lot more maintenance, such as chassis crack-testing, than a car with no such limitations. There was a theory that, in a perfect scenario, a racing car should be built to last only the duration of a race, having crossed the finish line it should fall to pieces. Unfortunately, Lotus had gained a reputation for not actually reaching the finish line.

The Team Lotus drivers did not start the race filled with great confidence following the practice failures. Ireland lined up on the third row of the grid in seventh, with Clark a further 2sec slower ninth and Stacey at the back 16th. The sun shone on a late, rather hurried start, the flag falling despite the presence of Lotus mechanics on the grid trying to start Clark's stalled engine. Ireland moved up into second behind Brabham on lap 2, only to drop out of contention within a couple more laps, with a recurrence of a practice clutch problem, leaving Phil Hill (Ferrari) to take up the chase of the Cooper. He rejoined after a pit stop down in 13th, but had pulled back up to tenth by lap 10, passing his team-mates who had started more gingerly. Clark tucked in behind him, whilst Stacey was happy to maintain his own pace. After two more pit stops, Innes spun

4: 1960 Formula 1 Season – Great Expectations

violently before Blanchimont on lap 13. Attempting to regain the circuit, he overdid it and lost control once more, this time diving off the road and bending the chassis against an embankment to end his afternoon. Clark's engine had not been running cleanly and he pitted on the following lap to clear a blocked carburettor jet, continuing without losing tenth, but falling a lap down on leader Brabham. He would eventually inherit fifth place to score his first Championship points, two laps behind by the finish.

Alan Stacey had taken Clark on lap 13 and worked his way steadily up the order to sixth by lap 20, as those ahead dropped out with mechanical problems. Then, on lap 24, he was apparently struck in the face by a bird and lost control of his Lotus, exiting the fast Malmédy curve. The car ran into the bank on the outside of the circuit, somersaulted across the road and plunged down an embankment bursting into flames. The unfortunate Stacey was flung out and killed instantly. Only five laps earlier, the promising Briton Chris Bristow had also been killed, after losing control of his Yeoman Credit Cooper.

The race continued unaware of these fatalities, Jack Brabham having led from start to finish, with Bruce McLaren second to complete a 1-2 for the Cooper team. Brabham's race speed of 133.63 mph made it the fastest race ever run at Spa. Lap times were calculated only to the nearest tenth of a second, allowing the fastest lap to be shared by Brabham, Phil Hill and Innes Ireland, with a time of 3min 51.9sec – over 6sec quicker than the 1958 lap record.

Team Lotus returned home somewhat subdued by the tragic death of Alan Stacey and the accidents to Stirling Moss and Michael Taylor. Moss' injuries were far more serious than had

ALAN STACEY
(b 29 August 1933, d 19 June 1960)

Alan Stacey had given the Lotus 18 its racing debut, albeit the Formula Junior version, at the 1959 Boxing Day Brands Hatch meeting. It was not generally realised that this popular, swarthy-complexioned Essex boy had an artificial limb, his right leg having been amputated below the knee following a childhood motorcycle accident. Despite what to some might have been a disability, Alan developed his own racing technique that involved a motorcycle twist grip throttle on the gearlever of his cars to overcome his inability to heel and toe. He made his name driving Lotus sports racing cars, notably the Eleven, prepared by veteran mechanic Bill Basson who only had one hand – a unique combination of driver and mechanic. His performances caught the eye of Colin Chapman, who invited him to join Team Lotus.

He made his Grand Prix debut in a one-off outing in the 1958 British Grand Prix in a Lotus 16, driving the unreliable car twice more in 1959, before assuming a more permanent role as number two to Innes Ireland for 1960. This coincided with the arrival of the rear-engined Lotus 18 into which he settled with ease. He realised that his place in Team Lotus was under threat, however, as John Surtees had been engaged to drive when his motorcycle commitments allowed.

Nevertheless, he drove the Lotus 18 sensibly and intelligently to hold third place in the Dutch Grand Prix before transmission failure, and was running steadily and consistently in the Belgian Grand Prix at Spa. With only 12 laps to complete, this quiet, popular and unassuming young man lost his life in an accident not of his making. Tragic though it was, he died doing something that he really enjoyed.

Alan Stacey with Colin Chapman in the pits at Zandvoort. (LAT Photographic)

at first been believed, and he would be out of racing for some months. Both drivers were flown back to Britain, where Moss was admitted to St Thomas's hospital. Although there was no public outcry over the deaths and injuries, it did focus attention on the speeds attained at Spa and the doubtful honour of possessing the fastest circuit in Europe. Phil Hill would comment: "back then safety was literally never discussed: for one thing there was a feeling that racing had never been safe – and never could be – and for another it was something you didn't really want to talk about, anyway, because if you did someone would start legislating, and then you wouldn't have your precious racing anymore."

Grand Prix de l'Automobile Club de France, Reims, 3 July 1960

Ferrari looked to the power advantage and outright speed of the front-engined Dino for a win on the long fast straights of Reims, a race it had dominated in both 1958 and 1959. Any such notions were immediately dispelled by Jack Brabham, using the better roadholding and lower frontal area of the latest rear-engined Cooper to advantage. He reeled off a succession of quick laps in the first practice session, culminating in a 2min 16.8sec for pole position, 2.4sec quicker than in 1959 and 5.8sec better than the lap record set that year by Stirling Moss in a BRM. Phil Hill was the closest challenger, his Ferrari 1.4sec slower.

Innes Ireland adjusts the mirror on '371' in the pits at Reims. Note the trunking feeding cool air from the nose to the carburettors, and the smaller, high-penetration radiator inlet to improve top speed. (Ferret Fotographics)

In the absence of Moss and the Walker team, there were just three Lotus 18s present, all entered by Team Lotus and all to be driven by Scotsmen, a source of much entertainment amongst their rivals. Following the loss of Alan Stacey, the show had to go on and Ron Flockhart, often seen in a BRM, was offered a one-off drive as a back-up to Innes Ireland and Jim Clark.

Flockhart's car was a brand new chassis (374), the last to be built by Team Lotus. In this chassis, the normally upright engine had been canted over to the right by some 17½° to bring the Weber carburettor inlets within the bodywork, out of turbulent air ahead of the left rear wheel. Team Lotus was being dogged by poor carburetion – Cooper had no such problems with its Climax engines. This development proved inconclusive, as no other chassis would be produced or modified in this way, although it would be adopted in 1961 for the Lotus 21.

Ireland's car (371) was fitted with trunking along its left flank to duct cool air from the nose to the carburettors, a tweak seen on the Walker car at Spa. All three 18s had longer, tapering nose cones with smaller, 'high penetration' radiator inlets to improve top speed along the long Reims straights. Significantly, the Cooper had the edge over the 18 in straightline speed, Ireland having found he lost 800rpm running in clean air on the flat out sections at Spa. Superior roadholding around and away from corners was insufficient to make up the difference, leaving Ireland quickest Lotus 18 driver yet only fourth on the grid, 1.7sec away from pole, despite improving his time by 1sec in the final session. Clark was 1.8sec slower in 12th, unspectacular yet competent, whilst Flockhart should have been 14th, but was classified eighth in error, having been credited with a time 3.9sec quicker than he actually achieved due to a mix up in race numbers.

The weather throughout practice had been untypically cool and cloudy, with hot coffee the order of the day rather than the traditional chilled champagne. Sunday was dull but dry, rather a relief to the drivers who would not have to put up with stifling cockpit temperatures, nor face the hazard of the road surface breaking up in the heat, as was the norm. Starter 'Toto' Roche caused chaos by dropping the flag 2sec after the 30sec board had been displayed. Nevertheless, the majority of the field roared away to complete the first lap, led by Brabham, shadowed by the Ferraris of Phil Hill and Wolfgang von Trips. Brabham and Hill dominated the first half of the race, swapping the lead lap after lap, until Hill's final drive failed at the end of lap 28 and then von Trips suffered a similar failure two laps later.

Meanwhile Ireland was engaged in an intense battle with Jo Bonnier over fourth, until the BRM dropped back with sagging oil pressure on lap 12. The Yeoman Credit Cooper of Gendebien and McLaren's works version now caught Ireland and the trio disputed every inch of road over the next 22 laps, the cars running nose to tail or side by side all around the circuit, in what became a battle for second place after the retirement of the Ferraris. Unfortunately Ireland was forced into the pits on lap 34, his left front wheel at an odd angle after the suspension ball joint failed allowing the anti-roll bar to come adrift. Repairs cost him four laps, but he resumed to finish a disappointing seventh. Clark had pulled up from 15th at the start to fifth by lap 35, with Flockhart steadily catching up in the latter half of the race, as he acclimatised to the Lotus and just failing to relieve Clark of the position as they crossed the finish line. Brabham won again, leading a Cooper 1-2-3-4, Team Lotus left with a disappointing 5-6-7.

RAC British Grand Prix, Silverstone, 16 July 1960

Two weeks later, the Grand Prix circus returned to the flat former WWII bomber airbase. Jack Brabham set the pace in practice,

Olivier Gendebien (Yeoman Credit Cooper) has the advantage over Innes Ireland (371) away from Thillois, during their intense mid-race duel at Reims. (LAT Photographic)

Lotus 18 – Colin Chapman's U-turn

as had become the norm, with a lap in 1min 34.6sec – 0.4sec outside the existing lap record. None of the front runners matched the times they set in May at the International Trophy. Team Lotus welcomed back John Surtees (373) for its customary three-car line up. He was plagued by a persistent misfire restricting him to 11th on the grid, found to be due to the plug leads chafing on the chassis. Ireland (371) retained the cool air ducting to the carburettors and the Reims nosecone, yet was once again unable to make the front row of the grid. Fifth fastest was his best, 1.6sec away from Brabham and 2sec slower than his May lap record. Clark was eighth quickest on 1min 37sec in the canted engine chassis (374) with Reims nosecone previously driven by Flockhart.

The sky was overcast, but with the promise of dry conditions, when no less a person than Stirling Moss dropped the Union flag to start the Grand Prix. Making his first outing from hospital since his accident at Spa just four weeks previously, he received a tremendous welcome as he stepped unaided from the BP helicopter, showing astonishing signs of progress on the road to recovery from his injuries.

The Grand Prix would be dominated by Graham Hill (BRM), who was left on the grid with a stalled engine at the start. In an adrenalin-fuelled performance, he drove right through the field to take the lead from a powerless Jack Brabham on lap 55. With just 17 laps remaining, it all came to nought when the BRM's three-point braking system typically faltered and the car spun on to the grass verge, damaging its right rear suspension against the earth bank at Copse corner.

Brabham had led the field away from the start, ahead of Bonnier, Ireland, McLaren, Surtees and Clark. By lap 20, Ireland was second, 5sec in arrears, with Clark and Surtees running

Jim Clark (374) has temporarily nipped ahead of John Surtees (373) who will finish a splendid second in the British Grand Prix. (LAT Photographic)

4: 1960 Formula 1 Season – Great Expectations

together a further 8sec back, Team Lotus running 2-3-4 and in numerical order 7, 8, and 9. Surtees established himself behind Ireland, despite Clark occasionally nipping back ahead of him. Around lap 53, Ireland became aware of a problem with one of his rear hubs and slowed, dropping back behind his team-mates. On lap 58, the Team Lotus trio was split when Clark pitted with his front nearside wheel at an odd angle – another broken ball joint. Although repairs were effected, he rejoined at a reduced pace to finish 16th and last, having lost 7 laps. With the Graham Hill drama out of the way, Surtees finished almost unnoticed in second, 50sec down on Brabham after a smooth and unspectacular race to consolidate his Grand Prix credentials. Ireland was third, constantly looking over his shoulder at the offending rear hub, the Cooper and the two Lotuses the only cars to complete the distance.

A notable omission from the Formula 1 schedule this year was the German Grand Prix normally held at the Nürburgring, the Automobil Club von Deutschland having decided to downgrade it to a Formula 2 event (see Chapter 5). This released the August Bank Holiday weekend for Brands Hatch to hold its first Formula 1 race, the Silver City Trophy, on the recently extended 2.65-mile circuit. The majority of the Grand Prix teams took part, even Scuderia Ferrari despatching two cars to a rare mid-season non-Championship race. Ireland was recorded as driving chassis 371, the same chassis he had driven at the Nürburgring the previous day in Formula 2 form. Was this a case of chassis plate swapping? It is quite possible that Team Lotus drove back from Germany to Kent overnight, changed the engine and had the car ready for Innes to practice the next day, yet it seems more likely that 372 was pressed into service at Brands Hatch.

Jim Clark (374) showed his worth on a familiar track by claiming pole position 0.2sec quicker than Jack Brabham, with Innes Ireland in third and John Surtees (373) sixth. For eight laps, Clark put Brabham under some pressure, before dropping back and then stopping on lap 21 with gearbox failure, but having shared the fastest lap with the Australian. Surtees was an early caller at the pits with clutch slip, recovering to finish sixth despite a misfire. Ireland was in trouble early, retiring on lap 6 with low oil pressure.

Gran Premio de Portugal, Porto, 14 August 1960

It seemed as though nothing could halt the Brabham/Cooper steamroller and it came as something of a surprise, therefore, when his name was not at the top of the timesheets after practice. John Surtees (373) was the man of the moment, taking the cobbles and tramlines of the Porto road circuit in his stride to record a time nearly 7sec quicker than Mike Hawthorn's 1958 lap record. His Friday practice session was fraught with gear selector problems and he spent most of the session waiting around while the Lotus mechanics tried to locate the cause. Shortly before the end of the session, he went out, only to have the final drive pinion break up. It was only then discovered that errant pieces of the pinion had been jamming the selector mechanism all the time.

Having missed most of Friday practice, Surtees needed to find his way around the circuit and, on Saturday afternoon, he latched onto the back of Dan Gurney's BRM. Their lap times steadily came down as Gurney tried to shake off the Lotus, until it was realised that Surtees had recorded a 2min 25.56sec lap, 0.07sec quicker than Gurney and nearly 0.5sec quicker than Jack Brabham. Before Brabham or anyone else could think of responding, it began to rain, preventing any further fast laps yet safeguarding the Motorcycle Champion's first four-wheel pole position.

JOHN SURTEES ON THE LOTUS 18

John Surtees made nine starts in a Lotus 18, eight in Formula 1 and one in Formula 2. He has recounted: "I think the Formula 1 Lotus 18 was much more of a motorcyclist's car, less forgiving than the Coopers perhaps but extremely efficient at high limits. You had to be precise with that car. That was an important factor. You needed to be very correct and economical.

"Colin, above everything else, wanted to win but his budget in those early years would have meant cutting many corners, part of the reason for the cars at times being referred to as frail. The fact that it fell apart didn't seem to matter to him provided it had gone quickly before it did. He was a brilliant engineer when it came to creating the concept of a racing car. I've often said that the 18 was probably the most competitive car that I drove relative to the opposition – in any of my motor racing years. Having said that though, his budget, and consequently the number of experienced personnel and the quantity and quality of the parts that were available, left something to be desired in the early sixties."

Lotus 18 – Colin Chapman's U-turn

There were three other Lotus 18s present, Stirling Moss making a welcome return to the Grand Prix scene only eight weeks after his Spa accident. The extensively-damaged Walker 18 had been rebuilt around a new chassis by Alf Francis and his crew up at Cheshunt. Although retaining the original chassis number 376 (for Customs carnet purposes), it was actually chassis number 906, the '900' designation indicating a Lotus Components built chassis. Nevertheless, the opportunity had been taken to connect the front anti-roll bar to the lower wishbone via drop links, rather than to eye-bolts in the top wishbone pivots, thus avoiding the problem encountered at Reims and Silverstone on the Team cars. A Colotti type 21 5-speed transmission had been substituted for the Lotus 'queerbox,' requiring modifications to the rear bulkhead and relocation of the rear brakes outboard. The larger section rear suspension radius rods were retained. In the first practice session, Moss was second fastest but, despite improving by around 2sec in the second session, he was relegated to fourth on the grid, 0.23sec away from Surtees on pole.

Aside from the problems with Surtees' 'queerbox,' Team Lotus was initially in some disarray with wrong gear ratios, although this was relatively simple to rectify by removing the transmission end cover, sliding the gears out and sliding in a revised set. Experimentation with rear brake location saw Ireland's car (371) plumbed with both inboard and outboard rear discs, allowing

COLOTTI TRANSMISSIONS

The first Colotti transmission had been a commission from Stirling Moss and Alf Francis in late 1958, when seeking a more robust unit for the Rob Walker team Coopers. Valerio Colotti was well known to Moss and Francis as the former Maserati chassis and transmission engineer who had recently set up his own Studio Tecnica Meccanica (TecMec) in Modena. After a hesitant start, due to inaccurate gear cutting by a sub-contractor, the Colotti type 10 transmission and its successor, the type 21, proved their worth. Colotti and Francis had identified a niche market for 'off-the-shelf' transmission units and went into partnership, during 1960, to form Gears Speed Developments SpA (GSD) in Modena to market and produce Colotti's transmissions. Although officially GSD transmissions thereafter, they remained popularly known by the 'Colotti' name and would attract a wide clientele over the early 1960s.

The Colotti type 21 5-speed transmission. (Author)

Right-hand gearchange for the Colotti transmission. (Author)

4: 1960 Formula 1 Season – Great Expectations

the mechanics to switch from one system to the other at will. The normal inboard mounted discs on either side of the 'queerbox' were always vulnerable to gearbox transmitted heat and oil leaks, yet there was no serious move to adopt the outboard location. The cool air trunking to the carburettors had been deleted from this car. Innes came to a halt out on the circuit with a fuel system failure, but would set seventh fastest time, nearly 2sec slower than Surtees, yet 0.4sec quicker than Clark.

On Saturday, trying a different line to avoid tramlines, Clark lost control of his car (374), clouted a left-hand kerb with a rear wheel and was flicked across the road into strawbales, bending the chassis extensively. He took no further part in practice, as a major chassis straightening exercise began in a local garage. With encouragement from Colin Chapman, work continued through the night right up to Sunday lunch time, not an unusual scenario for the hard-worked Team Lotus mechanics. The repaired Lotus looked somewhat secondhand with its glass-fibre nose section bound up with masking tape, and Clark was given strict instructions to take it easy in case the car's handling had been compromised.

The race started at 4.00pm to avoid the heat of the day, yet it remained very hot. At the 30-second signal, Graham Hill started to creep forward from the second row between Gurney and Brabham, who responded by edging forward as well. Confused by this behaviour, the starter dropped the national flag prematurely and the whole field roared off into the first corner to complete the opening lap in the order Gurney, Brabham, Moss, Surtees and Ireland, all in a tight bunch. By lap 4, Gurney had built a 4sec lead over Moss and Surtees, Brabham having run up an escape road and lost six places. Gurney eased off on lap 10, suspecting an oil leak, allowing Surtees into the lead, with Moss on his tail. Ireland made the first of a number of pit stops with a continuation of the fuel feed problem encountered during practice – resolved only by rebuilding the fuel system to run off the scuttle tank alone. He rejoined and ran quite well, but was too far in arrears to make any difference.

Jim Clark's rather secondhand-looking Lotus (374) sits in the pits, prior to the start of the Portuguese Grand Prix. (Sutton Images)

Lotus 18 | 57

Lotus 18 – Colin Chapman's U-turn

John Surtees (373) follows Stirling Moss (376) at Porto between a solid stone wall and trees 'protected' by strawbales. (LAT Photographic)

4: 1960 Formula 1 Season – Great Expectations

Innes Ireland (371) traverses the cobbles and tram lines of central Porto on his way to a delayed sixth place finish. (LAT Photographic)

Surtees looked calm and relaxed despite the presence of Moss in his mirrors and continued with a comfortable lead of 10sec, until lap 19 saw him running alone as Moss headed for the pits with a misfire. The Walker 18 completed a further lap on three cylinders and returned to the pits, where all four plugs were changed, before rejoining in ninth, although the engine was still not running cleanly. On lap 33, Surtees' lead was 22sec over Brabham, who was not attempting to catch him, seemingly quite content in second. All was not well, however, as Surtees had had a problem almost since the beginning of the race with fuel leaking on to his feet from a split seam in the large tank above his legs. On lap 36, his foot slipped off the brake pedal in the twisty section of the circuit and in a moment he lost control and spun off into the strawbales. He restarted behind Brabham, unaware that his radiator had been damaged, until it blew out a shower of water and steam on the following lap and he abandoned the Lotus at the roadside. It had been a convincing demonstration of the capabilities of both Surtees and the Lotus 18 and unfortunate that the only reward for the afternoon's work was having set the fastest lap.

Jim Clark was going extremely well in his patched-up Lotus, steadily gaining places as others ran into trouble. By lap 37, he found himself running third, yet some way behind the two works Coopers now leading. Ireland had to make a fuel stop because of his reduced capacity, but continued to finish sixth, seven laps in arrears. Moss, his Climax engine at last running cleanly, had moved back up to fifth, until a front brake locked approaching the sharp left-hander at the top of the circuit, causing him to spin on his 51st lap and stall his engine in the escape road. Unable to restart, he waited until the race was over before rolling downhill against the flow of traffic to bump start the engine, but was disqualified for his trouble – precisely the charge he had helped Championship rival Mike Hawthorn to escape without penalty, at Porto in 1958.

The Coventry Climax-powered Cooper had won its fifth Grand Prix on the trot and the sixth of the season, to secure the World Constructors' Championship for the second successive year, a disappointing outcome for Team Lotus after showing so much promise at the beginning of the season. Officially, there remained two qualifying rounds yet to run, but the British teams declined to take part in the Italian Grand Prix, as it was to be held for the first time since 1956 on the combined Monza road circuit and banking. The British constructors, including Team Lotus, objected to the bumpy and uneven banked section, considering it unsuitable for modern Grand Prix racing and would agree to race only on the road circuit. The Automobile Club d'Italia refused to back down and the race went ahead, providing a popular win for Ferrari on its home ground against minimal opposition. Reports in continental journals concluded that British cars were too fragile to run at Monza, the whole affair creating a rather unfortunate situation.

The Lotus 18 underwent a revival in fortunes in mid-September, when Innes Ireland (372) won the non-Championship Lombank Trophy at Snetterton, a month after the Portuguese Grand Prix. The three Team Lotus entries of John Surtees, Jim Clark and Ireland shared the front row of the grid with two BRMs. Team Lotus led the first lap in line astern, Clark heading Ireland and Surtees. At one third distance, Clark missed his braking point before the Esses and took to the escape road, allowing Ireland to win the 100-mile race by a margin of 13sec in the first 1-2 finish for the Lotus 18. Surtees retired early with a rough engine.

Of considerable interest at Snetterton was the appearance of a Lotus 18 chassis entered by Tony Vandervell, the purchase of which Harry Mundy had reported in *The Autocar* on 27 May. The performance of the Lotus at Goodwood on Easter Monday and in the Silverstone International Trophy had finally convinced

Lotus 18 – Colin Chapman's U-turn

JOHN SURTEES

(b 11 February 1934)

John Surtees is widely remembered as the only man to win World Championships on both two and four wheels – and never has the transition between the two disciplines been made with such ease. Between 1956 and 1960, he was the outstanding rider of the day, winning seven World titles in the 350cc and 500cc classes for MV Augusta, the *tifosi* dubbing him 'Le Grande John' in honour of his successes. In March 1960, he made his four-wheel debut, finishing second to an upcoming Jim Clark in a Formula Junior race at Goodwood. He signed to drive for Tony Vandervell, but in the absence of a Vanwall, made his Formula 1 debut in a Lotus 18, in May 1960, and competed in Grands Prix for Team Lotus when motorcycle commitments allowed. He scored an impressive second place in the British Grand Prix, and claimed pole position for the Portuguese Grand Prix, setting fastest lap and dominating the race until spinning off.

Surtees was reluctant to accept an offer from Team Lotus for 1961, and chose, instead, a drive for the Reg Parnell-run Yeoman Credit/Bowmaker team to gain further experience. He turned down an offer from Ferrari for 1962, to remain with Parnell in what was effectively the works Lola team, enabling him to mould the team around his own ambitions. He accepted a renewed offer from Ferrari for 1963, and was able to galvanise the Scuderia both as a driver and a source of technical input to bring Ferrari technology on to a par with its British rivals. This paid off with his first Grand Prix win that season followed by the World Championship title in 1964. After an acrimonious split from Ferrari in mid-1966, he continued to chase his personal ambitions through drives with Cooper and Honda, before a disastrous season with BRM convinced him to go it alone and become a constructor in his own right. This proved tougher than anticipated, bringing only odd moments of success. He retired from driving during 1972, to continue running Team Surtees in Grand Prix racing until sponsorship dried up in 1978 and he withdrew from the sport a disillusioned man.

At his best, he was a pure racer. Not one to mince his words, he was a man who honoured his commitments and stuck to his principles.

John Surtees – future world champion. (Author)

Vandervell that he should abandon front-engined developments and pursue the rear-engined route. The powerful 4-cylinder Vanwall engine had been squeezed into an extensively-reworked engine bay of a new chassis (901). Panel beaters Williams & Pritchard made up a special alloy tail cowling and the car ran on Vanwall alloy wheels. The engine stood some 2in taller than the Climax equivalent, and the additional circa 70lbs (24%) in engine weight would doubtless have upset the balance of the car. Tony Brooks practised the Lotus-Vanwall at Snetterton until the engine stretched its valves and consequently failed to start. Brooks had found it satisfactory and reasonably quick, despite a need for further testing and development. Unfortunately, this would fail to materialise and the car would never be seen again.

Guglielmo 'Mimo' Dei's wellknown Modena-based Scuderia Centro Sud, normally the entrant of Maseratis, appeared with a further engine variation for the non-Championship Oulton Park Gold Cup a week later. Another new chassis (902) had been fitted with a 4-cylinder Maserati 250S engine, derived from the 2-litre engine powering the Maserati 200S sports cars that had seen action in the Centro Sud Cooper T51 chassis during 1959. A power output of only 200-215bhp, allied to an inferior torque curve, ensured that it had never offered any challenge to Coventry Climax. The Centro

60 | Lotus 18

Sud entries missed practice (it had also entered two Cooper-Maseratis), as their transporter had crashed en route in Germany, but were allowed to start from the back of the grid. Driven by Ian Burgess, the Lotus-Maserati would last only 16 laps at the tail of the field, before succumbing to suspension failure.

Team Lotus faced a more representative Formula 1 entry for the Oulton Park Gold Cup, including Stirling Moss in the Rob Walker chassis (numbered 906 rather than 376 on this occasion). Moss and Clark shared the front row of the grid ahead of Brabham and Hill, with Ireland and Surtees on the second row. Ireland took an early lead from Brabham, Clark and Moss who had got away badly. Clark passed Brabham into second on lap 5 and closed on his team-mate. On lap 15, Ireland lapped the JBW of Brian Naylor who pulled across in front of Clark, unaware that he was following. Clark remonstrated angrily with Naylor after the resulting collision that eliminated both cars. On the following lap, Ireland went straight on at Cascades and dropped down to third, but within three laps had dramatically swept past both Moss and Brabham to regain the lead. Unfortunately, only 10 laps later, he lost the lead permanently with transmission failure. Meanwhile, Moss had managed to pass Brabham and, following Ireland's demise, pulled out a 21sec advantage in what had now become a procession. Surtees was out after only a single lap with fuel pump failure.

On 2 November, Team Lotus undertook a test session at Brands Hatch, running chassis 374 with anti-dive suspension settings front and rear. Five days later, a further test was undertaken at Silverstone with anti-dive on the front suspension only. These experiments appear to have proved inconclusive, as they were not pursued further.

On the way to the United States Grand Prix, Stirling Moss stopped off in upstate New York on 9 October for the extremely lucrative 230-mile Watkins Glen Formule Libre 'Grand Prix.' This attracted a mixture of Formula 1 cars, sports car and local built 'specials' and provided Moss and the Rob Walker Lotus 18 with another win by a margin of 6.5sec over Jack Brabham's Cooper.

United States Grand Prix, Riverside, 20 November 1960

This was the final Grand Prix to be run under the 2½-litre regulations and the final round of the 1960 World Championships, although both had already been decided of course. This Grand Prix had proved less than a success when held at Sebring in 1959 and had been switched to Riverside International Raceway in California for this year. Despite perfect weather conditions, the race failed to

20 November 1960: Stirling Moss (373) crests a rise at Riverside on the way to scoring the second Grand Prix win for Lotus. (LAT Photographic)

attract more than a small number of paying spectators due to an amazing reluctance by the circuit owners to pursue local publicity. It would not visit Riverside again.

The Lotus 18s present included the Rob Walker car (376) plus a recently acquired spare (912) for Moss, and the three regular chassis from Team Lotus, together with a new chassis (907), entered and driven by the talented Texan Jim Hall. Clark's car (371) had outboard rear disc brakes, whilst the Ireland (372) and Surtees (373) cars retained the inboard installation. Stirling Moss resumed his position as pacesetter, by lapping over 5.5sec quicker than the existing (sports car) lap record and, by the end of practice, had annexed pole position with a 1min 54.4sec – 0.6sec quicker than Brabham. Clark, Surtees and Ireland were 5-6-7 on the grid, between 1.2 and 2.6sec slower than Moss. Hall qualified well in 12th as fastest local driver and only 1.2sec slower than Innes Ireland.

Jim Hall's purchase of a Lotus 18 reflected the often offhand dealings and sharp practices Colin Chapman sometimes employed, here with a wealthy and potentially valuable customer.

Lotus 18 – Colin Chapman's U-turn

RIVERSIDE INTERNATIONAL RACEWAY

Set in the California desert near the San Bernardino Mountains, 60 miles east of Los Angeles, Riverside was a 3.275-mile artificial road course that held its first race on 22 September 1957. It became well known for the prestigious annual Los Angeles Times sports car Grand Prix.

The track featured a demanding uphill esses section after the start and a 1.1-mile long downhill straight, followed by a relatively slow, brake testing long right-hand 180° turn, prior to the pit straight. A low earth bank separated the pits from the track and many of the corners were disconcertingly marked out by upright car tyres set into the sandy soil. The weather was often hot, with almost gale force gusts of wind blowing sand across the track making it slippery, reducing visibility and getting in everything.

Riverside will not be remembered for much in Formula 1 terms – other than for another win for Stirling Moss, the second Grand Prix win for Lotus, a 1-2 finish and the 2½-litre Formula 1 finale. Formula 1 would never return to Riverside. Over subsequent years, the circuit would continue to host sports car races, rounds of the CanAm series, plus Indy Car, NASCAR, TransAm and IMSA and SCCA races, until the circuit closed in 1989 and the track was torn up to make way for a shopping mall.

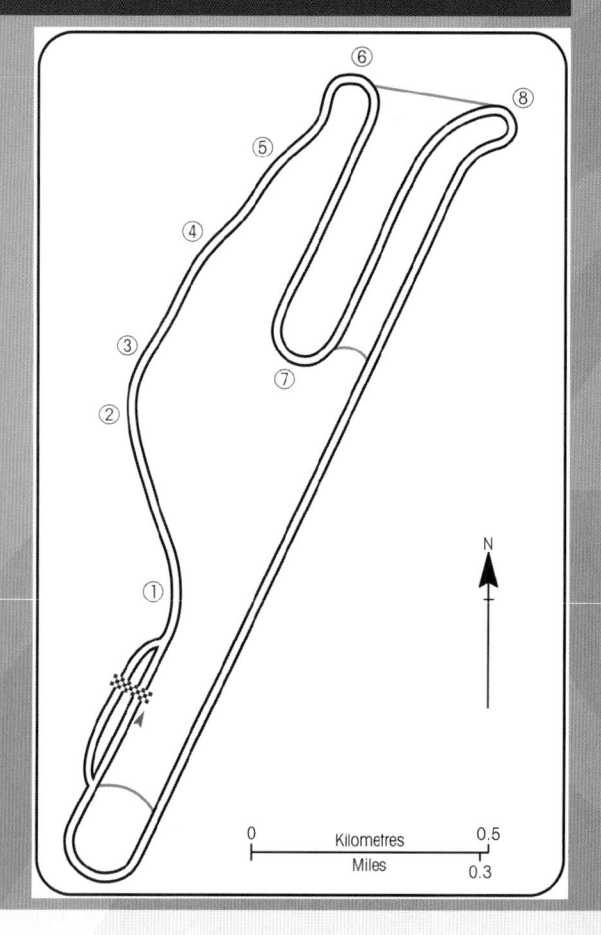

Hall had ordered an 18 with a 2½-litre Coventry Climax engine at an agreed price, only to discover it shipped to him with a 2-litre engine at a completely different price. Using his resourcefulness, Hall swapped the 2-litre engine for a 2½-litre Climax engine taken from a Cooper Monaco sports car that he subsequently sold on with the 2-litre engine.

Dead on 2.00pm the flag fell and Brabham shot away into the lead, hotly pursued by Moss, with Ireland third. Clark and Surtees tangled on lap 3, when the former motorcycle champion spun and took his team-mate with him. Surtees retired on the spot, but Clark made it to the pits for repairs, then stopped a second time with a leaking water pump that saw him trail home unclassified having completed 61 of the 75 lap distance. On lap 5, Brabham made the first of two pit stops with his car apparently on fire, to rejoin in 18th and begin to work his way back up the order.

Moss led Bonnier's BRM by 14sec at one third distance (25 laps) as the race settled into a pattern, the only interest concentrating on Brabham's hard driving back up the order to fourth. Around lap 50, Ireland was visibly gaining on Bonnier as the BRM began to lose power due to a broken valve spring and he swept past on lap 60. Moss won the second Grand Prix of the season for the Lotus 18, 38sec clear of Ireland, making it a Lotus 1-2. Jim Hall, who would become better known for his Chaparral sports cars in a few years, drove an extremely impressive race, only to be cheated out of fifth place by transmission failure three laps from the end.

A second Grand Prix win for Lotus: yet, frustratingly for Colin Chapman, it had been courtesy of Moss and Rob Walker once again, rather than Team Lotus. At the post-race celebrations, the organisers presented Stirling with a cake baked in the shape of a racing car. Recalling his Belgian accident, Stirling carefully sliced

4: 1960 Formula 1 Season – Great Expectations

Jim Clark (371) in the Riverside pits investigating a leaking water pump. (LAT Photographic)

Lotus 18 | 63

Lotus 18 – Colin Chapman's U-turn

Jim Hall (907) would have finished as high as fifth but for transmission failure three laps from the end of the United States Grand Prix. (LAT Photographic)

rate compared to an enviable 86% for Cooper. As Team Lotus' fortunes began to decline, so Stirling Moss stepped into the breach to score the marque's first Grand Prix win in the privately-entered Rob Walker Lotus 18. Had he not been seriously injured at Spa, it is certain that Stirling would have consistently challenged Cooper and prevented it from gaining five consecutive Grand Prix wins to claim a second successive Constructors' Championship.

Any likely challenge to either Cooper or Lotus from the other rear-engined debutant, the BRM P48, failed to materialise. Save for Graham Hill's adrenalin-fuelled performance at Silverstone, the BRM chassis proved lacking, its handling deficient, and the engine beset by valve gear failures. Ferrari, by contrast, retained the classic front-engined layout and even lost its edge in straight line speed over Cooper on the fast Spa and Reims circuits.

Lotus 18 Performance Summary – 1960

1960 Season	Starts	Finishes	1st	2nd	3rd	4th	5th	6th	PP	FL
Grands Prix	27	16	2	3	2	1	2	3	4	3
Other Formula 1	17	7	4	1	–	1	–	1	2	4
Total	44	23	6	4	2	2	2	4	6	7

off the left rear wheel and presented it to Chapman who, it seems, was not amused.

With another hectic season at an end, Colin Chapman's father Stanley, for so long the hard-working team manager for Team Lotus, decided it was time to retire to Devon, away from the frenzied life of motor racing. His place would eventually be filled by Andrew Ferguson, previously with Cooper and currently due to fill a similar role with Lucky Casner's Camoradi Formula 1 team, until it folded in mid-1961.

SUMMARY

The 2½-litre Formula 1 era drew to a close with Lotus having enjoyed a highly successful Grand Prix season compared to the failures of the Lotus 16, in 1958 and 1959. Two Grand Prix wins, three seconds and two thirds, plus six other placings put the marque into second place in the Constructors' Championship behind Cooper. In addition, there were four wins from five non-Championship Formula 1 races.

Yet the season had promised so much more after Innes Ireland's outstanding wins in the early non-Championship races had set new performance standards. Once the Grand Prix season was underway, however, the Lotus 18 began to experience reliability issues and also lacked the pace to make the front row of the grid. Over the season, the Lotus achieved a 59% finishing

Chassis Summary

Seven Lotus 18 chassis built by Team Lotus appeared in one or more Formula 1 events or Grands Prix during 1960, as follows:

369	Team Lotus – prototype chassis raced in Argentina. Acquired by Taylor & Crawley and written-off in Mike Taylor's accident at Spa.
370	Team Lotus – written-off in Alan Stacey's fatal accident at Spa.
371	Team Lotus – Innes Ireland's winner at Goodwood and the Silverstone International Trophy.
372	Team Lotus – mainly driven by Innes Ireland and Jim Clark.
373	Team Lotus – mainly driven by John Surtees.
374	Team Lotus – canted engine chassis mainly driven by Jim Clark.
376	RRC Walker Racing Team for Stirling Moss to win Monaco GP. Extensively damaged in practice accident at Spa. Rebuilt around new chassis (possibly 906). Winner of US GP.

Five production chassis built by Lotus Components for customer sale appeared, commencing from 901:

901	Vandervell Products Ltd. – modified to take Vanwall V254 4-cylinder engine.
902	Scuderia Centro Sud – fitted with 4-cylinder Maserati 250S engine.
906	RRC Walker Racing Team for Stirling Moss. Possibly rebuilt '376' – see above.
907	Jim Hall of Midland, Texas for US GP.
912	RRC Walker Racing Team for Stirling Moss. Not raced in 1960, practice only at US GP.

4: 1960 Formula 1 Season – Great Expectations

LOTUS 18 – Formula 1 Racing Record – 1960

Position	Driver	Entrant	Chassis	Engine	No	Grid	Comments
GRAN PREMIO de la REPUBLICA ARGENTINA, Buenos Aires, (RA), 6.2.60, 194.46 miles (312.886km)							
6th	Innes Ireland	Team Lotus	369	2.5 Climax FPF 4IL	20	Q2	
Glover Trophy, Goodwood (GB), 18.4.60, 100.80 miles (162.187km)							
1st	Innes Ireland	Team Lotus	371	2.5 Climax FPF 4IL	14	Q4	
	Alan Stacey	Team Lotus	369	2.5 Climax FPF 4IL	12	Q11	Engine lap 15/42
International Trophy, Silverstone (GB), 14.5.60, 146.35 miles (235.477km)							
1st	Innes Ireland	Team Lotus	371	2.5 Climax FPF 4IL	10	Q11	FL
4th	Alan Stacey	Team Lotus	370	2.5 Climax FPF 4IL	11	Q9	
	Mike Taylor	Taylor & Crawley Ltd	369	2.5 Climax FPF 4IL	19	Q24	N/C 32 laps/50
	John Surtees	Team Lotus	373	2.5 Climax FPF 4IL	12	Q6	Oil leak lap 9/50
GRAND PRIX de MONACO, Monte Carlo (MC), 29.5.60, 195.41 miles (314.147km)							
1st	Stirling Moss	RRC Walker Racing Team	376	2.5 Climax FPF 4IL	28	Q1	
	Innes Ireland	Team Lotus	371	2.5 Climax FPF 4IL	22	Q7	Misfire 56 laps/100
	Alan Stacey	Team Lotus	370	2.5 Climax FPF 4IL	24	Q13	Chassis lap 23/100
	John Surtees	Team Lotus	373	2.5 Climax FPF 4IL	26	Q15	Gearbox lap 18/100
GROTE PRIJS van NEDERLAND, Zandvoort (NL), 6.6.60, 195.41 miles (314.417km)							
2nd	Innes Ireland	Team Lotus	371	2.5 Climax FPF 4IL	4	Q3	
4th	Stirling Moss	RRC Walker Racing Team	376	2.5 Climax FPF 4IL	7	Q1	FL
	Alan Stacey	Team Lotus	370	2.5 Climax FPF 4IL	5	Q8	Final drive lap 57/75
	Jim Clark	Team Lotus	373	2.5 Climax FPF 4IL	6	Q11	Final drive lap 42/75
GRAND PRIX de BELGIQUE, Spa (B), 19.6.60, 315.41 miles (507.495km)							
5th	Jim Clark	Team Lotus	373	2.5 Climax FPF 4IL	18	Q9	34 laps/36
	Alan Stacey	Team Lotus	370	2.5 Climax FPF 4IL	16	Q16	Fatal accident lap 24/36
	Innes Ireland	Team Lotus	371	2.5 Climax FPF 4IL	14	Q7	Spin lap 13/36 (=FL)
DNS	Stirling Moss	RRC Walker Racing Team	376	2.5 Climax FPF 4IL	12		Accident in practice
DNS	Mike Taylor	Taylor & Crawley Ltd	369	2.5 Climax FPF 4IL	20		Accident in practice
GRAND PRIX de l'AUTOMOBILE CLUB de FRANCE, Reims (F), 3.7.60, 257.92 miles (414.993km)							
5th	Jim Clark	Team Lotus	373	2.5 Climax FPF 4IL	24	Q12	
6th	Ron Flockhart	Team Lotus	374	2.5 Climax FPF 4IL	22	Q8	
7th	Innes Ireland	Team Lotus	371	2.5 Climax FPF 4IL	20	Q4	Fr. Suspension 43 laps/50
RAC BRITISH GRAND PRIX, Silverstone (GB), 16.7.60, 225.37 miles (362.620km)							
2nd	John Surtees	Team Lotus	373	2.5 Climax FPF 4IL	9	Q11	
3rd	Innes Ireland	Team Lotus	371	2.5 Climax FPF 4IL	7	Q5	
16th	Jim Clark	Team Lotus	374	2.5 Climax FPF 4IL	8	Q8	Fr. Suspension 70 laps/77
Silver City Trophy, Brands Hatch (GB), 1.8.60, 122.50 miles (197.102km)							
6th	John Surtees	Team Lotus	373	2.5 Climax FPF 4IL	36	Q6	
	Jim Clark	Team Lotus	374	2.5 Climax FPF 4IL	34	Q1	Gearbox lap 21/50 (=FL)
	Innes Ireland	Team Lotus	372	2.5 Climax FPF 4IL	32	Q3	Oil pressure lap 6/50
GRAN PREMIO de PORTUGAL, Porto (P), 14.8.60, 253.15 miles (407.318km)							
3rd	Jim Clark	Team Lotus	374	2.5 Climax FPF 4IL	14	Q8	
6th	Innes Ireland	Team Lotus	371	2.5 Climax FPF 4IL	16	Q7	Fuel feed 48 laps/55
	John Surtees	Team Lotus	373	2.5 Climax FPF 4IL	18	Q1	Radiator lap 37/55 (FL)
	Stirling Moss	RRC Walker Racing Team	376	2.5 Climax FPF 4IL	12	Q4	DSQ lap 51/55
Lombank Trophy, Snetterton (GB), 17.9.60, 100.27 miles (161.334km)							
1st	Innes Ireland	Team Lotus	372	2.5 Climax FPF 4IL	6	Q5	
2nd	Jim Clark	Team Lotus	374	2.5 Climax FPF 4IL	8	Q2	FL
	John Surtees	Team Lotus	373	2.5 Climax FPF 4IL	7	Q4	Engine lap 11/37
DNS	Tony Brooks	Vandervell Products Ltd	901	2.5 Vanwall V254 4IL	15		Engine in practice
International Gold Cup, Oulton Park (GB), 24.9.60, 165.66 miles (266.547km)							
1st	Stirling Moss	RRC Walker Racing Team	906	2.5 Climax FPF 4IL	7	Q1	
	Innes Ireland	Team Lotus	372	2.5 Climax FPF 4IL	4	Q6	Gearbox lap 30/60
	Ian Burgess	Scuderia Centro Sud	902	2.5 Maserati 250S 4IL	22	NT	Suspension 16/60
	Jim Clark	Team Lotus	374	2.5 Climax FPF 4IL	5	Q2	Accident lap 13/60 (FL)
	John Surtees	Team Lotus	373	2.5 Climax FPF 4IL	6	Q7	Fuel pump lap 1/60
UNITED STATES GRAND PRIX, Riverside (USA), 20.11.60, 245.63 miles (395.187km)							
1st	Stirling Moss	RRC Walker Racing Team	376	2.5 Climax FPF 4IL	5	Q1	
2nd	Innes Ireland	Team Lotus	372	2.5 Climax FPF 4IL	10	Q7	
7th	Jim Hall	Jim Hall	907	2.5 Climax FPF 4IL	24	Q12	73 laps/75
	Jim Clark	Team Lotus	371	2.5 Climax FPF 4IL	12	Q5	N/C 61 laps/75
	John Surtees	Team Lotus	373	2.5 Climax FPF 4IL	11	Q6	Accident lap 3/75

Lotus 18 | 65

Lotus 18 – Colin Chapman's U-turn

POSTSCRIPT – FORMULE LIBRE IN AUSTRALIA AND NEW ZEALAND

Following the United States Grand Prix, the Team Lotus and Rob Walker 18s were shipped across the Pacific for the winter series of Formule Libre races in New Zealand and Australia, in early 1961. These races were supported by a number of European Grand Prix drivers who headed south for the relaxed atmosphere, yet no less serious racing against the best of the Antipodean drivers.

Stirling Moss (376) qualified on pole for the New Zealand Grand Prix and led for 25 laps, before a driveshaft failed on the extremely rough Ardmore airfield circuit. Innes Ireland (372), John Surtees (373) and Roy Salvadori (Reg Parnell 904) suffered transmission failures – only Jim Clark (371) surviving to finish seventh with a sick engine.

Seven days later, Clark finished second in the Hudson Trophy at Levin with Surtees failing to finish.

The Lady Wigram Trophy was shortened from 150 to 100 miles due to persistent heavy rain. Clark started from pole, but spun out on a large puddle and was unable to restart. Surtees ran in third, until dropping out with a misfire. Moss was hit by an errant backmarker, bending his left side rear suspension radius rods, yet managed to finish second. Stirling won the Warwick Farm International in Australia from pole position, as his potential challengers faded in the incredibly hot 110°F temperature. Innes Ireland made it a Lotus 1-2, despite the wrong gear ratios and a sluggish engine. Most of the 'international' contingent had returned home before the Teretonga International Trophy in New Zealand, leaving Roy Salvadori in the Parnell 18 to finish second to Jo Bonnier's Yeoman Credit Cooper.

Jo Bonnier (Yeoman Credit Cooper) beat Roy Salvadori (Reg Parnell entered 904) to win the Teretonga International Trophy in New Zealand. (LAT Photographic)

1960 FORMULA 2 SEASON – PROMISE UNFULFILLED 5

The 1½-litre Formula 2 category, introduced in 1957, proved to be extremely popular with race organisers, competitors, and the public, growing in profile over its four-year life. Races attracted full grids that were much cheaper to put on than a poorly-supported non-Championship Formula 1 race. For the competitors, it offered a genuine stepping-stone to Formula 1, and gave young racing talent the opportunity to compete on equal terms with the many established Grand Prix drivers who regularly took part. The public enjoyed some close racing, plus additional opportunities to see their heroes at work.

The formula came to be dominated by the rear-engined Cooper, powered by the 4-cylinder, 1½-litre Coventry Climax FPF engine. The V6 Ferrari Dino 156 made sporadic appearances, and Porsche would make a concerted effort in 1960 with its unique air-cooled, flat-4 engine. Lotus had not achieved any success with the Lotus 12 or 16, for the reasons already discussed in Chapter 1, but the Lotus 18 offered a new beginning, and Team Lotus would take in all the major events both at home and abroad, backed up by a gradually-increasing number of private entrants. It should be noted that Team Lotus did not build any 18 chassis specifically for Formula 2: designed as a multi-purpose chassis, it was used as such, alternating between Formula 1 and Formula 2 categories from one weekend to the next.

On its return from Argentina in February, the prototype Lotus 18

Stirling Moss (Porsche), Innes Ireland (369) and eventual winner Wolfgang von Trips (Ferrari 156) early in the Syracuse Grand Prix. (LAT Photographic)

Lotus 18 | 67

chassis (369) was hastily repaired, and the 2½-litre Climax FPF engine swapped for a 1½-litre version, before being transported to Sicily for the Syracuse Grand Prix on 19 March; the first Formula 2 event of the season. Innes Ireland took some time sorting out the travel-stained car before setting some fast laps. Following a change of final drive ratio, he turned in a 1min 58.1sec lap time – beaten only by Stirling Moss, by 0.5sec in the Rob Walker Porsche, in the final minutes of practice. Denis Jenkinson, *Motor Sport*'s legendary Continental correspondent, watching from a very fast right-hand curve during practice, reported that "… it was noticeable how much faster and steadier the rear-engined Lotus was, cornering on almost neutral-steer and showing no signs of being near the limit of adhesion. The Porsche seemed to be twitching all the time, not sure whether to be over-steering or under-steering …"

Ireland took the initiative at the start, but, at the end of the first lap, was third behind Moss and von Trips (front-engined Ferrari Dino 156), but ahead of Brabham (Cooper). Moss gradually eased away, leaving his three pursuers fighting over second place. On lap 25, the Lotus went on to three cylinders, making the first of two stops to cure a misfire. This lost Ireland a lap, but meanwhile Moss had retired with a dropped valve, donating the race to von Trips and Ferrari making a rare Formula 2 outing. Ireland managed to work his way back up the order to finish fourth, one lap in arrears.

Team Lotus entered three Lotus 18s for the 79-mile Oulton Park Trophy, although only two appeared. New chassis 370 was not yet race-ready, however, leaving only the original prototype for Innes Ireland to drive once again. Fourth fastest in practice behind three Coopers, Ireland was soon well out into a lead he never relinquished, taking an amazing 5sec off the previous Formula 2 lap record on the way to winning by a margin of 16sec over John Surtees. Surtees, who would shortly join Ireland in Team Lotus, performed outstandingly in his first Formula 2 race in a Ken Tyrell-entered Cooper that was no match for the Lotus.

The inaugural Brussels Grand Prix was held on a 4.552km road circuit around the suburb of Heysel to the north of the city.

Innes Ireland takes the Lotus 18 (369) to its first win – the Formula 2 Oulton Park Trophy. (Ferret Fotographics)

Esso was a principal backer of Team Lotus. (Author)

5: 1960 Formula 2 Season – Promise Unfulfilled

Stirling Moss (Porsche) is closely pursued by Innes Ireland (370), Roy Salvadori and Bruce Halford (Coopers) on the opening lap of the Lavant Cup at Goodwood on Easter Monday. (LAT Photographic)

Team Lotus now had two new race-ready type 18s to be driven by Alan Stacey (370) and Jim Clark (372), whilst Ireland was still in the prototype (369). The cars did not perform as well as might be expected, although 'new boy' Clark out-performed his senior team-mates to record fifth fastest practice time in 369 before being switched to his own car. Stacey was eighth, 1.2sec slower, and Ireland a further 0.8sec down in 11th. Held over two heats, both Clark and Stacey were out within five laps of Heat 1, Clark with a blown engine and Stacey with damaged offside front suspension after being rammed by Lucien Bianchi's Cooper. Ireland managed to finish seventh, despite gear selection problems. In the break between heats, Stacey's car was repaired with parts from Clark's, and Ireland's final drive ratio lowered. It was raining at the start of Heat 2. Ireland spun from fourth place to the tail of the field and would retire with a repeat of his gear selection problems after completing 10 laps. Stacey ran out of fuel due to a carburettor leak to complete a poor weekend for Team Lotus.

Lotus was back on form at Goodwood on Easter Monday, as Ireland, driving a new chassis (370) for the first time, beat Stirling Moss in the Rob Walker Porsche by 6.4sec, after 36 miles of the Lavant Cup. Having started from the pole, he set a new Formula 2 lap record on the way to victory at 97.3mph. Stirling recalled: "I drove as hard as I could and I think the Porsche had a slight edge under braking, but the Lotus had traction and cornering that were in another league." Later in the day, Innes beat Moss again, in the Formula 1 event, as recorded in Chapter 4.

Alan Stacey was able to demonstrate his considerable talents when he enjoyed a trouble-free practice session for the Aintree 200. He set equal third fastest time (370), 0.4sec away from Moss on pole in the Walker Porsche. Ireland (372) was 1.2sec slower in only tenth following clutch slip, whilst Clark (371) was a further 1.6sec down in an unrepresentative 12th. Ireland made up for his poor grid position by streaking through into third place on the opening lap. Two laps later, he momentarily took the lead from

Lotus 18 – Colin Chapman's U-turn

Brabham under braking for Tatts Corner, but went off the road in the process, dropping down to ninth. By lap 10, he was back up to fourth, only to pick up a rear puncture. Clark was brought in and Ireland took over his car, restarting in 21st. At almost the same time, Stacey slowed from a dice for third place with gear selection problems. He came into the pits where a wheel was taken off his car to replace the punctured rear on Ireland's car in which he went back into the race many laps in arrears. His race did not last too much longer before succumbing to a carburettor problem. Porsche took a 1-2-3 finish, with Ireland ninth, one lap down. This had been a round of the Formula 2 Constructors' Championship in which the Lotus challenge had failed once again, as at Syracuse and Brussels, just when it mattered.

Man of the moment, Innes Ireland, and the Lotus 18 make the front cover of Autosport after their Goodwood successes. (LAT Photographic)

Trevor Taylor (372) won against limited opposition in the Crystal Palace Trophy on Whit Monday, whilst everyone else of note was at Zandvoort for the Dutch Grand Prix. After a 12-week interval, the next important event was the Solitude Grand Prix on 24 July. Held on the magnificent circuit near Stuttgart in West Germany, it had previously been used only for motorcycle and latterly sports car races and the first major event at the circuit attracted entries from Ferrari, Porsche, Lotus, Cooper and many private teams. Much of practice was wet, but Jim Clark, entered for both the Formula 2 and Junior races, put his double practice sessions to good use to learn the circuit and began lapping faster and faster to take pole position by 0.5sec. Wolfgang von Trips was next up in the latest version of the rear-engined Ferrari followed by three Porsches. The Ferrari had been converted into Formula 2 form since its debut in the Monaco Grand Prix and would prove to be a prototype of the 1961 1½-litre Formula 1 car. Clark was driving the canted engine chassis (374) having its first Formula 2 race, leaving Innes Ireland a surprising 22sec slower in eleventh (373) with Clark's Formula Junior colleague Trevor Taylor a further 20sec down in 17th (371).

Conditions on race day were perfect, with a bunch of nine cars, including five Porsches, the Ferrari and Clark's Lotus circulating almost as one from the start. Clark emerged as the leader on lap 4 and drew away steadily into a 12.5sec lead by lap 8. His coolant temperature was rising due to a leaking head gasket, however, and he pitted at the end of lap 10 to take on water. Nine cars went past whilst he was stationery, but he would continue to finish the race eighth, 2min 32sec behind the leaders. Innes Ireland was chopping and changing places with the front-engined Ferrari of Phil Hill behind the leading group and beat him into sixth place by just 0.5sec as the first British car home. Taylor retired with broken valve gear at three-quarter distance. Von Trips managed to draw out a lead over four of the Porsches to run out the winner in the Ferrari, unknowingly providing a portent of the shape of things to come in 1961.

The following weekend, the German Grand Prix was held as a round of the Formula 2 Championship rather than the World Formula 1 Championship, the organisers seeking to provide the fans with a home win for Porsche. Instead of the full length Nürburgring, the race was held on the shorter 4.81-mile South circuit. Team Lotus entered 18s for Innes Ireland (371) and Jim Clark, but, when informed that Clark would have to qualify for a place on the grid, Colin Chapman sent him home in protest, to concentrate on the Brands Hatch Formula 1 race taking place the following day.

5: 1960 Formula 2 Season – Promise Unfulfilled

There was a second Lotus 18 on the grid nevertheless, this being entered by the American Louise Bryden-Brown for the Californian BRM Grand Prix driver Dan Gurney. Mrs Bryden-Brown was an occasional driver in her own right, but better known as an entrant, for whom Gurney had driven in his early days in California. This was the first Lotus Components-built customer chassis (903) to appear on track. Gurney went well on his first run in the pale blue and white Lotus although nearly 6sec off the pace, yet 0.3sec quicker than Ireland who was troubled by a locking front brake.

The second practice session was washed out by heavy rain and Gurney lined up eighth on the grid to Ireland's tenth. Race day was atrocious, with heavy rain and fog shrouding the circuit.

Dan Gurney's first race in Louise Bryden-Brown's new 18 (903) was a very wet Formula 2 German Grand Prix. (Ferret Fotographics)

Lotus 18 | 71

The race turned into a Porsche benefit, the German cars equipped with a German Dunlop SP road tyre that proved superior in the ghastly conditions. Colin Chapman obtained a set for Ireland, but he could not match the pace of the five Porsches and Brabham's Cooper ahead of him. As the fog became thicker, Ireland held a lonely seventh place to the finish, with Gurney in eighth, unable to keep up on ordinary racing Dunlops on the flooded track. Both were one lap behind and only too pleased to get out of the miserable weather.

With production of customer chassis now well under way at Lotus Components, the highest total yet of seven Lotus 18s appeared at Brands Hatch for the Kentish '100.' This included Team Lotus entries for Jim Clark (372), Innes Ireland (373) and John Surtees (374), Dan Gurney in Louise Bryden-Brown's car (903), new cars for Ian Burgess, entered in the name of Scuderia Centro Sud (905), and for British hill-climb expert Tony Marsh (909) and finally ex-motorcyclist Geoff Duke in Tim Parnell's car (904). Duke had already raced this car in minor events at Aintree and Snetterton at the beginning of August for Reg Parnell (Racing), retiring on both occasions with engine maladies. Dan Gurney really took to his Lotus and put it on pole position by 0.4sec from Stirling Moss in the Walker Porsche, with Clark third ahead of Bonnier's Porsche. Ireland was fifth, 0.6sec

DAN GURNEY ON THE LOTUS 18

Dan Gurney made five starts in a Lotus 18 (chassis 903), with a best finish of second to Jim Clark in the Kentish '100' Formula 2 race at Brands Hatch in August 1960, having started from pole position and made the fastest lap. He also raced the car in non-Championship Formula 1 and the Inter-Continental formula during 1961, when his commitments to Porsche allowed.

"I have fond memories of those races, though I was not that lucky but often fast. I suggested to Louise Bryden-Brown to buy a 1½-litre Lotus 18 as she wanted to set up her own team in Europe with mechanic Bill Basson. I had known Louise from my early racing days in California. The Lotus was one fantastic car with exceptional performance, amazing me at the speed and ease with which it cornered."

Gurney would subsequently race 903 in the USA when owned by the Arciero brothers, winning a couple of Formule Libre events.

Dan Gurney – a class act. (Author)

5: 1960 Formula 2 Season – Promise Unfulfilled

behind Clark, Surtees a further 0.4sec down in seventh and Marsh best of the other 18s in 16th.

Ireland anticipated the start from the second row and was penalised 60sec for his trouble. Bonnier took an initial lead until disposed of by Ireland, Clark and Gurney. Surtees appeared in fourth, before moving up into second as Ireland's engine began to misfire. Surtees and Clark were disputing the lead vigorously as they came up to lap Geoff Duke on lap 18. Surtees slid wide and the two motorcyclists collided, putting them both out. Clark gradually inched away from Gurney, until a few laps short of the finish his engine began to falter. Gurney quickly increased his pace to close on Clark's tail, but failed to catch him by 0.4sec, despite setting a new lap record at 92.98mph. Thus Lotus had finished 1-2, with Marsh (recovering splendidly from an early spin) in sixth. Innes Ireland was eighth after taking account of his penalty and a pit stop to check his engine. The Centro Sud Lotus struggled round to finish 13th four laps in arrears.

The first Danish Grand Prix was held on the 0.746-mile Roskildering and attracted 11 entries, including Stirling Moss in the Walker Porsche, a single works Cooper, two Lotus 18s from Team Lotus, plus Tim Parnell's private entry (904) for Geoff Duke. The three-heat event was marred by the death of George Lawton from New Zealand and all the heats shortened as a result. Innes Ireland (373)

A tight-lipped Jim Clark (372) scored his first Formula 2 victory in the Kentish 100 at Brands Hatch. (I AT Photographic)

finished second to Jack Brabham's Cooper with Graham Hill (374), making a one-off return to Team Lotus, third.

Team Lotus did not contest any further Formula 2 events, but Tony Marsh took in a number of minor Continental races with his Lotus (909) scoring a fifth place in the Flugplatzrennen at Zeltweg, seventh in the Modena Grand Prix, then fourth in the Preis von Tirol at Innsbruck. Tim Parnell had also appeared at Zeltweg and Innsbruck, driving his own 18 (904) but without scoring a finish.

Stirling Moss drove Parnell's car in the Modena Grand Prix to run with the leaders for 20 laps, before a stop to cure a misfire revealed a broken tappet. This event also saw Scuderia Centro Sud enter its 18 chassis (902) first seen in Formula 1 form eight days earlier at the Oulton Park Gold Cup. The 2½-litre Maserati engine had been replaced by a 1½-litre version developed from the Maserati 150S sports racing car of 1955. This engine reputedly produced around 140bhp at 7500rpm and was reasonably successful as a sports car unit, but had never been seriously contemplated for Formula 2. Ian Burgess drove the car once again until the engine failed before one third distance.

The 1960 Formula 2 season drew to a close with a win for Tony Marsh in the Lewis-Evans Trophy at Brands Hatch. A number of Formula Junior cars made up the numbers in this event, including the Ford 105E-engined Lotus 18 of John Mew that completed ten laps short of the race distance.

The four-year life of an extremely successful Formula 2 also drew to a close at the end of the year. New Formula 1 regulations, coming into effect on 1 January 1961, would adopt the Formula 2 engine capacity limit of 1½-litres and this stepping stone to Formula 1 would cease to exist until 1964, when a new 1.0-litre Formula 2 category would be introduced. Until then, the stepping stone would be Formula Junior.

SUMMARY

A Lotus 18 started in 16 Formula 2 races, of which it won five (31%), against six for Porsche, Cooper three and Ferrari two. The Lotus made an impressive start with two early season wins, including Easter Goodwood where Innes Ireland sensationally beat Stirling Moss in the Rob Walker-entered Porsche. Lotus would only beat Porsche once more, that being at Brands Hatch, another British circuit on which it was able to demonstrate its superior handling over the German marque. Ferrari raced only three times, enjoying perhaps a lucky win at Syracuse with the powerful Dino V6 front-engined chassis, but much more impressively at Solitude with the prototype rear-engined chassis. Cooper was supported by a multitude of private owners, but only appeared with a works-entered 1959 chassis in four events, in which it scored a single win.

The Lotus wins, apart from Brands Hatch, were all British sprint events of circa 50 miles, whereas Porsche concentrated on the more prestigious European events of over 100 miles. Lotus failed to make an impression at these events, other than at Solitude until Clark's engine ran short of coolant. As in Formula 1, Lotus seemed to lack the reliability necessary to succeed, which is not totally surprising considering the chassis were also being used for Formula 1.

Lotus 18 – Formula 2 Performance Summary – 1960

	Starts	Finishes	1st	2nd	3rd	4th	5th	6th	PP	FL
Total	35	20	5	2	1	2	1	2	5	6

Chassis Summary

All six Team Lotus built chassis appeared in Formula 2 guise over the season, as follows:

369	Team Lotus – prototype chassis. Winner Oulton Park Trophy prior to sale to Taylor & Crawley.
370	Team Lotus – Innes Ireland's winner at Goodwood.
371	Team Lotus – winner at Crystal Palace for Trevor Taylor.
372	Team Lotus – winner Kentish 100 for Jim Clark also starts for Innes Ireland and Trevor Taylor.
373	Team Lotus – mainly driven by Innes Ireland.
374	Team Lotus – canted engine chassis, starts for Jim Clark, John Surtees and Graham Hill.

Five customer chassis built by Lotus Components also appeared:

902	Scuderia Centro Sud – fitted with 4-cylinder Maserati 150S engine.
903	Mrs Louise Bryden-Brown – for Dan Gurney.
904	Reg Parnell (Racing) – driven by Geoff Duke, Tim Parnell and Stirling Moss.
905	Ian Burgess raced i.n.o. Scuderia Centro Sud.
909	Tony Marsh – winner Lewis-Evans Trophy.

LOTUS 18 – FORMULA 2 RACING RECORD – 1960

Position	Driver	Entrant	Chassis	Engine	No	Grid	Comments
Grand Premio di Siracusa, Syracuse (I), 19.3.60, 194.77 miles (313.38km)							
4th	Innes Ireland	Team Lotus	369	1.5 Climax FPF 4IL	8	Q2	55 laps/56
Oulton Park Trophy, Oulton Park (GB), 2.4.60, 79.03 miles (127.16km)							
1st	Innes Ireland	Team Lotus	369	1.5 Climax FPF 4IL	20	Q4	FL
	Alan Stacey	Team Lotus	370	1.5 Climax FPF 4IL	19	DNS	Car not ready
Grand Prix de Bruxelles, Brussels (B), 8.4.60, Aggregate of 2 Heats, 197.96 miles (318.64km)							
	Jim Clark	Team Lotus	372	1.5 Climax FPF 4IL	6	Q5	Engine Heat 1
	Alan Stacey	Team Lotus	370	1.5 Climax FPF 4IL	8	Q8	Out of fuel Heat 2
	Innes Ireland	Team Lotus	369	1.5 Climax FPF 4IL	4	Q11	Gear selector Heat 2
Lavant Cup, Goodwood (GB), 18.4.60, 36.00 miles (57.92km)							
1st	Innes Ireland	Team Lotus	370	1.5 Climax FPF 4IL	25	Q1	FL
BARC 200, Aintree (GB), 30.4.60, 150.00 miles (241.35km)							
9th	Clark/Ireland	Team Lotus	371	1.5 Climax FPF 4IL	3	Q12	49 laps/50
	Ireland/Stacey	Team Lotus	372	1.5 Climax FPF 4IL	1	Q9	Carburettor lap 21/50
	Alan Stacey	Team Lotus	370	1.5 Climax FPF 4IL	2	Q4	Gear selector lap 10/50
Crystal Palace Trophy, Crystal Palace (GB), 6.6.60, 50.04 miles (80.51km)							
1st	Trevor Taylor	Team Lotus	372	1.5 Climax FPF 4IL	1	Q1	=FL
Großer Preis der Solitude, Solitude (D), 24.7.60, 141.78 miles (228.34km)							
6th	Innes Ireland	Team Lotus	373	1.5 Climax FPF 4IL	16	Q11	
8th	Jim Clark	Team Lotus	374	1.5 Climax FPF 4IL	17	Q1	
	Trevor Taylor	Team Lotus	371	1.5 Climax FPF 4IL	18	Q17	Engine lap 15/20
Großer Preis von Deutschland, Sudschliefe Nürburgring (D), 31.7.60, 155.47 miles (250.20km)							
7th	Innes Ireland	Team Lotus	371	1.5 Climax FPF 4IL	11	Q10	31 laps/32
8th	Dan Gurney	Mrs L Bryden-Brown	903	1.5 Climax FPF 4IL	21	Q8	31 laps/32
Aintree Trophy, Aintree (GB), 1.8.60, 75.00 miles (120.67km)							
	Geoff Duke	Reg Parnell (Racing)	904	1.5 Climax FPF 4IL	1	N/A	DNF - engine
Vanwall Trophy, Snetterton (GB), 6.8.60, 67.75 miles (109.01km)							
	Geoff Duke	Reg Parnell (Racing)	904	1.5 Climax FPF 4IL	74	N/A	Engine lap 7/25
Kentish 100, Brands Hatch (GB), 28.8.60, 106.00 miles (170.55km)							
1st	Jim Clark	Team Lotus	372	1.5 Climax FPF 4IL	48	Q3	
2nd	Dan Gurney	Mrs L Bryden-Brown	903	1.5 Climax FPF 4IL	50	Q1	FL
6th	Tony Marsh	AE Marsh	909	1.5 Climax FPF 4IL	28	Q16	39 laps/40
8th	Innes Ireland	Team Lotus	373	1.5 Climax FPF 4IL	46	Q5	39 laps/40
13th	Ian Burgess	Scuderia Centro Sud	905	1.5 Climax FPF 4IL	44	Q21	36 laps/40
	John Surtees	Team Lotus	374	1.5 Climax FPF 4IL	16	Q7	Accident lap 18/40
	Geoff Duke	RHH Parnell	904	1.5 Climax FPF 4IL	52	Q20	Accident lap 18/40
Danske Grand Prix, Roskildering (DK), 11.9.60, 3 Heats 86.99 miles (139.97km)							
2nd	Innes Ireland	Team Lotus	373	1.5 Climax FPF 4IL	2	N/A	
3rd	Graham Hill	Team Lotus	374	1.5 Climax FPF 4IL	11	N/A	FL
	Geoff Duke	RHH Parnell	904	1.5 Climax FPF 4IL	4	N/A	DNF
Flugplatzrennen, Zeltweg (A), 18.9.60, 117.29 miles (188.72km)							
5th	Tony Marsh	AE Marsh	909	1.5 Climax FPF 4IL	10	Q3	57 laps/59
	Tim Parnell	RHH Parnell	904	1.5 Climax FPF 4IL	11	Q7	DNF
Gran Premio di Modena, Modena (I), 2.10.60, 147.14 miles (236.60km)							
7th	Tony Marsh	AE Marsh	909	1.5 Climax FPF 4IL	22	Q10	94 laps/100
	Ian Burgess	Scuderia Centro Sud	902	1.5 Maserati 150S 4IL	4	Q7	Engine lap 29/100
	Stirling Moss	Reg Parnell (Racing)	904	1.5 Climax FPF 4IL	16	Q2	Engine lap 21/100
Preis von Tirol, Innsbruck (A), 8.10.60, 42.25 miles (67.52km)							
4th	Tony Marsh	AE Marsh	909	1.5 Climax FPF 4IL	162	N/A	39 laps/40
	Tim Parnell	RHH Parnell	904	1.5 Climax FPF 4IL	167	N/A	DNF
Lewis-Evans Trophy, Brands Hatch (GB), 16.10.60, 52.08 miles (83.80km)							
1st	Tony Marsh	AE Marsh	909	1.5 Climax FPF 4IL	40	Q1	FL

Lotus 18 – Colin Chapman's U-turn

Tony Marsh in his privately-run 18 (909) finished seventh in the Modena Grand Prix. (Ferret Fotographics)

1961 FORMULA 1 SEASON – AGAINST THE ODDS 6

New Formula 1 Regulations came into force on 1 January 1961, reducing engine capacity from 2½ to just 1½ litres – identical to the outgoing Formula 2 category. When first announced in October 1958, by the CSI of the FIA, these regulations were greeted with uproar from British interests, suspicious that the 'continentals' were ganging up on them, as, by 1958, Britain had at last gained supremacy in Grand Prix racing, with Mike Hawthorn as World Champion and Vanwall the Constructors' Champion. British manufacturers favoured retention of the 2½-litre Regulations they now dominated. The only redeeming factor was that the CSI had authorised Britain and other concerned countries to propose another formula to suit their mutual interests. This would lead to the ill-fated proposal for an 'Inter-Continental' formula with a 3-litre engine capacity limit – see Chapter 7.

Throughout 1959 and 1960, and with only months to run before the new regulations came into force, British interests continually tabled protests and objections against the 1½-litre Formula 1, mostly on the grounds that the cars would be underpowered and unspectacular. The Society of Motor Manufacturers and Traders (SMMT), representing all the British constructors, drivers, fuel and oil companies, accessory and tyre manufacturers, announced that its members would not support the FIA proposals. It recommended that the new regulations should be rescinded and that the current Formula 1 and Formula 2 regulations should continue unchanged. The CSI made no response to the SMMT. Meanwhile, Ferrari, having initially opposed the new Formula, found itself with a potential world-beater in the 1½-litre V6-powered rear-engined Formula 2 chassis that had won at Solitude in 1960, and had begun readying it for 1961. Similarly, Porsche had enjoyed a successful 1960 Formula 2 season and was preparing for the step up to Formula 1 by developing a new flat-8 air-cooled engine.

Gradually the realisation dawned on the British motor racing industry that the new Formula 1 would be implemented whether it liked it or not. All the strong words and self-imposed uncertainty had served only to distract Coventry Climax and BRM from starting the design of new 1½-litre engines that would not now be ready until late in the 1961 season – at the earliest. As an interim measure, Coventry Climax produced a Mk II version of the 4-cylinder 1½-litre FPF engine (see panel) and was in the unique position of powering all the British Grand Prix contenders – including BRM, until its own purpose built V8 was up and running.

Colin Chapman's response to the new regulations was to design the Lotus 21 for 1961, in which the box-shaped bodywork of the Type 18 gave way to slim and attractive elliptical section panels of much reduced frontal area. Contrary to normal practice, however, the 21 would not to be available for customer purchase. During 1960, Stirling Moss had won two Grands Prix with his Rob Walker, BP-contracted Lotus 18, whereas the Esso-backed Team Lotus had failed to score. Having effectively financed the Lotus 18, Esso was not impressed and ruled that neither Moss nor any other customer should benefit from this latest Lotus until the 1961 season was over. Meanwhile, delays in development and construction of the Type 21 left Team Lotus having to rely on type 18s for the opening non-Championship races of the season.

Where did this leave existing Lotus customer, Rob Walker, and Stirling Moss, the best driver in the world? With no competitive alternative chassis available on the market, they had little option other than to continue to race the year-old Lotus 18. The Dorking-based team had two chassis available: 376 rebuilt as 906 (the 376 chassis number was not used in 1961) campaigned through 1960 and an as-yet-unraced 912, acquired towards the end of the year. Stirling faced a season competing against Cooper and BRM with equal engines, against Lotus with an equal engine in a potentially superior chassis and both Ferrari and Porsche with superior engines in chassis of uncertain ability. Clearly Moss would be competing against the odds. Not for the first time was he to be cast in the role of the underdog, a challenge he positively relished.

Other potential Lotus customers were also directed to the 18,

Lotus 18 | 77

Lotus 18 – Colin Chapman's U-turn

TECHNICAL UPDATE: COVENTRY CLIMAX FPF – 1½-LITRE – MK II

Coventry Climax had made no promises as to when the new 1½-litre V8 engine would be ready and, as an interim measure, produced a Mk II version of the original 1475cc 4-cylinder FPF Formula 2 engine. This incorporated the improvements and developments successfully applied to the 2495cc version of the FPF in 1959, including the cross-braced crankcase. Cylinder bore was enlarged from 81.2mm to 81.9mm and, by retaining the original stroke of 71.1mm, capacity increased to 1498cc. A new cylinder head was developed, with modified inlet and exhaust ports, with the same stud centres as the larger engine, making it incompatible with pre-1961 engines. Larger diameter tappets were incorporated, as the valve springs were increased in size to extend the operating range from 7600rpm to approximately 8200rpm.

Maximum power output on two twin choke Weber 45DCOE9 carburettors rose to 151bhp at 7500rpm on 100-octane petrol but, more significantly, output increased by between 8 and 10bhp in the mid-range between 5000 and 7000rpm. The Mk II FPF retained the Climax tradition of a good spread of power over a wide speed range, yet there remained a deficit of circa 30bhp to the contemporary Ferrari Dino V6 engine.

The first batch of 8 Mk II engines was delivered in time for the 1961 Monaco Grand Prix, including single examples going to power the Lotus 18s of Rob Walker and UDT-Laystall. By July, production was well under way, with examples becoming available to all private Lotus 18 owners.

Henry Taylor (UDT-Laystall 916) kept a tail-wagging Jim Clark (371) behind him in the 1961 season opener at Snetterton. (LAT Photographic)

6: 1961 Formula 1 Season – Against the Odds

Jim Clark (371) led from start to finish in the 1961 Pau Grand Prix, the first of his many Formula 1 wins. (Ferret Fotographics)

Lotus Components continuing to satisfy demand for additional examples into 1961. Working on the build of customer 18s at that time was Bob Dance, whose meticulous attention to detail would eventually see him promoted to become Team Lotus chief mechanic in 1968. Bob had joined Team Lotus in August 1960, to be trained on the build and maintenance of the 'queerboxes,' and was working in Lotus Components before moving on to involvement in the development of the Lotus-Ford twin-cam 'LF' engine that would power the Elan sports car.

A new customer for the 18 was the UDT-Laystall Racing Team. Financed by the United Dominions Trust Hire Purchase Company and its Laystall engineering subsidiary, the team was managed by the British Racing Partnership (BRP), the team run by Ken Gregory and Alfred Moss, respectively the manager and father of Stirling. This arrangement left BRP particularly well-funded and posed a potential threat to the regular factory teams in driver contract negotiations. BRP had traditionally been a Cooper customer until Ken Gregory approached Cooper works driver Bruce McLaren to join BRP. Charles Cooper took umbrage at this and became evasive about selling new cars to Gregory. In the event, McLaren stayed with Cooper, but BRP turned to Colin Chapman, and the UDT-Laystall Racing Team ordered four new Lotus 18 chassis.

For the first time, the World Championship was to be run to a set of rigid rules to which the Lotus 18 could be adapted relatively easily. The minimum weight limit of 450kg (991lb), excluding fuel, was unlikely to be a problem, nor was the fitting of an electric starter. This would typically be powered by a compact 12-volt Varley battery located on its side on the cockpit floor. A safety roll-protection bar had to be provided behind the driver's head, yet there were no further definitions as to the gauge of metal or requirements for it to be braced or supported. A simple tubular hoop was the order of the day – little protection in the event of the car overturning. The fuel/oil tank fillers of the 18 stood proud of the body panels and would henceforth have to be concealed beneath them. Finally, fuel was restricted to 100-octane petrol, having previously been AvGas 130-octane Aviation spirit, and no oil could be added to the engine during a race.

The 1961 season began in late March, at a cold Snetterton, for the Lombank Trophy, held as a combined Formula 1/Inter-Continental event, attracting just nine assorted Formula 1 entries. Of these, three were 18s – former Monaco Formula Junior Grand Prix winner Henry Taylor finishing second in one of the new UDT-Laystall chassis (916). Plagued by a misfire, Jim Clark finished a lowly fourth (371) for Team Lotus, followed by Tim Parnell (904) in fifth, two laps in arrears.

The Pau Grand Prix traditionally clashed with the Goodwood Easter Monday meeting, Team Lotus opting to split its resources between both the French and British events. The Team 18s were described by Denis Jenkinson of *Motor Sport* as looking a little tired when they appeared at Pau, but that did not prevent Jim Clark (371) from winning the first Formula 1 race of his career on this tortuous street circuit. This would be the first of many such victories in which he would start from pole position, lead from start to finish, set fastest lap and remain unchallenged throughout the race. Trevor Taylor, in the second Team entry (374), retired before half distance. Nearly a lap in arrears, in second, was Jo Bonnier, the works Porsche driver having a one-off outing in a new 18 (914) for the German Scuderia Colonia, also fielding an ex-Team Lotus chassis (373) for Wolfgang Seidel that failed to finish due to an oil leak.

A second new 18 (908) appeared in the name of Camoradi International, driven by Ian Burgess, but it had broken its transmission

Lotus 18 | 79

by quarter distance. Formed in 1959 by American pilot/motor trader/amateur driver Lloyd 'Lucky' Casner, the Casner Motor Racing Division (hence 'Camoradi') had run a team of 'Birdcage' Maserati T61s in 1960 endurance racing, winning the Nürburgring 1000kms with Stirling Moss and Dan Gurney. Camoradi was now trying its luck in Formula 1 with a pair of Lotus 18s, the second being a chassis (905) that Burgess had first raced as a Scuderia Centro Sud entry in the 1960 Kentish 100 at Brands Hatch.

Meanwhile at Goodwood, Innes Ireland found he was unable to repeat his 1960 success in the Glover Trophy, finishing fifth (372) behind two Coopers, a BRM and Stirling Moss in the newer Walker 18 chassis (912). Moss had chased the Yeoman Credit team Cooper of eventual winner John Surtees hard until his engine went off song, slipping back to fourth. Lotus 18s finished in fourth to eighth places, the UDT entries of Henry Taylor and Cliff Allison sandwiching the Tony Marsh privately run entry.

JIM CLARK

(b. 4 March 1936, d. 7 April 1968)

Jim Clark's talent shown in Club racing took him into Formula Junior with the Lotus 18 in 1960, a category he quickly dominated. He also drove the 18 in Formula 2 for Team Lotus, and Colin Chapman would have promoted him to the Formula 1 team sooner had not John Surtees become available. Nevertheless, like Surtees, he made his Grand Prix debut in the Lotus 18. He completed a steady, unspectacular 1960 season, always more at home on British circuits with which he was, of course, more familiar. Apart from Formula Junior, he also won in Formula 2 at Brands Hatch with a Lotus 18, and then, into 1961, he showed more confidence by easily winning the Pau Grand Prix. 1961 was a relatively unspectacular season with the Lotus 21 until he succeeded in beating Stirling Moss twice in the South African Springbok series in December.

Into 1962, Clark would show a new confidence now as No 1 driver for Team Lotus and, following the accident to Stirling Moss at Goodwood on Easter Monday 1962, he quickly adopted from him the role of 'the man to beat.' A constant challenger for the 1962 World Championship, he drove with a smooth, precise and elegant style in an apparently unhurried fashion. Out of the cockpit, however, the shy, introverted Scot lacked confidence, was never really relaxed, chewed his fingernails and was indecisive. From 1962, the combination of Jim Clark, Colin Chapman and the revolutionary Lotus 25 and its successor the 33, developed into the greatest driver/constructor combination of all time. Clark had complete trust in Chapman, whilst Chapman had complete faith in Clark and was able to provide him with a vastly superior car throughout his career.

The results, a total of 25 Grand Prix wins and two World Championships (which could have been more given better engine reliability) speak for themselves. That his career should come to an untimely end at a grey Hockenheim on 7 April 1968 in a relatively insignificant Formula 2 race seemed inconceivable to everyone.

Jim Clark accepts the bubbly.
(LAT Photographic)

6: 1961 Formula 1 Season – Against the Odds

Start of the Glover Trophy at Goodwood on Easter Monday. Stirling Moss (7) is on pole, with Innes Ireland (5) just behind him. The 18s of Cliff Allison (15), Tony Marsh (29) and Henry Taylor (17) are also visible. (LAT Photographic)

Lotus 18 – Colin Chapman's U-turn

Ten 18s were entered for the three-heat Brussels Grand Prix: two each from Team Lotus, UDT-Laystall and Scuderia Colonia, with single entries from Rob Walker, Tony Marsh, Tim Parnell and Camoradi International. Tony Marsh finished a splendid third on aggregate in his privately-run 18, with other examples filling fifth to eighth places. Denis Jenkinson noted that Stirling Moss was driving the spare Walker 18 fitted with a Lotus 'queerbox.' Moss was classified seventh, after a frustrating afternoon in which his engine refused to run consistently on all four cylinders. Only after a change of fuel pump prior to Heat 3 did it run properly, enabling him to finish second to Jack Brabham's winning Cooper. Jim Clark retired the canted engine chassis (374) on lap 1 of Heat 1 with a broken gearbox input shaft, whilst team-mate Innes Ireland spun out of the lead on lap 1 of Heat 3, severely damaging his rear suspension, yet was classified sixth overall. Other finishers were Cliff Allison (915) in fifth, and Ian Burgess (908) eighth.

Tony Marsh had carried out a number of modifications to his 18 chassis (909) over the winter. The addition of a top link in the rear suspension relieved the half-shafts of lateral wheel location duties, splined half-shafts replacing the fixed length type, to accommodate changes in length due to suspension movement. Stronger steering arms were fitted, and the front anti-roll bar was coupled to the lower wishbone via a drop link, rather than the top wishbone ball joint, so as to eradicate failures seen on the Team Lotus cars during 1960. Finally, he installed a Cooper C5S 5-speed transmission to replace the potentially troublesome Lotus 'queerbox.'

Stirling Moss scored his first Formula 1 win of the season, in the Preis von Wien at Aspern in Austria, Lotus 18s filling the first three places, admittedly against a small, unrepresentative field. Wolfgang Seidel was second, ahead of a new 18 from Scuderia Dolomiti for Ernesto Prinoth (913). Two entries from Tim Parnell retired,

Wolfgang Seidel (ex-Team Lotus '373'), about to be lapped in a rural section of the Syracuse Grand Prix, by Innes Ireland (371) and Jack Brabham (Cooper). (LAT Photographic)

including another new chassis (919) entered for Gerry Ashmore.

What would be the largest number of 18s to appear on a grid, gathered at Aintree, when 11 Lotuses faced 11 Coopers for an extremely wet and dismal BARC 200. Equality of numbers was insufficient, however, Coopers filling five of the top six places. Once again, Tony Marsh in seventh was the top finisher for Lotus. On this occasion, Moss was driving a Rob Walker Cooper, his regular 18 on its way to Sicily for the Syracuse Grand Prix. Team Lotus found its cars a handful in the wet, Clark (372) and Ireland (371) finishing ninth and tenth, two laps down on the winning Cooper of Jack Brabham. Gerry Ashmore (919) was 11th, three places ahead of Dan Gurney in the Bryden-Brown 18 (903), followed by Cliff Allison in the surviving UDT entry (915), all three-or-more laps behind.

The Syracuse Grand Prix was the first race under the new Formula 1 regulations with a fully representative grid, and would give an indication of the prospects for the new season. Besides the first appearance of the Porsche team, albeit with 1960 former Formula 2 cars, it marked the race debut of the new rear-engined Ferrari Dino 156. First seen at the annual Maranello news conference in February, its dominant visual feature was twin 'nostril' radiator inlets in the nose that quickly earned it the nickname 'Sharknose.' Otherwise, it was a refined version of the V6-engined car that had won at Solitude in 1960. In the hands of 'new boy' Giancarlo Baghetti, it began lapping very quickly during practice without any apparent effort.

Held on Tuesday 25 April, a public holiday in Sicily, and just three days after the Aintree race, the British teams and drivers only arrived in time for the final day of practice. Dan Gurney managed to put his Porsche on pole just 0.1sec quicker than the Ferrari, with Surtees' Cooper next up, 0.8sec slower. Of five Lotus 18s entered, Moss (906) was the fastest in seventh (2.3sec off the pace with a misfire), Ireland (371) was ninth (0.9sec sec slower), and Clark (374) a further 2.8sec slower, in twelfth. Wolfgang Seidel (373) was nineteenth, whilst Ernesto Prinoth (913) failed to start after his Climax engine blew a gasket.

From the start, Baghetti's Ferrari and the Porsches of Gurney and Bonnier quickly annexed the top three positions to dominate the entire race. Ireland's Lotus battled with Brabham (Cooper) and Graham Hill (BRM) for fourth, until a sticking throttle and a lack of fuel pressure sidelined him before half distance. Jim Clark's was the only 18 running at the end, down in a lowly sixth, lapped three times, whilst Moss suffered a misfire all afternoon, eventually pushing his car over the line with a dead engine to be classified eighth. Significantly, all the British teams had followed powerless in the wake of the Ferrari and two Porsches.

Grand Prix de Monaco, Monte Carlo, 14 May 1961

The 1½-litre Formula 1 era opened in earnest at Monte Carlo on 14 May 1961. The entry list included four Lotus 18s – Stirling Moss in the Rob Walker car (912) with GSD type 32 transmission, two UDT-Laystall cars, for Cliff Allison (916) and Henry Taylor (915), and the Swiss fuel-injection expert Michael May, entered by Scuderia Colonia (914). The UDT 18s were equipped with a new Laystall-built 5-speed gearbox, overhung behind the final drive in a ribbed, barrel shaped casing, replacing the usual Lotus 'queerbox.' Moss

This Laystall-built transmission replaced the 'queerbox' on one of the UDT team cars at Monaco. (LAT Photographic)

had a guaranteed place on the 16-car grid by reason of being a past winner, but the others would have to qualify for a place. Moss had one of an initial batch of eight Coventry Climax Mk II FPF engines, but UDT-Laystall only had one between its two cars.

The Walker Lotus initially experienced a fuel feed problem. A high speed misfire had afflicted the engine at both Brussels and Syracuse, and was not rectified until Alf Francis discovered a minor manufacturing flaw in a Weber carburettor causing the floats to stick intermittently. He eradicated this by hand-finishing the inside of the float chamber castings. The fault had arisen following the introduction of mass production at the Weber factory, replacing an almost-entirely handmade and expensive manufacturing process. Now at Monaco, Francis and the Weber representative stripped down a new carburettor overnight and matched it against a Walker team version to discover that a tiny drilling had been omitted.

The new 'Sharknose' Ferraris of Phil Hill, Richie Ginther and Wolfgang von Trips were running fast and impressively, but it was Moss who claimed the pole, with a lap in 1min 39.1sec in the final session, 0.2sec quicker than Ginther. The Walker 18 was now running beautifully, after curing the carburettor problem and installing twin Bendix electric fuel pumps. Moss had tried the Walker Cooper briefly, but soon decided that the Lotus was quicker and easier to drive around the twisty circuit. Michael May was 13th on the grid, having latched on to two faster cars that towed him around the circuit in their slipstream to record a time 1sec quicker than he could manage on his own. Of the UDT cars, only Allison managed to qualify, scraping onto the back of the grid, the Mk II Climax engine worth 1sec per lap.

There was panic on the grid when Moss spotted a slight crack in a chassis tube on the Walker 18. Alf Francis calmly welded the offending tube, his torch flame barely inches away from the fuel tank, swathed in wet towels to catch any errant sparks. Everyone else in the vicinity beat a hasty retreat!

At the fall of the starter's flag, Ginther, driving the only Ferrari with the more powerful 120° V6 engine, took the initiative from the middle of the front row to lead the opening laps through the Monte Carlo streets. Moss, driving with the cockpit side panels removed, in anticipation of a long hot race, followed 5sec in arrears. He really needed to take the lead and open up a gap over the Ferraris and made his move on lap 14 to nip ahead of Ginther. Bonnier moved his Porsche up to second, as Ginther dropped to fourth to allow the slower-starting Phil Hill to take up the Ferrari challenge. On lap 26, Hill took second from Bonnier, 10sec down the road from Moss.

Ginther got ahead of Bonnier on lap 41, so that by half distance the two Ferraris were running nose to tail 7secs behind Moss.

Ginther pushed Hill along very hard, to within 3.8sec of Moss by lap 60. Forced on to the defensive as the Ferraris grew large in his mirrors, Moss was holding on by sheer skill and brilliance and, appreciably quicker and luckier through traffic, began to draw away again. They were lapping consistently at around 1min 37sec, over 2sec quicker than in practice. On lap 75, Ginther, obviously able to lap faster than Hill, was signalled to pass him and go for Moss. He managed to reduce the deficit to 4.5sec by lap 80 and, on lap 84, set an inspired new lap record of 1min 36.3sec, nearly 3secs faster than pole position and only a tenth off the old 2½-litre record. Moss immediately responded by equalling Ginther's time, driving to the absolute limit to keep his lead. The vast crowd was

14 May 1961: Master and commander – Stirling Moss (912) sweeps down into the Station Hairpin on his way to a memorable Monaco Grand Prix victory. (Author)

6: 1961 Formula 1 Season – Against the Odds

Michael May smokes the Scuderia Colonia 18 (914) out of the Monaco Station Hairpin into retirement. Bruce McLaren (Cooper) follows. (LAT Photographic)

Lotus 18 | 85

MONTE CARLO

The original round-the-houses circuit, the event was first held in 1929. Despite being an unlikely location for a World Championship Grand Prix, Monte Carlo became the most glamorous of them all, due to its location in the Principality of Monaco on the shores of the Mediterranean, playground of the rich and famous.

The 1.94-mile circuit wound around the narrow, hilly and twisting streets of Monte Carlo, before descending through hairpin bends to the sea front, through a 400-yard tunnel and around the harbour. The start/finish line was situated on the promenade, only a short dash away from the Gasometer hairpin, until a multiple accident there on the first lap of the 1962 Grand Prix prompted its relocation inland to the other side of the hairpin.

It was a very demanding circuit, its endless succession of corners calling for approximately 20 gear changes per lap, and was consequently very hard on transmissions. Limited to just 16 starters, never more than around half a dozen would see the finish.

Stirling Moss had won for Maserati in 1956 and then scored the first Grand Prix win for the Lotus 18 in 1960. Its second consecutive win, in 1961 against overwhelming odds, confirmed the status of Moss and the Lotus 18 as masters of Monaco.

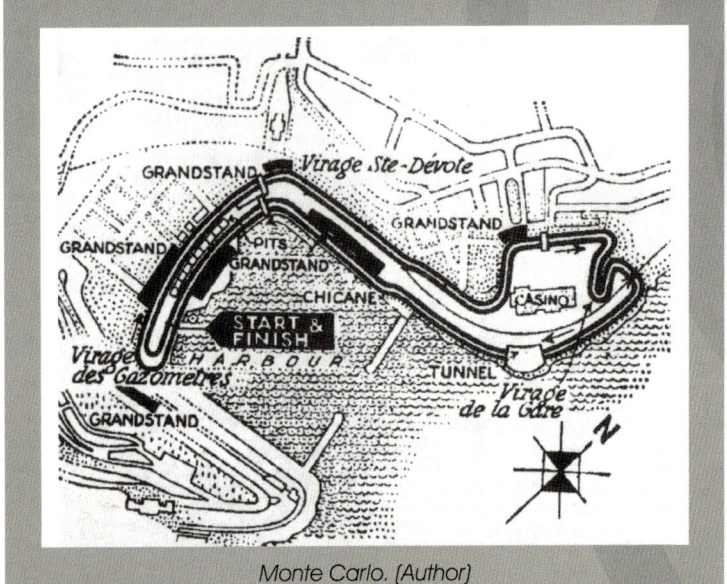

Monte Carlo. (Author)

gripped by the duel, as Ginther closed to within 4sec of Moss on entering the final lap, yet could finish no closer than 3.6sec to the 'maestro' after 2¾ hours of racing.

Denis Jenkinson summed it all up for *Motor Sport*: "What a race!" Like Moss, Ginther would describe this as the race of his life, commenting: "that son of a gun! If you did well against him then you'd really done something special." Moss, however, would recall that it was not a race he thought he could win. He believed that the Ferraris were biding their time and would eventually use the additional 30bhp of their V6 engines to power past on the hill up to Casino Square. He was going as hard as he could, but was never able to get away from them. As it turned out the Ferraris were also on the limit.

Baghetti's win at Syracuse had shown the potential of the Ferraris, yet, against all the odds, Moss had used his amazing abilities to the full to extract the maximum from the better-handling Lotus to beat them. It would go down in history as one of the greatest Grands Prix of all time and the third, and most memorable, Grand Prix win for the Lotus 18.

The non-Championship Naples Grand Prix held on the same day as Monaco attracted a 13-car entry, including four 18s and a 'Sharknose' Ferrari for Giancarlo Baghetti once again. After a slow start, Baghetti outpaced Gerry Ashmore's Tim Parnell-run 18 (919) by a whole lap, with Ian Burgess fourth, two laps down in the Camoradi car (905), and Parnell himself (904) eighth. Whilst the major teams were invited to take part in the Dutch Grand Prix just seven days later, UDT-Laystall was relegated to Crystal Palace to compete for the London Trophy. Roy Salvadori's Yeoman Credit Cooper dominated both practice and the race, ahead of the UDT 18 of Henry Taylor (916), and Tony Marsh in his privately run car (909).

Grote Prijs van Nederland, Zandvoort, 22 May 1961

How much better would Ferrari perform on the sweeping curves between the sand dunes of Zandvoort on Whit Monday? The organising club had chosen to invite 15 cars to take part in the race, plus two reserves should an invitee not survive practice. The favoured 15 included just two Lotus 18s: Moss in his Monaco winner and Trevor Taylor for Team Lotus (371), filling in for Innes Ireland, who had crashed heavily during practice at Monaco and broken a leg. A Camoradi International entry (905) for Ian Burgess was present as one of the reserves.

6: 1961 Formula 1 Season – Against the Odds

BP cashes in on its support for the 'maestro.' (Author)

Autosport celebrates "the incomparable Stirling Moss" and the Lotus 18, with its traditional green cover for a British Grand Prix win. (LAT Photographic)

Lotus 18 | 87

STIRLING MOSS ON THE LOTUS 18

In *Stirling Moss – My Cars, My Career* (Patrick Stephens 1992/Haynes Publishing 1999), Stirling recalled to Doug Nye how he "found the car staggeringly fast and responsive, so responsive that it became an extension of its driver – a real driver's car par excellence. That's not to say it was easier to drive than the Cooper, because it was not. It was never as forgivable nor as 'chuckable.' The Cooper really allowed one to take enormous liberties and get away with them, whereas the Lotus was a far more delicate instrument demanding precision. You had to keep it operating within a very tight envelope and if you could maintain it within those limits its ultimate braking, cornering and traction were all superior to the Cooper's.

"With experience I quickly found that if it wasn't doing just what I wanted it to, then there were a host of adjustments which could be made. Once we started racing the car I found there were perhaps too many. In some ways it was curiously insensitive. For example, we could change the camber on the rear wheels, or their toe-in, without me noticing very much difference on the road. It was all too easy to make a change and find an improvement and so do something else which made it worse, and so on until time ran out and I had merely worn out an engine trying different things.

"So eventually I tended to work on the Lotus so that starting with the same tyre pressures front and rear I could get a little more oversteer or understeer by changing pressures and then we refined this by altering the damper settings. I seldom changed the ant-roll bars."

Close attention: Stirling Moss (912) chasing Richie Ginther (Ferrari) during their battle for fourth that the Englishman will win on the last lap. (Sutton Images)

6: 1961 Formula 1 Season – Against the Odds

The circuit had never suited Ferrari's handling characteristics, but, after spending some time sorting out the suspension, the Scuderia excelled in the final practice session to annex the front row of the grid, all three cars now equipped with 120° V6 engines. Moss once again tried the Walker Cooper, but could not approach the times he set in his 18 (912), taking fourth place on the grid as fastest Climax user, 0.3sec off the front row. Taylor was 14th, whilst Burgess would not be able to fill any vacancy, after bending his chassis against an embankment when his throttle jammed open.

The Ferraris of von Trips and Phil Hill took the lead from the start, with Moss squeezed down to ninth on the opening lap. He moved up to fifth on lap 3, before being taken by Ginther (Ferrari), who had not made a good start either. Ginther's V6 engine was not running well, and Moss re-passed him, on lap 21, into what was now fourth place. The Ferrari engine cleared itself, allowing Ginther to retake Moss on lap 38, but he remained unable to shake off the Lotus that was keeping up only by virtue of Moss' skill. Ginther was in a precarious position, as his throttle return spring had broken, requiring him to lift the accelerator pedal with his foot as he slowed for corners. Come the final lap, he misjudged his throttle closure on the approach to the hairpin behind the pits, the Ferrari slid wide and Moss was through into fourth in a flash. Ginther used the slipstream of the Lotus to gain speed on the finishing straight, but lost fourth to Moss by a matter of inches (officially 0.1sec) as they crossed the line. Trevor Taylor was lapped twice, down in 13th.

As the dust settled on a dominant Ferrari 1-2 finish, it was realised that all 15 starters had finished the race and there had not been a single pit stop, earning the event a unique place in the history books as the only Grand Prix with a 100% finishing record.

The non-Championship Formula 1 Silver City Trophy at Brands Hatch attracted nine 18s in a field of 24 starters. These included single car entries from Tony Marsh in his regular 18 (909), Tim Parnell (904), and Dan Gurney in Louise Bryden-Brown's car (903), now with pannier fuel tanks along its flanks. Scuderia Colonia had entries for Michael May (914) and Wolfgang Seidel (373); Team Lotus for Trevor Taylor (371); and UDT-Laystall for Stirling Moss, Henry Taylor and Jo Bonnier (like Gurney, on release from Porsche, which was not represented).

The 18s of Moss (918) and Bonnier (917) were new chassis, looking unfamiliar in a set of more slippery body panels that bore more than a passing resemblance to the Lotus 21. The similarity did not end there: the rear suspension had been modified in line

Dan Gurney (903) could only manage fifth at Brands Hatch, having finished second with the same car in 1960. Note the car now has pannier fuel tanks alongside the driver. (Ferret Fotographics)

Jo Bonnier at Druids Corner in the new UDT-Laystall 18/21 (917), during the Silver City Trophy. Bruce McLaren's Cooper is perched precariously on the embankment, in the background. (Ferret Fotographics)

Lotus 18 – Colin Chapman's U-turn

with the 21 as well – such upgraded chassis became known as the Lotus '18/21' (see panel). Moss was suitably impressed, taking pole position ahead of John Surtees (Yeoman Credit Cooper) and Jim Clark in a Team Lotus 21. Gurney was only 12th, 4sec slower than the pole time he had achieved in the same chassis in 1960. Since then it had been damaged in accidents in Inter-Continental races at Goodwood and Silverstone, and would never handle quite as well again.

TECHNICAL UPDATE: LOTUS 18/21

The Lotus 21 epitomised the state-of-the-art 4-cylinder Formula 1 car of 1961, but there was no likelihood of an example falling into the hands of a privately run team until the end of the season. The Lotus 18 was by no means totally outclassed, at least in the hands of Stirling Moss, but could conceivably be updated to incorporate features of the 21, specifically Colin Chapman's latest thinking on rear suspension layout and improved aerodynamics. UDT-Laystall Racing Team chief mechanic Tony Robinson, always keen to improve the performance of the cars in his charge, took up the challenge to incorporate these features on the team's 18s.

Chapman had adapted the rear suspension of the 18 to accommodate Dunlop's latest 6.00 section tyres for the 21, dictating the addition of a transverse top link to generate the required roll centre height and adding another option for adjustability. Robinson modified the UDT chassis rear bulkheads to accept an upper transverse link with a shorter upright. Relieved

The new UDT-Laystall 18/21 (918) Stirling Moss will drive to victory in the Silver City Trophy in the Brands Hatch pits. (Ferret Fotographics)

of lateral wheel location duties, the former fixed length half-shafts required provision for changes in their length as the rear wheels rose and fell under suspension movement. Robinson opted for replacing them with the orthodox Hardy Spicer sliding spline type, whilst Chapman, who always had a horror of sliding splines, took advantage of newly developed Metalastik flexible rubber couplings. Interestingly, Tony Marsh had already made similar modifications to the rear suspension of his privately run 18 (909) over the winter of 1960/61 – see above.

Since the Coventry Climax Mk II would be considerably down on power compared to the Ferrari 156 V6, Colin Chapman had reduced the frontal area of the Lotus 21 to the minimum, to decrease aerodynamic drag. The 18

Stirling Moss chats with UDT-Laystall chief mechanic and Lotus 18/21 creator, Tony Robinson, on the grid at Brands Hatch. (LAT Photographic)

6: 1961 Formula 1 Season – Against the Odds

Moss settled into third from the start, behind the battling Clark and Surtees, until the ex-motorcycle champion missed a gear and went off the road, crushing the nose of his Cooper. Moss now closed on Clark, who managed to hold onto the lead, until caught and passed in front of the pits on lap 48 of the 76. The young Scotsman tried hard to regain the lead, but the edge had gone off his engine and Moss ran out the winner by 10sec. Gurney was fifth, two laps down, lacking a Mk II Climax. Marsh, delayed

had been sadly lacking in straight line speed and more slippery, rounded body panelling might well improve its performance. Robinson consulted Chapman on the subject and they liaised with body builders Williams & Pritchard to devise new panels that, unsurprisingly, bore a striking resemblance to those of the Lotus 21, albeit necessarily wider to accommodate the 18's more substantial frame. Frank Coltman of the Progress Chassis Company, long-time chassis sub-contractor to Lotus, carried out the necessary chassis work that included re-profiling the upper section of the seatback and scuttle bulkheads. Fuel was relocated from above the driver's legs to pannier tanks alongside the cockpit.

The Lotus 21-style body panels and 21-type rear suspension led to Lotus 18s so modified becoming known as 'Lotus 18/21s.' UDT modified chassis 916 in this way, whilst 917 and 918 were raced from new as 18/21s. Reflecting the close relationship with the BRP managed team, the Rob Walker chassis 906 and 912 were also upgraded. Walker chief mechanic Alf Francis chose to anchor the upper radius rods of the rear suspension to a lower point on the uprights than the UDT cars. By the end of the season, Team Lotus had converted 371 and 372 to 18/21 specification prior to their disposal.

18/21 rear suspension upright, incorporating a top transverse link. (Author)

Re-profiled upper sections of the seat back and scuttle bulkheads – compare these with the photographs in Chapter 2. (Author)

Whether or not the new body panels made any appreciable difference to performance is difficult to say, as there was never an opportunity to compare the two shapes. Wind tunnel testing remained very much in the future during the 1960s, thus any advantage was somewhat hypothetical. At the very least, the 18's appearance was transformed. Nevertheless, Stirling Moss appeared to like the result – although he possessed the skill to extract the most from the 18 whatever the specification, and remained the only driver to achieve any worthwhile results with the car.

Lotus 18 | 91

Lotus 18 – Colin Chapman's U-turn

SPECIFICATION: LOTUS 18/21 (1961) – AS FOR LOTUS 18 (1960) EXCEPT:
Engine: Rear-mounted Coventry Climax FPF Mk II 4-cylinder in line 1498cc, 151bhp at 7500rpm.
Transmission: Lotus 5-speed in unit with final drive and ZF differential with sequential gear change, or GSD type 32 5-speed in unit with final drive and ZF differential.
Fuel tanks: Fabricated aluminium tanks alongside and behind driver. Capacity 30 gallons approx.
Suspension: Rear: single upper link with long, low mounted reversed tubular wishbones. Combined coil spring/damper unit and anti-roll bar. Cast alloy hub carrier located by twin parallel radius arms.

by overheating, was sixth, followed by Parnell in seventh, and the Taylors (Henry and Trevor respectively) eighth and ninth. This race marked the first Formula 1 win for the UDT-Laystall Racing Team and for the Lotus 18/21.

Grand Prix de Belgique, Spa-Francorchamps, 18 June 1961

Whilst there might have been some lingering uncertainty as to the outcome of the Dutch Grand Prix, few would have doubted that the extra power of the Ferraris would be a decisive factor in the Belgian Grand Prix held on the super-fast Spa Francorchamps circuit. This proved to be the case, as the scarlet cars were never challenged, either in practice or the race. Moss' regular Walker Lotus had been brought up to 18/21 specification in the four week break since the Dutch Grand Prix and was joined by four other 18s on the entry list. UDT-Laystall was fielding only a single 18/21 (918), for either Cliff Allison or Henry Taylor, the pair having the unenviable task of competing against each other for the drive.

Stirling Moss (912) leads Tony Brooks (BRM) into La Source hairpin at Spa, in a race in which he would finish an uncharacteristically low eighth.
(LAT Photographic)

6: 1961 Formula 1 Season – Against the Odds

This was decided on the opening lap of practice, when Allison crashed heavily on the fast approach to Blanchimont corner, sustaining serious leg injuries and severely damaging the Lotus. He had crashed heavily at Monaco in 1960, when driving for Ferrari, and this second serious accident would prompt his retirement from motor racing.

Moss found his engine was not pulling sufficient revs down the straights, so the Walker team fitted trunking along the side of the car to feed cool air to the carburettors from the nose. He could lap no better than 4min 8.2sec for eighth on the grid, beaten by four Ferraris, a Cooper and two BRMs. Even though he was almost 9sec off the pace, he was at least 9.5sec quicker than the struggling Team Lotus 21s. Equipe Nationale Belge withdrew its two Emeryson-Maseratis, due to persistent chassis failures, and came to arrangements with Tony Marsh and Wolfgang Seidel (who had failed to qualify) for the loan of their Lotus 18s, to keep their Belgian drivers on the grid. Willy Mairesse would drive Marsh's car (909) and Lucien Bianchi Seidel's Colonia entry (373), both cars distempered overnight in Belgian racing yellow.

All the entries were weighed during practice to ensure they complied with the regulation minimum weight limit of 450kg. The BRM was heaviest at 520kg, the lightest Ferraris was 505kg, Porsche and Cooper were 500kg each, with the Lotus 21 lightest at 455kg. Of the Lotus 18s, the Walker 18/21 was heaviest at 500kg, the Marsh 18 465kg and, strangely, the Scuderia Colonia 18 455kg.

The Ferraris ran as they pleased in the race, finishing 1-2-3-4 in the order Hill, von Trips, Ginther and guest driver, the Belgian, Olivier Gendebien. The latter was a Ferrari endurance racing specialist who had recently won his third Le Mans 24 Hours, and was not often seen in single-seaters. Best of the rest was John Surtees in a Yeoman Credit-run Cooper in fifth. Stirling Moss initially ran in company with Masten Gregory's Camoradi Cooper, before breaking free to finish an uncharacteristically low eighth. His was the first Lotus home, pulling only 146mph, utterly outclassed in terms of straight line speed. The two hired 18s were both out within nine laps with engine-related problems, having trailed around at the tail of the field. Ian Burgess had appeared for practice in his Camoradi 18, but failed to qualify. This all put *Autosport* into a rather downbeat mood, editor Gregor Grant declaring that "the domination begun by Vanwall and carried on by Cooper Climax is at an end. Until British drivers receive new equipment, particularly engines, they will continue to tail along behind the red cars from Maranello."

Grand Prix de L'Automobile Club de France, Reims, 2 July 1961

The long, slipstreaming straights of the Reims circuit were regarded as another certain walkover for Ferrari, fielding a four-car entry once again. The fourth car was for Giancarlo Baghetti, the victor of the Syracuse and the Naples Grands Prix for Ferrari. UDT-Laystall entered 18/21s for Henry Taylor (916), joined by Lucien Bianchi (917), who replaced the injured Cliff Allison. These cars were back on Lotus 'queerboxes,' the Laystall-built versions now abandoned having not proved a success. Stirling Moss was in the Walker 18/21, and numbers were made up to five by Michael May for Scuderia Colonia and Ian Burgess for Camoradi in standard 18s.

Ferrari dominated the typically hot Reims practice sessions, Phil Hill leading von Trips and Ginther, to take over the front row of the grid, with Baghetti back in twelfth. Moss was unhappy with the handling of his 18/21, but managed to pick up a tow from von Trips' Ferrari. The German lapped faster and faster, trying to break the tow, but the Lotus remained firmly tucked into his slipstream. Von Trips failed to appreciate that he was towing Moss around to an outstanding lap time of 2min 27.6sec, 2.4sec quicker than he could achieve on his own. This put him fourth on the grid, some 1.4sec better than Clark, in the next Climax-powered car. Ferrari team manager Tavoni, now wise to this ruse, kept a careful eye on his cars to ensure that no other British drivers tried the same trick. The UDT cars were well down, Bianchi 8sec off the pace in 19th, with Taylor 25th – May and Burgess between them on 22nd and 24th.

The weather remained hot for race day, the three Ferraris surging forwards from the front row as one on the fall of the starter's flag. Moss tucked himself right into their slipstream, crouched down behind his windscreen to minimalise his frontal area. These four pulled away from the pack, Phil Hill leading von Trips and Ginther. On lap 4, Ginther spun at Muizon, letting Moss up to third. Within a couple of laps Ginther was back ahead of Moss and the Ferraris gradually drew away, leaving Moss 10sec in arrears. Moss began to slow visibly under braking and, by lap 13, a pack of seven cars hotly disputing fifth place was right on his tail. He quickly sank within it, his braking uneven and the pedal spongy. On lap 19, he drew into the pits, where it was discovered that the balance pipe between the two pads of the right rear disc brake had fractured, allowing pressure and fluid to escape. Repairs consumed four laps before he could continue, only to experience a violent vibration from the right rear wheel. He stopped again on the next lap to ensure the wheel was secure,

Lotus 18 | 93

Lotus 18 – Colin Chapman's U-turn

Start of the French Grand Prix: the Ferrari boys set the pace – Richie Ginther (18) is slightly ahead of Phil Hill (16) and Wolfgang von Trips (20), with Stirling Moss (26) latching onto their slipstream. (Author)

6: 1961 Formula 1 Season – Against the Odds

Stirling Moss drifts the Walker Lotus 18/21 (912) through Thillois Corner at Reims over a deteriorating road surface. (LAT Photographic)

rejoined, but was back in again within a few more laps. It took some time to discover that molten tar flung up from the road surface had centrifuged around the inside of the wheel rim, then run down to the bottom when the car was stationary and coagulated into a globule, putting the wheel out of balance. Moss was now many laps behind, but the drama was not yet over. On lap 38, leader Phil Hill spun on wet tar at Thillois in front of Moss, the two cars collided bending the front suspension of the 18/21. Hill lost two laps before restarting his stalled engine, whilst Moss crept up the road to the pits to retire.

The Ferrari team had been decimated as, aside from Hill, both von Trips and Ginther had suffered engine failures. Meanwhile Giancarlo Baghetti, in the fourth Ferrari, had been holding his own in an intense slipstreaming battle with the Porsches and Team Lotus

Lotus 18 | 95

Lotus 18 – Colin Chapman's U-turn

Phil Hill spins his Ferrari in front of Stirling Moss on wet tar at Thillois. The two cars collide, the Lotus suffering terminal suspension damage as a result.
(LAT Photographic)

for what was now the lead. Displaying the coolness of a veteran in only his first Grand Prix, he ducked out of the slipstream of Dan Gurney's Porsche to snatch a sensational victory by just 0.1 sec.

RAC British Grand Prix, Aintree, 15 July 1961

From the hot Champagne region of France, the Championship moved to the bleak and wet suburbs of Liverpool and the Aintree circuit, laid out in and around the famous steeplechase course. Lotus 18s were out in force, with nine entries, including 18/21s for Moss (912), and the UDT-Laystall pair of Taylor (916) and Bianchi (917). Standard 18s came from Louise Bryden-Brown (903) for South African Formula Junior newcomer Tony Maggs, Ian Burgess was in the Camoradi car (905) (now running with a longer, more streamlined nosecone), Wolfgang Seidel had his Scuderia Colonia car (373), with Tony Marsh (909), Tim Parnell (904) and Gerry Ashmore (919) in their own examples.

Somewhere under the tarpaulin is Tony Maggs, about to make his Grand Prix debut driving for Louise Bryden-Brown (903). (Ferret Fotographics)

Lotus 18 – Colin Chapman's U-turn

Any hopes that the circuit would favour the British teams were quickly dispelled, when the Ferraris of Hill and Ginther annexed the first two places on the grid, with Bonnier's Porsche third. Von Trips was relegated to the second row, 0.2sec quicker than Moss, the timekeepers having adjudged that the first four drivers had recorded identical times, as their watches read only to the nearest one fifth of a second. The best other 18 was Taylor down in 17th, 2.8sec slower. After dry practice sessions on Thursday, Friday was washed out: wind and rain lashed the circuit, making any improvement in times impossible.

It was raining heavily at the start of the race, as Phil Hill led von Trips, Ginther and Moss away in a vast plume of spray. The huge crowd was hoping that the conditions would act as an equaliser and offer Moss an opportunity to mix it with the Ferraris and cheered loudly when he moved up to third, as Ginther had a big slide on lap 6. On the following lap, von Trips nipped into the lead after Hill was held up by a tail-ender. On lap 10, another huge cheer erupted as Moss moved up to second, when Hill had a hairy moment on a large puddle at the Melling Crossing. Moss closed onto von Trips' tail in the hope of worrying the German into an error. He maintained his position in the Ferrari's mirrors from laps 16 until 24, when he too was caught out on the Melling Crossing puddle. The tail of the Walker Lotus slid out to the left, was corrected, slid to the right, then back again then through a full 360°, Moss catching it at the end of the spin, selecting a lower gear and accelerating away, as if nothing had happened. This put Moss 10sec behind von Trips as the rain began to ease. Ginther had taken third from Hill, and began to close on Moss, demoting him to third on lap 40. Moss now seemed to be in trouble, no longer able to stay with the Ferraris, and was taken by Hill four laps later. Sure enough, he pulled into the pits – to a huge groan from the crowd. Quite extraordinarily, he had suffered a similar brake balance pipe failure to the one at Reims, this time on the left rear rather than the right rear disc. The race ran its course in drying conditions as another Ferrari 1-2-3, von Trips followed by Hill and Ginther.

Of the other Lotus 18s, Tony Maggs was the top finisher, well beaten down in 13th, followed by Ian Burgess, both lapped six times. The remaining 18s failed to finish, including Henry Taylor who crashed heavily into hoardings on the outside of the track on lap 5, after hitting the Melling Crossing puddle, demolishing the UDT-Laystall 18/21 and injuring himself.

Four 18s turned out for the Solitude Grand Prix, one week later, that would be dominated by a race-long duel between the Porsches of Jo Bonnier and Dan Gurney and the Lotus 21 of Innes Ireland, the decision going to the Scot in the last few yards. Stirling Moss was driving a UDT-Laystall 18/21 (917), and was joined by Seidel and May in the Scuderia Colonia 18s, and Lucky Casner making a one-off appearance in one of his Camoradi 18s (908). Moss was unhappy with his car in practice, apparently down on power and 2.6sec off the pace, in fifth place on the grid. In the race, he ran seventh, well behind the leading bunch, before retiring with a broken final drive. Seidel gave up, having broken his steering wheel, May went off the road, damaging his chassis, on the opening lap, whilst Casner never started due to a practice engine failure.

Lotus 18s scoop the British Grand Prix programme cover. (Author)

6: 1961 Formula 1 Season – Against the Odds

Wet start at Aintree: Phil Hill is already out of shot, ahead of Ferrari team-mates Wolfgang von Trips (4) and Ritchie Ginther (6), with the persistent Stirling Moss (28) following closely. (Sutton Images)

Lotus 18 | 99

Moss (912) splashes away from the Melling Crossing in his relentless hounding of the Ferraris. (LAT Photographic)

Großer Preis von Deutschland, Nürburgring, 6 August 1961

The German Grand Prix returned to the magnificent 14.5-mile Nürburgring after a gap of two years. The ultimate test of driver and car, the circuit would provide another opportunity for Stirling Moss to match his skills against the Ferrari team as an acknowledged 'Ringmeister,' or even 'Regenmeister' should the weather be wet. Besides the Walker 18/21, the two Scuderia Colonia 18s (373 and 914) were out again, together with Tony Marsh (909) and Gerry Ashmore (919) in their privately run 18s, and Tony Maggs in Louise Bryden-Brown's pale blue example (903). The UDT-Laystall team 18s had not been invited.

Practice was notable for the appearance of the first 'proper' British 1½-litre Formula 1 car, a Cooper, powered by the new Coventry Climax FWMV V8 engine. Predictably, a Ferrari was quickest in practice, Phil Hill lapping in an almost unbelievable time of 8min 55.2sec on soft Dunlop D12 rain tyres. The first sub-nine minute lap of the circuit left him both physically and mentally drained. Jack Brabham was next up, some 6secs slower, after numerous problems with the Climax V8. Moss was down on maximum speed and troubled by his GSD gearbox jumping out of third gear. Trying really hard he put in a best lap of 9min 1.7sec for third on the grid, only 0.3sec slower than Brabham, but some 6.5sec slower than Hill. Marsh was fastest of the other 18s, down in 20th, with Maggs 22nd and Ashmore 25th. May lost control of his Colonia car, turning it over and bending it too extensively to start. Seidel had his front suspension collapse, but it was repaired with parts salvaged from May's car and he started 23rd.

Race day dawned hot and sunny, but weather forecasters predicted rain. This proved to be the case: it rained at midday, soaking the circuit, but as the cars formed up on the grid, the sky cleared and the sun returned. The circuit remained wet enough for the teams to have to decide whether or not to run the D12 rain tyre. Dunlop advised against the D12s, as they would not last the distance on a drying track, but Moss went against this, seeking to gain an advantage over the Ferraris with their extra grip, should it rain again or the track not dry out completely. The green identification 'spots' on his D12s, were blacked over to conceal his tactics.

Dunlop had introduced the D12 soft compound nylon carcase R5 tyre at the start of the 1961 Grand Prix season, specifically for really bad weather conditions. Extensive development work had created the first race tyre to feature a synthetic rubber tread in a high hysteresis (capacity to absorb energy) compound. It offered startling degrees of grip in the wet, with a 20% increase in braking efficiency and considerable improvements in reducing rear-end breakaway in corners. Whilst the synthetic rubber could tolerate

6 August 1961: Stirling Moss (912), in stylish pose, leans into the Nürburgring Karussel on his way to a sensational defeat of the Ferrari team. (LAT Photographic)

6: 1961 Formula 1 Season – Against the Odds

The Walker Lotus (912) becomes airborne on a dry patch of the Nürburgring, as Moss endeavours to maintain his lead. (LAT Photographic)

higher temperatures, it needed the cooling effect of a wet track to keep the temperature and wear rate under control, otherwise there was the ever-present danger of the tread 'chunking.' All the R5 tyres, including the D12, featured identical construction and tread pattern, normal usage being the D9 for dry and D12 for wet conditions; both mounted on 15in diameter wheels.

At the start, Brabham jumped into the lead from Moss, but his race lasted barely 5km before he lost the new V8 Cooper on a damp patch of track, and went off into the shrubbery. With a clear road ahead of him, Moss drew on all his skill and experience of the Nürburgring to complete the first long lap with a 2sec lead over Hill, who had shaken his Ferrari free of the pack. Through sheer brilliance, Moss extended his lead over Hill to 11sec by lap 4. Von Trips was 7.5sec further back in third, rapidly gaining ground after a slow start. Moss had been making full use of his softer D12s, but the track had now dried and the Ferraris were able to put on the pressure. Moss maintained his lead, however, making up on the corners what he lost on the straighter bits. Von Trips took Hill for second on lap 8, and began stringing together a series of fast laps around the nine-minute mark to bring him within 10sec of Moss. On lap 10, he became the first driver to break the nine-minute barrier in a race, with a lap of 8min. 59.9secs,

Lotus 18 – Colin Chapman's U-turn

THE NÜRBURGRING

Perhaps the finest circuit on the Grand Prix calendar, the 14.17-mile Nürburgring circuit was carved out of the forest-clad slopes of the Eifel mountains near Koblenz, western Germany. Opened in 1927, it incorporated almost every conceivable variation of corner – 88 left-handers, 84 right-handers – as the road twisted, climbed and plunged through the forest, with a variation in altitude of 1,000ft between the lowest and highest points.

It provided the driver with a roller coaster of a ride through swoops and swerves between hedgerows and overhanging trees. Many corners were entered blind, or over the brow of a hill, on a surface often made damp by the frequent appearance of mist or fog. It soon became the ultimate 'driver's circuit,' one he could 'get his teeth into,' the yardstick against which a driver's true skill was measured.

Although he had never won a Grand Prix at the Nürburgring, Stirling Moss had always set the pace and had won three consecutive 1000km sports car events, ably demonstrating the outstanding skills of a 'Ringmeister.' Underlining those skills to the full in the 1961 Grand Prix, he once again overcame the odds to beat the Ferrari team in changeable conditions. He even inspired Phil Hill to break the magic nine-minute lap barrier in his desperate pursuit of the Rob Walker Lotus 18/21.

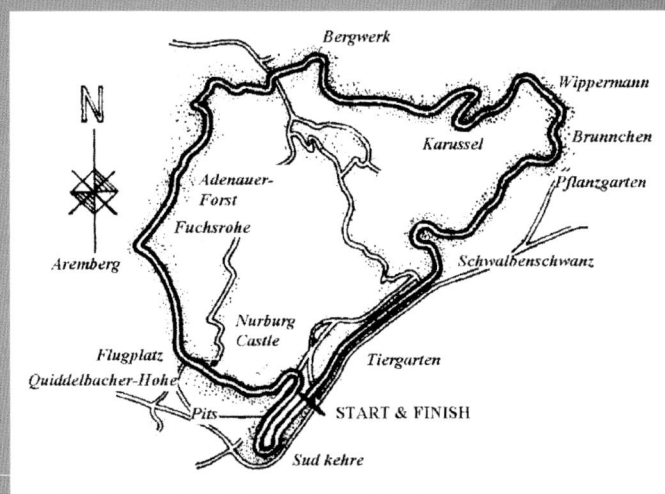

The Nürburgring. (Author)

yet barely had he done so, than Hill recorded 8min 57.8sec, set to remain the fastest lap of the race. Despite this, the Ferraris were still 6.9secs in arrears, yet it seemed ever more likely that they would catch Moss, as his tyres became more marginal lap by lap. He held on purely by virtue of his superior skill, and then, on lap 13, it started to rain again, giving his tyres the break they needed. Without rain tyres, the Ferraris were unable to keep pace and the race was over.

Moss won by 21.4 sec after another display of masterly driving to match that seen at Monaco, to give the Lotus 18 its second Grand Prix victory of the season and fourth in total. The Ferraris were left to dispute second place, von Trips slithering across the line 1.1sec ahead of Hill. *Autosport* celebrated with its traditional green cover for a British win and enthused over the ability of Moss to match "... the superior power of the Ferraris with driving virtuosity and an uncanny appreciation of the situation that had both von Trips and Hill baffled" – this with a year-old Lotus 18 chassis.

Of the other 18s, Maggs brought his home 11th, one lap behind, with Marsh two laps behind in 15th, after stops to repair a broken ignition wire. Ashmore was 16th, whilst Seidel had retired on lap 3 with broken steering.

Phil Hill (Ferrari) tries his damnedest to close up on 'Ringmeister' Moss. (Author)

6: 1961 Formula 1 Season – Against the Odds

STIRLING MOSS

(b. 17 September 1929)

By 1961, Stirling Moss was 31 and at the peak of his career. His first regular Grand Prix season had been in 1953 and, since then, he had been runner-up in the World Championship four times, never quite favoured with that extra element of luck to take the title for himself. He was rightly regarded as 'the man to beat,' the standard against which all drivers measured themselves, a position that he had inherited on the retirement of the great five-times Champion Juan Fangio in 1958. In such circumstances, the lack of a Championship title seemed of little consequence. He was an outstanding ambassador for the sport and for Britain and rightly regarded by its public as 'Mr Motor Racing.'

Moss was an immaculate stylist at the wheel, who never gave less than 100% and, whatever the conditions or situation, he was always a potential winner if the car could match his commitment. Even if it could not, he had the ability to compensate for any mechanical deficiencies and still win. He was a true all-rounder, brilliant in a wide variety of cars and categories of racing, slipping easily from Formula 1 to Formula 2, sports cars, GT and saloon cars in the space of a single afternoon.

Moss would have been welcomed into any factory team, yet preferred to drive cars in the relaxed atmosphere of the private team run by his friend Rob Walker. Following Walker's purchase of a Lotus 18 during 1960, Stirling quickly assumed the role of 'team leader' for the marque, exercising his superiority over the Team Lotus entries. He gave Lotus its first World Championship win at Monaco and, but for the serious accident in Belgium, might well have made 1960 his Championship year. Racing for Walker did not allow him the most competitive chassis in 1961, due to conflicting fuel contracts, leaving him in the position of something of an underdog. He accepted the challenge with relish and continued to drive the Lotus 18 to defeat the Ferraris memorably in his all-time great Grand Prix drives at Monaco and the Nürburgring.

Whilst Team Lotus failed to score a Championship victory with the Lotus 18 for various reasons, Moss in the Walker-prepared cars won four Grands Prix, plus six non-Championship wins for the marque up to the end of 1961. He opened his 1962 season with the 18/21 V8 Special, that he drove forcefully despite its shortcomings, and it was unfortunate that it should have been in this car that Stirling ended his career on Easter Monday 1962.

Stirling Moss is congratulated by Colin Chapman on another win for Lotus. (Author)

Lotus 18 – Colin Chapman's U-turn

Three non-Championship Formula 1 races were held in the four-week period before the next Grand Prix at Monza. Stirling Moss drove a UDT-Laystall 18/21 (918) to victory in the Kanonloppet at Karlskoga in central Sweden from the back of the grid, after missing practice due to the clashing Goodwood RAC Tourist Trophy the previous day. The ever-present privateer Tim Parnell finished fifth in his 18 (904), in a race in which Innes Ireland, in the absence of a 21, had transmission failure on his Team Lotus 18 (371). The following weekend, Moss drove another UDT-Laystall 18/21 (916) to win all three heats of the Danish Grand Prix held at the Roskildering. Henry Taylor, recovered from his British Grand Prix injuries, was fourth and Tim Parnell fifth. Finally, Moss completed a hat trick by winning the Modena Grand Prix, driving his usual Walker 18/21 (912). Despite an entry list of 28 cars, the regulations allowed only 14 starters, of which four were 18s. These included two UDT 18/21s for Taylor (918) and Masten Gregory (917) – the American taking a regular drive with the British team following the folding of Camoradi International. Finally, Giorgio Scarlatti was down to drive the ex-Scuderia Centro Sud chassis (902), powered by the 4-cylinder Maserati 150S engine and now owned by Prince Gaetano Starrabba. Moss led unchallenged from lap 12 to 100, his the only 18 to finish.

TECHNICAL UPDATE: LOTUS 18/21 V8 SPECIAL

The first of the new Coventry Climax FWMV V8 engines was allocated to the Cooper team, but the second unit went to the Rob Walker racing team for Stirling Moss. In the absence of an up-to-date chassis, the spare Walker Lotus 18/21 chassis (906) was extensively rebuilt and modified to take the engine, thereby creating the ultimate version of the Lotus 18.

A Team Lotus draughtsman detailed the chassis modifications in a drawing dated 5 June 1961, entitled 'Modifications to 1960 Formula 1 chassis to suit 1961 rear suspension and V8 Coventry Climax engine (S Moss Esq).' The actual rebuilding work was carried out by Harry Ferguson Research, with whom Rob Walker already had a working relationship, having race-prepared and entered the experimental four-wheel-drive Ferguson P99 in the 1961 British Grand Prix. The existing engine bay of the 18 chassis was cut away and a new bay constructed in 1in diameter 18swg tubing. This terminated in a substantial,

The Lotus 18/21 V8 Special (906) on its debut at Monza with 'gun-turret' above the carburettors – possibly the only way of defeating the Ferraris. (LAT Photographic)

104 | Lotus 18

6: 1961 Formula 1 Season – Against the Odds

Gran Premio d'Italia, Monza, 10 September 1961

The Italian Grand Prix was to take place on the combined, high speed Monza road and banked circuit, as it had in 1960. On that occasion, the event had been boycotted by the British teams, deeming that the roughness of the banking made it unsuitable for a modern Grand Prix car. The banking remained rough, but the British teams only voiced objections this time, hoping perhaps that it might cause the Ferraris to falter on their home ground.

Showing how seriously it was taking this event, Ferrari arrived for practice with five Dino 156 chassis plus a spare, to be driven by the usual team of Hill, von Trips and Ginther, joined by Baghetti and debutant Ricardo Rodriguez. This 19-year-old Mexican had made a name for himself as a charger in Ferrari sports cars, but showed little mechanical sympathy for his cars. Cooper had its new Climax V8-engined car once again and, in the intervening period since the German Grand Prix, Coventry Climax had produced a second FWMV V8, allocated to Stirling Moss for installation in the Walker team's spare Lotus 18/21 chassis (906) – see panel.

fabricated tubular rear bulkhead, supporting both the V8 engine, the GSD type 32 5-speed transmission and the 18/21-type rear suspension mounting points. The whole structure was bolted to the front half of the frame and was completely detachable, to permit engine removal and installation.

Colin Chapman reckoned that chassis rigidity had been compromised by the modifications, but there was probably an element of professional jealousy involved, as he felt aggrieved that the Climax V8 had been allocated to Rob Walker rather than to Team Lotus. The hybrid chassis was readied using a standard 18/21 rear body section, incorporating an ugly turret-shaped hump above the V8's downdraught Weber carburettors, whilst still retaining the left side carburettor bulge of the 4-cylinder engine. The car was completed, somewhat hurriedly, in time for the Italian Grand Prix on 10 September, and arrived at Monza completely untried.

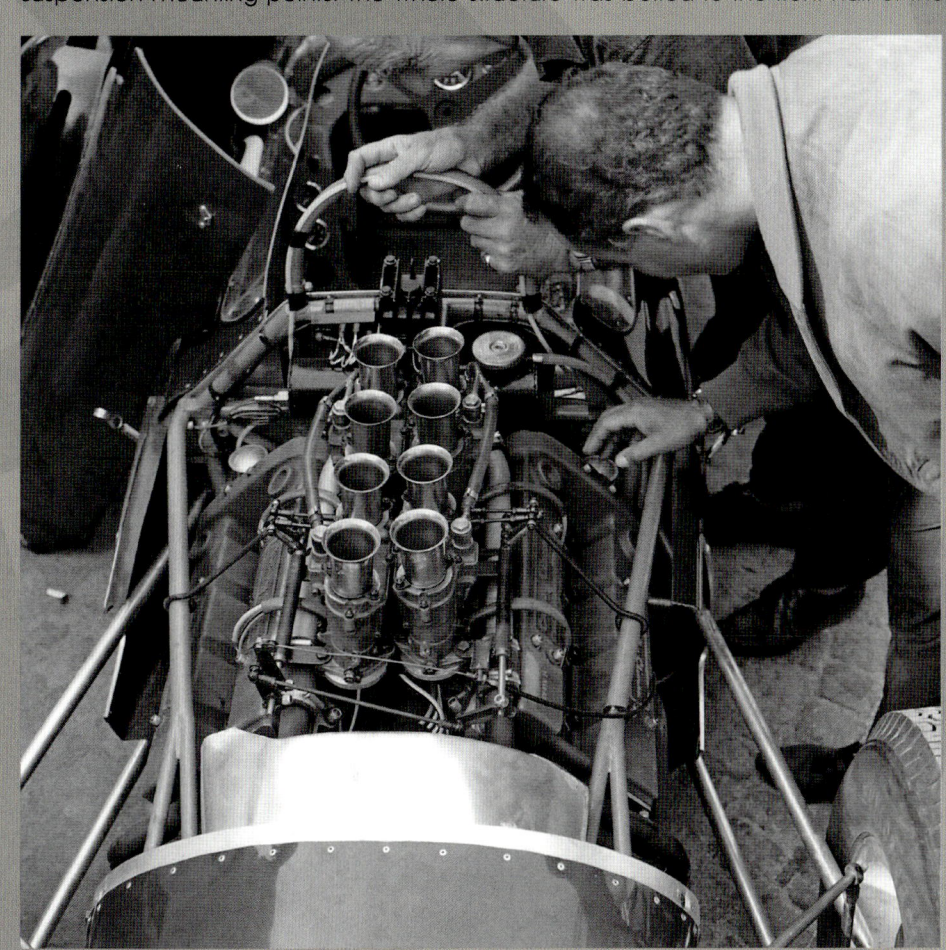

The installation of the new Coventry Climax FWMV V8 in the Walker team 18/21 Special chassis. (Author)

Lotus 18 | 105

Lotus 18 – Colin Chapman's U-turn

SPECIFICATION: LOTUS 18/21 V8 SPECIAL (1961) CHASSIS 906
– as for Lotus 18/21 except:
Engine: Rear-mounted Coventry Climax FWMV V8 cylinder 1494cc, 181bhp at 8500rpm.
Chassis: Fully-triangulated Lotus 18 multi-tubular space frame constructed in mainly 1in diameter 18 and 16 gauge steel tubing. Fabricated perforated hoop-type bulkhead at scuttle, fabricated tubular rear bulkhead. Engine bay extensively redesigned and rebuilt to accommodate Climax V8 engine
Transmission: GSD type 32 5-speed in unit with final drive and ZF differential.

Moss on the Monza banking with the 18/21 V8 Special during practice. (LAT Photographic)

Rob Walker also had the Monaco and Nürburgring winning 18/21 (912) as a backup, and there were two UDT-Laystall 18/21s for Henry Taylor (918) and Masten Gregory (917). Four standard 18s completed the entry, including Wolfgang Seidel for Scuderia Colonia, the regular duo of Tim Parnell and Gerry Ashmore, together with Prince Gaetano Starrabba driving his Maserati-powered chassis (902).

Making its first public appearance was the impressive and beautifully executed new V8-engined BRM P578, but it was Ferrari that dominated practice – as anticipated – taking the top four places. Both the Climax V8s suffered chronic overheating, consuming gallons of water. Brabham persevered with his to lap 0.2sec quicker than Moss in 11th, but over 5sec away from pole position. The V8 was clearly not yet raceworthy and Moss decided to fall back on his familiar 4-cylinder-engined 18/21 chassis for the race, despite having set his grid time with the V8.

Overnight, Innes Ireland made the noble gesture of offering his Team Lotus 21 to Moss, to aid the chances of Lotus in the Constructors' Championship. Both Colin Chapman and Rob Walker were agreeable, so the cars were swapped and Ireland appeared at the start in the Walker 18/21, with a spare pale green UDT-Laystall upper body panel (the Team 21 equivalent would not fit), dark blue Walker side panels and his race number 38. The 21 for Moss looked equally bizarre, with a dark blue Walker nose/upper section, green Team Lotus side panels and yellow wheels.

The grid formed on a two-by-two basis, instigated by the organisers to allow the Ferraris to pull clear from would-be slipstreamers in the lower ranks. Those at the back of the massive 16-row, 32-car grid passed the start line some seconds after the front rows had departed. The Ferraris were fitted with higher final drive ratios for this circuit and were slow getting away, allowing Clark and Brabham to get amongst them, so that Hill led the first lap, followed by Ginther, Rodriguez, Clark, Brabham and von Trips. On lap 2, tragedy struck entering the Parabolica, when von Trips and Clark collided. The Ferrari spun, overturned and careered along the spectator enclosure before bouncing back onto the road, leaving 14 spectators and von Trips dead or dying.

The race continued unaware of the tragedy, Phil Hill leading from start to finish to scoop the 1961 Drivers' World Championship, the first American ever to hold the title. Lacking Stirling Moss in the cockpit, the 18s failed to make any impression. Innes Ireland, in the Walker car, maintained 13th place in the second bunch behind the Ferraris, before pitting on lap 5, unable to select gears properly. Investigation revealed that the chassis had cracked and was flexing, putting the gear selectors out of phase with the lever. Moss, in Ireland's 21, fought a race-long duel with Gurney's Porsche, latterly for second place, until a left front wheel bearing failed seven laps short of the finish, the legacy of the punishment meted out by the banking.

Of the remaining 18s, Seidel's engine expired on the opening lap, whilst Ashmore entered the Parabolica too quickly and shot over a grass bank into the woods beyond. Masten Gregory stopped for a change of plugs in the vain hope of improving his engine's performance, only to retire on lap 11 with a broken rear suspension wishbone. Starrabba's Maserati engine failed on lap 19, leaving only Parnell and Taylor to finish in 10th and 11th, trailing three and four laps behind respectively.

Another seven days and another Formula 1 race later, Innes Ireland had reclaimed his Lotus 21 from Moss to win the Flugplatzrennen at Zeltweg. Three 18s appeared for this event, of which Tim Parnell (904) was the sole finisher in seventh. The persistent Wolfgang Seidel retired with engine failure, whilst Ernesto Prinoth in his Scuderia Dolomiti 18 (913) went off the road. The Oulton Park Gold Cup attracted five 18s, but not Stirling Moss, who chose to drive the four-wheel-drive Ferguson P99 to its one and only victory. The UDT-Laystall 18/21s of Gregory and Taylor were outrun by the Coopers and a BRM to finish fifth and eighth respectively, with Wolfgang Seidel tenth. Trevor Taylor made another appearance in a Team Lotus 18 (371), but retired with a broken exhaust. With the main teams on their way to the USA, Tim Parnell was the only 18 driver to contest the Lewis-Evans Trophy at Brands Hatch, the last Formula 1 event of the British season. Tony Marsh had deserted the 18 ranks in favour of a Climax-engined 1960 BRM P48 chassis, with which he won the event, with Parnell third in an unrepresentative field.

United States Grand Prix, Watkins Glen, 8 October 1961

The introduction of Formula 1 to the USA had not exactly been a roaring success, the event being held at Sebring in 1959 and Riverside on the West coast in 1960. It was decided to take a chance on holding the event in upstate New York, at Watkins Glen, for 1961, a location that would prove to be a success for a good number of years. Unfortunately, Ferrari failed to show, denying new World Champion Phil Hill the opportunity to race in front of his fellow countrymen. Consequently, the entry resembled a British non-Championship race, with only the Porsche team adding a little international flavour.

Lotus 18 – Colin Chapman's U-turn

Tim Parnell in his privately-run 18 (904) rounds Bottom Bend at Brands Hatch, on his way to third in the Lewis Evans Trophy. (LAT Photographic)

Lotus 18s numbered seven, of which two 18/21s were on hand from Rob Walker for Stirling Moss, both the conventional Monaco/Nürburgring winner and the V8 Climax-engined 'Special' seen at Monza. UDT-Laystall had a pair of 18/21s for Masten Gregory and Olivier Gendebien (filling in for Henry Taylor, who had decided to retire from racing). Team Lotus delivered two of its long-serving 18s, upgraded to 18/21 specification, to new owners Jim Hall (371) and J Wheeler Autosport (372) for Canadian Peter Ryan. Finally, Indianapolis driver Lloyd Ruby was down to drive the ex-Jim Hall 1960 standard chassis (907).

The absence of Ferrari gave Jack Brabham the opportunity to take pole position in the V8 Climax-engined Cooper T58. Stirling Moss was only 0.2sec slower in his V8-engined Lotus, both V8s having been back to Coventry Climax since Monza to diagnose, and hopefully cure, the cooling problems experienced to date. Nevertheless, the Moss V8 developed a persistent misfire that defied all attempts to cure it. He swapped over to his 4-cylinder car, achieving a best time 1sec slower than with the V8 car. As practice drew to a close, he elected to drive his more reliable 4-cylinder example in the race and forego second spot on the

6: 1961 Formula 1 Season – Against the Odds

Lloyd Ruby, in the J Frank Harrison entered 18 (907), would retire from the United States Grand Prix at Watkins Glen with a failed magneto drive. (LAT Photographic)

grid for third. Gregory was back in 11th for UDT, ahead of Peter Ryan in 13th, who had driven very smoothly after a magneto change. Gendebien overturned his car in a ditch, but it was repaired in time for him to qualify 15th, although he was somewhat shaken. Hall and Ruby were at the back of the 19-car field.

The start of the race was performed by the lavender-suited, cigar-chewing Tex Hopkins, whose antics of leaping in the air whilst waving the flag would become a familiar feature at the Glen. Moss took an initial lead, but was taken by Brabham after five laps, the improved Climax V8 running well. These two swapped the lead over the next 40 laps, Moss doing everything he could to stay with the V8 Cooper. Meanwhile Masten Gregory was disputing sixth place with Dan Gurney's Porsche, until the duel ended abruptly on lap 23, when the 18/21 had a gear selector break. Gregory was not finished yet, however, as he took over team-mate Gendebien's 18/21 on lap 33, the Belgian still suffering the after effects of his practice accident.

On lap 39, Brabham dropped behind Moss, the Climax V8 trailing wisps of smoke from the left-hand exhaust and then spurting water from the overflow pipe. Brabham pitted with a recurrence of the Monza overheating problem, leaving Moss in a comfortable lead. As the race settled into its second half, to everyone's astonishment, Moss coasted in on lap 58 with a dead engine, the main bearings of the 4-cylinder Climax engine having failed. The lead now passed to the Lotus 21 of Innes Ireland, who saw out the remaining laps to score the first Grand Prix victory for himself and for Team Lotus, all other Lotus successes having been achieved by Moss with the Rob Walker 18, of course. The only 18s to finish were those of Peter Ryan in ninth, four laps behind, and the Gregory/Gendebien car in 11th, eight laps behind. Lloyd Ruby and Jim Hall had both retired at around three-quarter distance, with a fuel leak and sheared magneto drive respectively.

The European season drew to a close in October with the Coppa Italia, a national event contrived to decide the Italian Championship in favour of Giancarlo Baghetti over Lorenzo Bandini. Two Italian-owned 18s were entered, the Scuderia Dolomiti example (913) of Ernesto Prinoth finished second in both heats to Baghetti's Porsche, whilst Gaetano Starrabba (902) failed to finish the second heat, when his Maserati engine failed.

South African Formula 1 Series

The South African National 'Gold Star' Series had been based around European Formula 2 regulations and strongly supported by local drivers in a variety of imported Coopers and several

Moss (912) could have won his third Grand Prix of the season at Watkins Glen but for bearing failure on his Climax engine. (LAT Photographic)

Lotus 18 | 109

Lotus 18 – Colin Chapman's U-turn

home-built derivatives powered by mainly 4-cylinder Coventry Climax or Alfa Romeo engines. Now that the National Series effectively complied with the current Formula 1 regulations, the RAC of South Africa decided to organise a four-race 'Springbok' series in December, for which it succeeded in attracting Porsche, Team Lotus and the UDT-Laystall team, the latter taking three 18/21 chassis to be driven by Masten Gregory and Stirling Moss.

The most competitive local driver was Syd van der Vyver, the 1960 and 1961 South African National Champion. He had purchased a Formula 2 Lotus 18 chassis from the factory as a kit of parts and, as such, it was never allocated an appropriate factory chassis number. In addition, a number of Formula Junior Lotus 18 chassis sold to South Africa over the course of the year appeared in the series, powered by a variety of engines. As these were not pure Lotus 18 Formula 1/2 chassis in the accepted sense, they are detailed in Chapter 11 – Lotus 18 chassis in South African Formula 1.

A local driver with a 'genuine' Lotus 18 was Helmut Menzler. He had imported a new chassis (911) into South Africa in the latter part of 1960, into which he installed an ex-works Borgward 4-cylinder, 16-valve fuel-injected sports car engine. This engine had been campaigned very successfully by Stirling Moss during 1959 in European Formula 2 events when powering Cooper chassis. Distinctive for its ducting of cool air from the nose to the inlet system, the Lotus-Borgward would prove to be well off the pace, however, finishing only once, five laps in arrears in tenth place in the South African Grand Prix.

Masten Gregory (917) dropped out of third place during the Rand Grand Prix with overheating, an event won by Jim Clark in a Lotus 21. Stirling Moss (918) joined Gregory for the following two events, but missed practice for the Natal Grand Prix and had to start from the back of the 22-car grid. By lap 15, he had charged through to fourth place and, eight laps later, he was second to the Lotus 21 of Jim Clark. He drove as hard as he could, setting the fastest lap, but could not get within 30sec of Clark over the remaining 63 laps. Moss followed this with second spot on the grid for the South African Grand Prix, just 0.2sec slower than Clark. Gregory (916) was fifth, but would last only nine laps before a brake pipe fractured. Clark led Moss from the start, until spinning on lap 6 to avoid a back marker. This enabled Moss to build a 20sec lead, but Clark piled on the pressure, catching, then passing, the 18/21 relatively easily to draw away and win by 15sec.

Moss had been beaten twice by Jim Clark in the space of ten days and now realised that, if he wanted to keep ahead of the talented Scotsman in future, he would need at least an equal car. Clark was becoming that good. The series ended with the Cape Grand Prix on 2 January 1962. Masten Gregory, in the sole 18/21 in the race (917), finished in fourth place despite gear selection problems, behind the Team Lotus 21s and Jo Bonnier's Porsche. Menzler finished tenth in his 18-Borgward once again, this time only three laps behind.

SUMMARY

By rights, the Lotus 18 should not have featured significantly in 1961. It was, after all, a year old and somewhat bulky when compared to its successor, the Lotus 21. That it did so was down to the superior driving skill of Stirling Moss in the Rob Walker-entered chassis, whose defeat of the Ferraris at Monaco and the Nürburgring was sensational by any standards.

Monaco and the Nürburgring apart, Ferrari fulfilled the early indications that it would be the car to beat, as it began to accumulate the five wins out of the seven Grands Prix that it contested. More was expected of Porsche than it delivered, proving disappointing on its Formula 1 debut, despite a successful season of Formula 2 during 1960. The main challenge to Ferrari should then have come from Colin Chapman's latest offering, the Lotus 21, the state-of-the-art 4-cylinder Climax-engined Grand Prix car, yet it also failed to meet expectations.

Moss and the immaculately-prepared Walker 18/21 were always going to be in contention, and might even have also won at Reims when the Ferraris encountered problems. As it was, fractured brake balance pipes robbed the Lotus of victory there, and a fourth place at Aintree. An engine bearing failure at Watkins Glen denied Moss and the 18/21 a third win. It is interesting to speculate on the outcome of the Championship without these retirements: four wins and one third place would have given Moss 39 points and the 1961 World Championship against all the odds, five points ahead of Phil Hill!

As it was, the Rob Walker-entered Lotus 18 and Moss accumulated 18 of the marque's 35 points total, Lotus finishing the season as runner-up to Ferrari in the Constructors' Championship. No other Lotus 18 – and there were 20 examples in circulation – managed to finish in the points.

The Lotus 18 also won six non-Championship Formula 1 races compared to five for the Lotus 21 and five for Cooper. Once again, Moss was the principle scorer, but, by the end of the season in South Africa, Jim Clark and the Lotus 21 had gained an edge in performance over the well-prepared Lotus 18/21.

Helmut Menzler's Borgward-engined 18 (911) has been lapped by the Porsche of Edgar Barth (No 4) during the South African Grand Prix (www.motoprint.co.za).

Moss, with the oversteering UDT-Laystall 18/21 (918), in pursuit of Jim Clark in South Africa. (LAT Photographic)

Stirling Moss (UDT-Laystall 18/21) leads Jo Bonnier (Porsche) during the South African Grand Prix at East London. They would finish in this order behind the Lotus 21 of Jim Clark. (www.motoprint.co.za).

Lotus 18 Performance Summary – 1961

	Starts	Finishes	1st	2nd	3rd	4th	5th	6th	PP	FL
Grands Prix	40	18	2	–	–	1	–	–	1	1
Other Formula 1	96	56	6	8	4	4	8	4	6	8
Total	136	74	8	8	4	5	8	4	7	9

Chassis Summary

21 Lotus 18 chassis made one or more starts in 1961 Grands Prix/Formula 1 races, as follows:

371	Retained by Team Lotus – winner Pau GP for Jim Clark. Rebuilt as 18/21 then to Jim Hall for US GP.
372	Retained by Team Lotus – two early season F1 races only. Rebuilt as 18/21 prior to acquisition by J Wheeler Autosport (Peter Ryan) for US GP.
373	Ex-Team Lotus acquired by Scuderia Colonia (Wolfgang Seidel). 13 starts including three GPs.
374	Retained by Team Lotus – canted engine chassis. Four early season F1 races only.

Production chassis built by Lotus Components:

902	Acquired by Prince Gaetano Starrabba from Scuderia Centro Sud with Maserati 150S engine.
903	Mrs Louise Bryden-Brown retained from 1960 for Dan Gurney and Tony Maggs.
904	Tim Parnell retained from 1960.
905	Ian Burgess from 1960 to Camoradi International.
906	RRC Walker Racing Team retained from 1960. Rebuilt as 18/21 'Special' to take Climax FWMV V8 – practice only for Italian and US GPs.
907	To J Frank Harrison ex-Jim Hall 1960. US GP only.
908	Camoradi International new 1961.
909	Tony Marsh retained from 1960.
911	Ecurie Wolman (South Africa) new 1960. Fitted with Borgward RS engine.
912	RRC Walker Racing Team new autumn 1960 for Stirling Moss. Winner Monaco and German GPs.
913	Scuderia Dolomiti new for 1961 for Ernesto Prinoth.
914	Scuderia Colonia new for 1961 for Michael May.
915	UDT-Laystall Racing Team new for 1961 – not raced after July.
916	UDT-Laystall Racing Team new for 1961. Rebuilt as 18/21 July. Winner Danish GP for Stirling Moss.
917	UDT-Laystall Racing Team new for 1961 as 18/21.
918	UDT-Laystall Racing Team new for 1961 as 18/21. Winner Silver City Trophy and Kanonloppet for Stirling Moss.
919	Tim Parnell new for 1961 for Gerry Ashmore. Acquired by Ashmore in August.

6: 1961 Formula 1 Season – Against the Odds

LOTUS 18 – FORMULA 1 RACING RECORD – 1961
(* signifies chassis converted to 18/21 specification)

Position	Driver	Entrant	Chassis	Engine	No	Grid	Comments
Lombank Trophy, Snetterton (GB), 26.3.61, 100.27 miles (161.334km)							
2nd	Henry Taylor	UDT-Laystall Racing Team	916	1.5 Climax FPF 4IL	5	Q4	
4th	Jim Clark	Team Lotus	371	1.5 Climax FPF 4IL	7	Q3	35 laps/36
5th	Tim Parnell	RHH Parnell	904	1.5 Climax FPF 4IL	19	Q7	34 laps/36
Grand Prix de Pau, Pau (F), 3.4.61, 171.40 miles (276.00km)							
1st	Jim Clark	Team Lotus	371	1.5 Climax FPF 4IL	6	Q2	FL
2nd	Jo Bonnier	Scuderia Colonia	914	1.5 Climax FPF 4IL	18	Q10	
	Trevor Taylor	Team Lotus	374	1.5 Climax FPF 4IL	8	Q6	Transmission lap 41/100
	Wolfgang Seidel	Scuderia Colonia	373	1.5 Climax FPF 4IL	20	Q15	Oil leak lap 40/100
	Ian Burgess	Camoradi International	908	1.5 Climax FPF 4IL	16	Q16	Gearbox lap 25/100
Glover Trophy, Goodwood (GB), 3.4.61, 100.80 miles (162.18km)							
4th	Stirling Moss	RRC Walker Racing Team	912	1.5 Climax FPF 4IL	7	Q1	
5th	Innes Ireland	Team Lotus	372	1.5 Climax FPF 4IL	5	Q5	41 laps/42
6th	Henry Taylor	UDT-Laystall Racing Team	916	1.5 Climax FPF 4IL	17	Q7	41 laps/42
7th	Tony Marsh	AE Marsh	909	1.5 Climax FPF 4IL	29	Q9	41 laps/42
8th	Cliff Allison	UDT-Laystall Racing Team	915	1.5 Climax FPF 4IL	15	Q8	40 laps/42
Grand Prix de Bruxelles, Bruxelles (B), 9.4.61, Aggregate of 3 Heats, 186.68 miles (300.43km)							
3rd	Tony Marsh	AE Marsh	909	1.5 Climax FPF 4IL	26	Q8	
5th	Cliff Allison	UDT-Laystall Racing Team	915	1.5 Climax FPF 4IL	14	Q12	
6th	Innes Ireland	Team Lotus	371	1.5 Climax FPF 4IL	20	Q13	Accident Heat 3
7th	Stirling Moss	RRC Walker Racing Team	906	1.5 Climax FPF 4IL	18	Q9	
8th	Ian Burgess	Camoradi International	908	1.5 Climax FPF 4IL	12	Q18	
	Jim Clark	Team Lotus	374	1.5 Climax FPF 4IL	22	Q6	Gearbox Heat 1
	Wolfgang Seidel	Scuderia Colonia	373	1.5 Climax FPF 4IL	28	Q11	Gearbox Heat 1
	André Pilette	RHH Parnell	904	1.5 Climax FPF 4IL	24	Q17	Gear selector Heat 1
	Henry Taylor	UDT-Laystall Racing Team	916	1.5 Climax FPF 4IL	16	Q10	Fr suspension Heat 1
	Maurice Trintignant	Scuderia Colonia	914	1.5 Climax FPF 4IL	10		DNS Final drive
Preis von Wien, Aspern (A), 16.4.61, 93.30 miles (150.12km)							
1st	Stirling Moss	RRC Walker Racing Team	906	1.5 Climax FPF 4IL	7	Q1	FL
2nd	Wolfgang Seidel	Scuderia Colonia	373	1.5 Climax FPF 4IL	5	Q6	
3rd	Ernesto Prinoth	Scuderia Dolomiti	913	1.5 Climax FPF 4IL	8	Q7	
	Tim Parnell	RHH Parnell	904	1.5 Climax FPF 4IL	10	Q5	N/C 34 laps/55
	Gerry Ashmore	RHH Parnell	919	1.5 Climax FPF 4IL	11	Q3	Brakes lap 5/55
BARC 200, Aintree (GB), 22.4.61, 150.00 miles (241.35km)							
7th	Tony Marsh	AE Marsh	909	1.5 Climax FPF 4IL	27	Q8	49 laps/50
9th	Jim Clark	Team Lotus	372	1.5 Climax FPF 4IL	19	Q5	48 laps/50
10th	Innes Ireland	Team Lotus	371	1.5 Climax FPF 4IL	18	Q7	48 laps/50
11th	Gerry Ashmore	RHH Parnell	919	1.5 Climax FPF 4IL	26	Q12	48 laps/50
14th	Dan Gurney	Mrs L Bryden-Brown	903	1.5 Climax FPF 4IL	23	Q15	47 laps/50
15th	Cliff Allison	UDT-Laystall Racing Team	915	1.5 Climax FPF 4IL	21	Q11	46 laps/50
	Trevor Taylor	Team Lotus	374	1.5 Climax FPF 4IL	20	Q14	N/C 41 laps/50
	Henry Taylor	UDT-Laystall Racing Team	916	1.5 Climax FPF 4IL	22	Q17	Gearbox lap 26/50
	Tim Parnell	RHH Parnell	904	1.5 Climax FPF 4IL	25	NT	Engine lap 7/50
	Michael May	Scuderia Colonia	914	1.5 Climax FPF 4IL	24	Q21	Engine lap 7/50
	Ian Burgess	Camoradi International	908	1.5 Climax FPF 4IL	16	Q25	DSQ lap 34/50
Gran Premio di Siracusa, Sicily (I), 25.4.61, 192.77 miles (308.00km)							
6th	Jim Clark	Team Lotus	374	1.5 Climax FPF 4IL	20	Q12	53 laps/56
8th	Stirling Moss	RRC Walker Racing Team	906	1.5 Climax FPF 4IL	18	Q7	Engine lap 52/56
	Wolfgang Seidel	Scuderia Colonia	373	1.5 Climax FPF 4IL	40	Q19	N/C 49 laps/56
	Innes Ireland	Team Lotus	371	1.5 Climax FPF 4IL	38	Q9	Throttle lap 26/56
	Ernesto Prinoth	Scuderia Dolomiti	913	1.5 Climax FPF 4IL	4	DNS	Gasket in practice
GRAND PRIX de MONACO, Monte Carlo (MC), 14.5.61, 195.42 miles (314.50km)							
1st	Stirling Moss	RRC Walker Racing Team	912	1.5 Climax FPF 4IL	20	Q1	=FL
8th	Cliff Allison	UDT-Laystall Racing Team	916	1.5 Climax FPF 4IL	32	Q14	93 laps/100
	Michael May	Scuderia Colonia	914	1.5 Climax FPF 4IL	8	Q13	Oil leak lap 42/100
	Henry Taylor	UDT-Laystall Racing Team	915	1.5 Climax FPF 4IL	34		DNQ

Lotus 18 | 113

Lotus 18 – Colin Chapman's U-turn

Position	Driver	Entrant	Chassis	Engine	No	Grid	Comments
Gran Premio di Napoli, Posillipo (I), 14.5.61, 92.86 miles (149.41km)							
2nd	Gerry Ashmore	The Three Musketeers	919	1.5 Climax FPF 4IL	10	Q1	59 laps/60
4th	Ian Burgess	Camoradi International	905	1.5 Climax FPF 4IL	30	Q5	58 laps/60
8th	Tim Parnell	The Three Musketeers	904	1.5 Climax FPF 4IL	8	Q12	54 laps/60
	Ernesto Prinoth	Scuderia Dolomiti	913	1.5 Climax FPF 4IL	40	Q6	N/C 34 laps/60
GROTE PRIJS van NEDERLAND, Zandvoort (NL), 22.5.61, 195.41 miles (314.47km)							
4th	Stirling Moss	RRC Walker Racing Team	912	1.5 Climax FPF 4IL	14	Q4	
13th	Trevor Taylor	Team Lotus	371	1.5 Climax FPF 4IL	16	Q14	73 laps/75
	Ian Burgess	Camoradi International	905	1.5 Climax FPF 4IL	18		DNS – reserve entry
London Trophy, Crystal Palace (GB), 22.5.61, 51.43 miles (82.75km)							
2nd	Henry Taylor	UDT-Laystall Racing Team	916	1.5 Climax FPF 4IL	22	Q2	=FL
3rd	Tony Marsh	AE Marsh	909	1.5 Climax FPF 4IL	24	Q5	
5th	Wolfgang Seidel	Scuderia Colonia	373	1.5 Climax FPF 4IL	26	Q6	36 laps/37
8th	Cliff Allison	UDT-Laystall Racing Team	915	1.5 Climax FPF 4IL	20	Q4	35 laps/37
Silver City Trophy, Brands Hatch (GB), 3.6.61, 201.40 miles (324.05km)							
1st	Stirling Moss	UDT-Laystall Racing Team	*918	1.5 Climax FPF 4IL	26	Q1	FL
5th	Dan Gurney	Mrs L Bryden-Brown	903	1.5 Climax FPF 4IL	32	Q12	74 laps/76
6th	Tony Marsh	AE Marsh	909	1.5 Climax FPF 4IL	34	Q13	71 laps/76
7th	Tim Parnell	RHH Parnell	904	1.5 Climax FPF 4IL	38	Q19	71 laps/76
8th	Henry Taylor	UDT-Laystall Racing Team	916	1.5 Climax FPF 4IL	28	Q10	69 laps/76
9th	Trevor Taylor	Team Lotus	371	1.5 Climax FPF 4IL	22	Q11	69 laps/76
	Jo Bonnier	UDT-Laystall Racing Team	*917	1.5 Climax FPF 4IL	30	Q15	N/C 57 laps/76
	Michael May	Scuderia Colonia	914	1.5 Climax FPF 4IL	52	Q14	Overheating lap 16/76
	Wolfgang Seidel	Scuderia Colonia	373	1.5 Climax FPF 4IL	48	Q16	Gearbox lap 12/76
GRAND PRIX de BELGIQUE, Spa Francorchamps (B), 18.6.61, 262.84 miles (423.00km)							
8th	Stirling Moss	RRC Walker Racing Team	*912	1.5 Climax FPF 4IL	14	Q8	
	Lucien Bianchi	Equipe Nationale Belge	373	1.5 Climax FPF 4IL	12	NT	Oil pipe lap 9/30
	Willy Mairesse	Equipe Nationale Belge	909	1.5 Climax FPF 4IL	10	NT	Engine lap 7/30
	Cliff Allison	UDT-Laystall Racing Team	*918	1.5 Climax FPF 4IL	16		DNS accident in practice
	Ian Burgess	Camoradi International	905	1.5 Climax FPF 4IL	50		DNQ
GRAND PRIX de l'AUTOMOBILE CLUB de FRANCE, Reims (F), 2.7.61, 268.25 miles (431.70km)							
10th	Henry Taylor	UDT-Laystall Racing Team	*916	1.5 Climax FPF 4IL	30	Q25	49 laps/52
11th	Michael May	Scuderia Colonia	914	1.5 Climax FPF 4IL	46	Q22	48 laps/52
14th	Ian Burgess	Camoradi International	905	1.5 Climax FPF 4IL	38	Q24	42 laps/52
	Stirling Moss	RRC Walker Racing Team	*912	1.5 Climax FPF 4IL	26	Q4	Brake pipe lap 31/52
	Lucien Bianchi	UDT-Laystall Racing Team		1.5 Climax FPF 4IL	28	Q19	Clutch lap 21/52
RAC BRITISH GRAND PRIX, Aintree (GB), 15.7.61, 225.00 miles (362.10km)							
13th	Tony Maggs	Mrs L Bryden-Brown	903	1.5 Climax FPF 4IL	50	Q24	69 laps/75
14th	Ian Burgess	Camoradi International	905	1.5 Climax FPF 4IL	44	Q25	69 laps/75
	Wolfgang Seidel	Scuderia Colonia	373	1.5 Climax FPF 4IL	52	Q22	N/C 58 laps/75
	Lucien Bianchi	UDT-Laystall Racing Team	*917	1.5 Climax FPF 4IL	32	Q30	Gearbox lap 45/75
	Stirling Moss	RRC Walker Racing Team	*912	1.5 Climax FPF 4IL	28	Q5	Brake pipe lap 44/75
	Tony Marsh	AE Marsh	909	1.5 Climax FPF 4IL	48	Q27	Ignition lap 25/75
	Tim Parnell	RHH Parnell	904	1.5 Climax FPF 4IL	38	Q29	Clutch lap 12/75
	Gerry Ashmore	G Ashmore	919	1.5 Climax FPF 4IL	40	Q26	Ignition lap 7/75
	Henry Taylor	UDT-Laystall Racing Team	*916	1.5 Climax FPF 4IL	30	Q17	Accident lap 5/75
Großer Preis der Solitude, Solitude (D), 23.7.61, 177.23 miles (285.16km)							
	Stirling Moss	UDT-Laystall Racing Team	*917	1.5 Climax FPF 4IL	17	Q5	Gearbox lap 22/25
	Wolfgang Seidel	Scuderia Colonia	373	1.5 Climax FPF 4IL	15	Q14	Steering lap 7/25
	Michael May	Scuderia Colonia	914	1.5 Climax FPF 4IL	16	Q12	Accident lap 1/25
	Lloyd Casner	Camoradi International	908	1.5 Climax FPF 4IL			DNS – engine in practice
GROSSER PREIS von DEUTSCHLAND, Nürburgring (D), 6.8.61, 212.60 miles (342.15km)							
1st	Stirling Moss	RRC Walker Racing Team	*912	1.5 Climax FPF 4IL	7	Q3	
11th	Tony Maggs	Mrs L Bryden-Brown	903	1.5 Climax FPF 4IL	33	Q22	14 laps/15
16th	Tony Marsh	AE Marsh	909	1.5 Climax FPF 4IL	37	Q20	13 laps/15
17th	Gerry Ashmore	G Ashmore	919	1.5 Climax FPF 4IL	27	Q25	13 laps/15
	Wolfgang Seidel	Scuderia Colonia	373	1.5 Climax FPF 4IL	26	Q23	Steering lap 3/15
	Michael May	Scuderia Colonia	914	1.5 Climax FPF 4IL	25		DNQ
Kanonloppet, Karlskoga (S), 20.8.61, 55.89 miles (89.88km)							
1st	Stirling Moss	UDT-Laystall Racing Team	*918	1.5 Climax FPF 4IL	1	NT	FL

6: 1961 Formula 1 Season – Against the Odds

Position	Driver	Entrant	Chassis	Engine	No	Grid	Comments
5th	Tim Parnell	RHH Parnell	904	1.5 Climax FPF 4IL	12	Q7	28 laps/30
	Innes Ireland	Team Lotus	371	1.5 Climax FPF 4IL	9	Q5	Transmission lap 10/30
	Carl Hammarlund	UDT-Laystall Racing Team	*917	1.5 Climax FPF 4IL	6	Q8	Spin lap 4/30
Danske Grand Prix, Roskilde (DK), 27.8.61, 3 Heats 59.65 miles (95.98km)							
1st	Stirling Moss	UDT-Laystall Racing Team	*916	1.5 Climax FPF 4IL	7	Q1	FL
4th	Henry Taylor	UDT-Laystall Racing Team	*917	1.5 Climax FPF 4IL	9	Q4	
5th	Tim Parnell	RHH Parnell	904	1.5 Climax FPF 4IL	10	Q7	
	Jim Clark	Team Lotus	371	1.5 Climax FPF 4IL	4	NT	N/C 60 laps/80
	Masten Gregory	UDT-Laystall Racing Team	*918	1.5 Climax FPF 4IL	8	Q8	Gearbox Heat 2
Gran Premio di Modena, Modena (I), 3.9.61, 147.14 miles (236.75km)							
1st	Stirling Moss	RRC Walker Racing Team	*912	1.5 Climax FPF 4IL	26	Q1	FL
	Masten Gregory	UDT-Laystall Racing Team	*917	1.5 Climax FPF 4IL	32	Q7	N/C 71 laps/100
	Henry Taylor	UDT-Laystall Racing Team	*918	1.5 Climax FPF 4IL	30	Q11	Head gasket lap 42/100
	Giorgio Scarlatti	Prince G Starrabba	902	1.5 Maserati 150S 4IL	18	Q14	Engine lap 4/100
	Wolfgang Seidel	Scuderia Colonia	373	1.5 Climax FPF 4IL	24		DNQ
	Tim Parnell	RHH Parnell	904	1.5 Climax FPF 4IL	48		DNQ
GRAN PREMIO d'ITALIA, Monza (I), 10.9.61, 267.19 miles (430.00km)							
10th	Tim Parnell	RHH Parnell	904	1.5 Climax FPF 4IL	16	Q27	40 laps/43
11th	Henry Taylor	UDT-Laystall Racing Team	*918	1.5 Climax FPF 4IL	20	Q23	39 laps/43
	Gaetano Starrabba	Prince G Starrabba	902	1.5 Maserati 150S 4IL	72	Q30	Engine lap 19/43
	Masten Gregory	UDT-Laystall Racing Team	*917	1.5 Climax FPF 4IL	22	Q17	R. wishbone lap 11/43
	Innes Ireland	Team Lotus	*912	1.5 Climax FPF 4IL	38	Q9	Chassis lap 5/43
	Wolfgang Seidel	Scuderia Colonia	373	1.5 Climax FPF 4IL	56	Q28	Engine lap 1/43
	Gerry Ashmore	G Ashmore	919	1.5 Climax FPF 4IL	18	Q25	Accident lap 1/43
	Stirling Moss	RRC Walker Racing Team	*906	1.5 Climax FWMV V8	28		Practice only
Flugplatzrennen Zeltweg, Zeltweg (A), 17.9.61, 159.07 miles (255.94km)							
7th	Tim Parnell	RHH Parnell	904	1.5 Climax FPF 4IL	15	Q12	74 laps/80
	Wolfgang Seidel	Scuderia Colonia	373	1.5 Climax FPF 4IL	16	Q6	Engine lap 36/80
	Ernesto Prinoth	Scuderia Dolomiti	913	1.5 Climax FPF 4IL	18	Q9	Accident lap 6/80
International Gold Cup, Oulton Park (GB), 23.9.61, 165.66 miles (266.55km)							
5th	Masten Gregory	UDT-Laystall Racing Team	*917	1.5 Climax FPF 4IL	14	Q8	58 laps/60
8th	Henry Taylor	UDT-Laystall Racing Team	*918	1.5 Climax FPF 4IL	15	Q12	56 laps/60
10th	Wolfgang Seidel	Scuderia Colonia	373	1.5 Climax FPF 4IL	28	Q18	56 laps/60
	Trevor Taylor	Team Lotus	371	1.5 Climax FPF 4IL	6	Q13	Exhaust lap 40/60
	Tim Parnell	RHH Parnell	904	1.5 Climax FPF 4IL	18	Q21	Fuel pump lap 1/60
Lewis-Evans Trophy, Brands Hatch (GB), 1.10.61, 79.50 miles (127.92km)							
3rd	Tim Parnell	RHH Parnell	904	1.5 Climax FPF 4IL	11	Q4	
UNITED STATES GRAND PRIX, Watkins Glen (USA), 8.10.61, 230.00 miles (370.10km)							
9th	Peter Ryan	J Wheeler Autosport	*372	1.5 Climax FPF 4IL	16	Q13	96 laps/100
11th	Gendebien/Gregory	UDT-Laystall Racing Team	*918	1.5 Climax FPF 4IL	21	Q15	92 laps/100
	Lloyd Ruby	J Frank Harrison	907	1.5 Climax FPF 4IL	26	Q19	Magneto drive lap 76/100
	Jim Hall	J Hall	*371	1.5 Climax FPF 4IL	17	Q21	Fuel pipe lap 76/100
	Stirling Moss	RRC Walker Racing Team	*912	1.5 Climax FPF 4IL	7	Q3	Engine lap 58/100
	Masten Gregory	UDT-Laystall Racing Team	*917	1.5 Climax FPF 4IL	22	Q11	Gear selector lap 23/100
	Stirling Moss	RRC Walker Racing Team	*906	1.5 Climax FWMV V8	7T		Practice only
Coppa Italia, Vallelunga (I), 12.10.61, 2 Heats 66.22 miles (106.55km)							
2nd	Ernesto Prinoth	Scuderia Dolomiti	913	1.5 Climax FPF 4IL	2	Q3	
	Gaetano Starrabba	Prince G Starrabba	902	1.5 Maserati 150S 4IL	4	Q5	Engine Heat 2
Rand Grand Prix, Kyalami (ZA), 9.12.61, 190.88 miles (307.13km)							
	Masten Gregory	UDT-Laystall Racing Team	*917	1.5 Climax FPF 4IL	6	Q3	Overheating lap 42/75
	Helmut Menzler	Ecurie Wolman	911	1.5 Borgward RS 4IL	16	Q10	Overheating lap 24/75
Natal Grand Prix, Westmead (ZA), 17.12.61, 200.21 miles (322.14km)							
2nd	Stirling Moss	UDT-Laystall Racing Team	*918	1.5 Climax FPF 4IL	7	NT	FL
	Helmut Menzler	Ecurie Wolman	911	1.5 Borgward RS 4IL	16	Q14	DNF Suspension
	Masten Gregory	UDT-Laystall Racing Team	*917	1.5 Climax FPF 4IL	6	Q4	Head gasket lap 14/89
South African Grand Prix, East London (ZA), 26.12.61, 194.80 miles (313.43km)							
2nd	Stirling Moss	UDT-Laystall Racing Team	*918	1.5 Climax FPF 4IL	7	Q2	
10th	Helmut Menzler	Ecurie Wolman	911	1.5 Borgward RS 4IL	16	Q14	75 laps/80
	Masten Gregory	UDT-Laystall Racing Team	*916	1.5 Climax FPF 4IL	6	Q5	Brake pipe lap 9/80
Cape Grand Prix, Killarney (ZA), 2.1.62, 123.47 miles (198.66km)							
4th	Masten Gregory	UDT-Laystall Racing Team	*917	1.5 Climax FPF 4IL	6	Q4	
10th	Helmut Menzler	Ecurie Wolman	911	1.5 Borgward RS 4IL	16	Q11	57 laps/60

Lotus 18 | 115

7 1961 INTER-CONTINENTAL FORMULA SEASON – A DAMP SQUIB

As detailed in Chapter 6, the announcement of the new 1½-litre Formula 1 regulations were greeted with outrage by British interests. Representatives from Britain, Italy and the USA had voted against the proposal, preferring to continue with the existing 2½-litre regulations, and they were authorised by the CSI, by way of compensation, to propose another formula to suit their mutual interests. As a result, a proposal was submitted for an 'Inter-Continental' formula, with a 3-litre engine capacity limit, that would both prolong the life of existing 2½-litre machinery and draw in interest from American professional track racing, typified by the Indianapolis 500. British interests assumed that the 1½-litre Formula 1 regulations would fail due to a lack of support from constructors and a lack of interest from the paying public. As a result, the World Championship would be run to Inter-Continental regulations, with its much more powerful, and supposedly spectacular, machinery. The reality was somewhat different: in the event, the Inter-Continental Formula began to collapse before it had even started.

The professional US racing industry showed little or no interest in racing outside its domestic environment – and then Ferrari, realising that it had a potential world beating 1½-litre Grand Prix car, decided to set aside any Inter-Continental Formula aspirations that it might have had. For many continental race organisers, Ferrari was the deciding factor. Spectators would turn up in droves to see a scarlet Ferrari, rather than a collection of British racing green cars. Add in the attraction of the German Porsche team, and the established Grand Prix organisers began committing to Formula 1 in preference to the Inter-Continental Formula. By the latter part of the 1960 season, it was obvious that the 1½-litre Formula 1 would be implemented, and fully supported, by constructors and accessory manufacturers alike, and that it was the Inter-Continental Formula that lacked support.

The British found themselves out of step with their continental rivals and the CSI. Nevertheless, a handful of races were organised, all in Britain – with only one of the unsuccessful front-engined American Scarabs from 1960 providing an 'Inter-Continental' flavour. To add a further nail to the Inter-Continental coffin, Coventry Climax announced, in early 1961, that it would not support further development of its 2½-litre FPF engine, choosing instead to concentrate on the new 1½-litre V8 for Formula 1. Similarly, none of the constructors produced anything new for the Formula, preferring only to prolong the life of existing 1960 machinery. Team Lotus fielded Lotus 18s, the chassis living a double life by fulfilling a role as a Formula 1 chassis until the Lotus 21 came on stream, running in Inter-Continental races as a sideline. The UDT-Laystall Racing Team utilised two of its brand new 18s in a dual Formula 1/Inter-Continental role.

Dan Gurney (903) leads Bruce McLaren (Cooper), Chuck Daigh (Scarab) and the rest into Madgwick at the start of the Lavant Cup at Goodwood. (LAT Photographic)

7: 1961 Inter-Continental Formula Season – a Damp Squib

The first event of the 1961 European calendar was a combined Formula 1/Inter-Continental Formula race, held at a cold Snetterton in late March. Innes Ireland was one of just five entries, his Team Lotus 18 (374) leading until its transmission failed, leaving Jack Brabham to win an uneventful race for Cooper. Cliff Allison finished second in one of the new UDT-Laystall Racing Team 18s (915), nearly a lap in arrears. There was but a single 18 entered for the Lavant Cup at Goodwood on Easter Monday, that being the powder blue version (903) of Mrs Louise Bryden-Brown for Dan Gurney. Taking the lead from the start, he slipped back to fourth, then spun off backwards, into an embankment protecting an observers post between Woodcote and the Chicane, on the final lap when attempting to retake third from the BRM of Graham Hill.

The British Racing Drivers Club (BRDC), as stalwart supporters of the Inter-Continental Formula, decided to run their prestigious May International Trophy at Silverstone over a full 80-lap, 234-mile distance in a bid to demonstrate its viability. Unfortunately, the weather worked against them, heavy rain falling throughout

It was wet for the Silverstone International Trophy – Jack Brabham heads Innes Ireland (371), sandwiched between the Coopers of Bruce McLaren and eventual winner Stirling Moss, just entering the picture. (LAT Photographic)

Lotus 18 | 117

the event and making the track extremely slippery. The chassis of Gurney's 18 had been straightened since Goodwood, but its handling had been compromised and Dan went off the road once again during practice, ending up on top of the Beckett's corner embankment. Damage was sufficient to render him a non-starter. Similarly, Mike Parkes damaged a Reg Parnell-entered 18 during practice and would not be able to take the start. The identity of this chassis is something of a mystery. It has been recorded as 901, although this was still in the hands of Tony Vandervell at the time, complete with Vanwall engine. It has also been recorded as 904, even though Tim Parnell was apparently racing this chassis himself at Silverstone.

Five other 18s made the grid, however, including two each from Team Lotus and UDT-Laystall, one of the latter (906) being borrowed from the Rob Walker Racing Team. Innes Ireland was the fastest 18 (371) driver in the dry practice session, fifth behind three Coopers and a BRM. On the opening lap, Ireland and team-mate Clark (374) spun in the treacherous conditions at Abbey, but continued. Henry Taylor in the Walker/UDT 18 worked his way steadily up to third place, whilst Clark pitted with falling oil pressure, but rejoined. Ireland spun at Abbey again, later in the race, taking some 15min to get the car back on to the track, then pitted for a further 2min for the suspension to be checked over. Shortly after, Ireland found himself off on the grass once again, this time at Maggots, in the company of Cliff Allison in the second UDT car (915). Allison had been struggling around at the back of the field with a rough sounding engine and was unable to restart. Ireland managed to get going, but had lost 20 laps by the end of the race. Meanwhile, at the front, Stirling Moss was excelling in the conditions in Rob Walker's Cooper, to win by over a lap, after a miserable, overly long 2hr 41min of racing. Henry Taylor survived to finish fourth – as top 18, even *his* car ailing.

The BRDC remained keen enough on the Inter-Continental formula to put on a second event at Silverstone, two months later: the British Empire Trophy. The entry was similar to that in May, with the addition of the race debut of the Ferguson P99 four-wheel-drive car to add technical interest. The Lotus 18 was represented by the usual duos from Team Lotus and UDT-Laystall, with a fifth for Tim Parnell (904). Innes Ireland was the fastest 18 driver, qualifying fifth (371) behind four Coopers. Once again, the weather was wet as Stirling Moss stormed off into an unchallenged lead, in front of a much-reduced crowd compared to May. Henry Taylor (916) was initially fourth, but Ireland was straight into the pits with a slipping clutch, losing two laps. Taylor lasted only three laps before his transmission failed, but he took over the 18 of team-mate Lucien Bianchi (915) to finish tenth despite the engine smoking badly. Jim Clark (372) duelled with Tony Brooks' BRM, eventually relieving him of sixth place. As the race drew to a close, he caught Salvadori's gearless Cooper, to snatch fifth two laps before the end of an otherwise dull and processional race.

August Bank Holiday Monday saw Brands Hatch put on a 200-mile race for the Guards Trophy. The usual complement of Inter-Continental Formula runners was on hand, most drivers having returned overnight from the Nürburgring, where Stirling Moss had trounced the Ferrari team with his 18/21 in the German Grand Prix. Would the Guards Trophy prove as exciting? Probably not.

Five Lotus 18s were entered, Innes Ireland (371) and Jim Clark (372) for Team Lotus, together on the second row of the grid, with Masten Gregory (916) and Dan Gurney (915), representing UDT-Laystall on this occasion, behind them on the third. Bruce Halford handled the fifth chassis (374), recently acquired from Team Lotus by Jim Diggory. Gregory was eliminated on lap 4, shunted off by Bruce McLaren's Cooper, but Ireland was running fifth, Clark seventh and Gurney ninth. Ireland and Gurney retired with gearbox problems, leaving Clark, the remaining 18 runner, in third behind

Jim Clark (372) duelled with the BRM of Tony Brooks during the British Empire Trophy at Silverstone and would eventually finish fifth. (Ferret Fotographics)

7: 1961 Inter-Continental Formula Season – a Damp Squib

Brabham's Cooper and Hill's BRM. On lap 66, Hill spun, letting Clark into second, in which place he finished, a lap down on winner Brabham.

SUMMARY

There were no further Inter-Continental Formula races scheduled, and the category quietly petered out, its passing hardly noticed, let alone mourned. It had failed to provide the alternative to Grand Prix racing expected of it, lacking both the international flavour of the premier category and any excitement. The category had been dominated by Cooper – two second places the only reward for the 18s that were only mid-field runners at best. After a full season of both Formulae 1 and 2 in 1960, and then Formula 1 and Inter-Continental in 1961, the Team Lotus 18s were tired and past their best, and little time was expended preparing them, at a time when Formula 1 was the priority. While Formula 1 had taken on a new lease of life, the Inter-Continental Formula had achieved little more than that expected of a British Formule Libre Club race.

Lotus 18 – Intercontinental Formula Performance Summary – 1961

Starts	Finishes	1st	2nd	3rd	4th	5th	6th	PP	FL
18	6	–	2	–	1	1	–	1	1

Chassis Summary

The eight Lotus 18 chassis making one or more starts in 1961 Inter-Continental races were as follows:

371	Team Lotus – driven by Innes Ireland.
372	Team Lotus – driven by Jim Clark.
374	Team Lotus – Ireland/Clark. Acquired by SJ Diggory for Guards Trophy at Brands Hatch for Bruce Halford.
903	Mrs Louise Bryden-Brown retained from 1960 for Dan Gurney. Damaged at Easter Goodwood, repaired and damaged again in practice for Silverstone International Trophy.
904	Tim Parnell retained from 1960 for two starts.
906	RRC Walker Racing Team retained from 1960. Loaned to UDT-Laystall for International Trophy.
915	UDT-Laystall Racing Team new for 1961.
916	UDT-Laystall Racing Team new for 1961.

LOTUS 18 – INTERCONTINENTAL FORMULA RACING RECORD – 1961

Position	Driver	Entrant	Chassis	Engine	No	Grid	Comments
Lombank Trophy, Snetterton (GB), 26.3.61, 100.27miles
2nd	Cliff Allison	UDT Laystall Racing Team	915	2.5 Climax FPF 4IL	4	Q3	
	Innes Ireland	Team Lotus	374	2.5 Climax FPF 4IL	6	Q1	Gearbox lap 14/37 (FL)
Lavant Cup, Goodwood (GB), 3.4.61, 50.40miles
	Dan Gurney	Mrs L Bryden-Brown	903	2.5 Climax FPF 4IL	18	Q5	Accident lap 20/21
International Trophy, Silverstone (GB), 6.5.61, 234.16 miles
4th	Henry Taylor	UDT Laystall Racing Team	906	2.5 Climax FPF 4IL	14	Q17	78 laps/80
	Cliff Allison	UDT Laystall Racing Team	915	2.5 Climax FPF 4IL	12	Q11	Spun off lap 68/80
	Innes Ireland	Team Lotus	371	2.5 Climax FPF 4IL	7	Q5	N/C 60 laps/80
	Jim Clark	Team Lotus	374	2.5 Climax FPF 4IL	8	Q9	Clutch lap 55/80
	Tim Parnell	RHH Parnell	904	2.5 Climax FPF 4IL	22	Q18	Accident lap 8/80
	Mike Parkes	Reg Parnell (Racing)	?	2.5 Climax FPF 4IL	9	Q10	DNS accident in practice
	Dan Gurney	Mrs L Bryden-Brown	903	2.5 Climax FPF 4IL	21	NT	DNS accident in practice
British Empire Trophy, Silverstone (GB), 8.7.61, 152.36 miles
5th	Jim Clark	Team Lotus	372	2.5 Climax FPF 4IL	9	Q10	50 laps/52
9th	Innes Ireland	Team Lotus	371	2.5 Climax FPF 4IL	10	Q5	50 laps/52
10th	Bianchi/Taylor	UDT Laystall Racing Team	915	2.5 Climax FPF 4IL	3	Q16	48 laps/52
	Tim Parnell	RHH Parnell	904	2.5 Climax FPF 4IL	23	Q15	Spin lap 10/52
	Henry Taylor	UDT Laystall Racing Team	916	2.5 Climax FPF 4IL	4	Q9	Transmission lap 3/52
Guards' Trophy, Brands Hatch (GB), 7.8.61, 201.32 miles
2nd	Jim Clark	Team Lotus	372	2.5 Climax FPF 4IL	16	Q7	75 laps/76
	Innes Ireland	Team Lotus	371	2.5 Climax FPF 4IL	14	Q6	Gearbox lap 34/76
	Dan Gurney	UDT Laystall Racing Team	915	2.5 Climax FPF 4IL	20	Q9	Gearbox lap 26/76
	Bruce Halford	SJ Diggory	374	2.5 Climax FPF 4IL	22	Q14	Final drive lap 26/76
	Masten Gregory	UDT Laystall Racing Team	916	2.5 Climax FPF 4IL	18	Q11	Accident lap 5/76

Lotus 18 | 119

8 1962 FORMULA 1 SEASON – SECOND DIVISION

The 1962 season heralded the long-awaited arrival of V8 engines from BRM and Coventry Climax, destined to relegate the 4-cylinder Climax FPF-powered Lotus 18s to the rear of the grid. Although the BRM engine was offered for sale, most constructors/teams opted for the Coventry Climax FWMV V8, for which deliveries were slow, as the solution to the overheating problem encountered in 1961 had consumed valuable production time. New V8 engines required new chassis and, in an apparent reversal of the policy adopted in 1961, Colin Chapman was making his 1962 chassis available for customer purchase. Delays in the production of both this Lotus 24 chassis and the Climax engine left existing Lotus customers, such as the UDT-Laystall Racing Team, having to prolong the lives of their 4-cylinder Lotus 18/21s into the early part of the season. Stirling Moss and the Rob Walker Racing Team were in a similar position, but could at least fall back on the as-yet-unraced 18/21 V8 Special (906) seen in the latter part of 1961, for which they had an FWMV engine.

The Brussels Grand Prix on 1 April was the first Formula 1 event of the 1962 European calendar, the result decided on the aggregate of three heats. The prototype Lotus 24 was on hand from Team Lotus for Jim Clark, as was the Rob Walker 18/21 V8 Special for Stirling Moss: the only teams in possession of a Climax FWMV V8. UDT-Laystall entered two 4-cylinder 18/21s, returned from South Africa, for Innes Ireland (916) and Masten Gregory (917). Innes' appearance in the UDT team resulted from him having been unceremoniously dropped by Colin Chapman from Team Lotus, despite scoring several wins in 1961 and achieving the Team's first Grand Prix victory in the USA. A fourth 18/21 entered was the ex-Walker/Moss 1961 Monaco and Nürburgring winner (912), looking unfamiliar in the red colour scheme of the wealthy young Italian Count Giovanni Volpi's Scuderia SSS Republica de Venezia, for Sicilian Nino Vaccarella.

Jim Clark proved fastest in practice, driving the new Lotus 24; just 0.2sec quicker than Moss, who was finding the rear suspension of the now much tidier-looking 18/21 Special "unpleasant." Graham Hill took the remaining place on the

A fine shot of Stirling Moss driving a much neater-looking 18/21 V8 Special (906) during the Brussels Grand Prix. (Author)

8: 1962 Formula 1 Season – Second Division

front row of the grid with the new BRM P578 V8, whilst Ireland and Gregory were seventh and ninth respectively in the UDT-Laystall 18/21s. Vaccarella damaged his 18/21 during Saturday's wet practice session and would not make the start.

Stirling Moss led the opening lap of Heat 1 before sliding up an escape road when his front brakes locked. Completing that first lap 18th and last, he set about retrieving the situation as only he could, and was back up to second behind leader Hill's BRM within 15 laps. On his way, however, Stirling had inadvertently missed a gear and over-revved the Climax V8 and it began to lose power, allowing the BRM to win the heat by 5.5sec. The UDT-Laystall 18/21s were engaged in a battle with Bonnier's Porsche, sixth place going to the Swede ahead of Ireland, whilst Gregory's car collapsed on the side of the road with a broken suspension wishbone. The new Climax engine in Clark's Lotus 24 had expired on the opening lap.

The 18/21 V8 Special was fitted with a higher final drive ratio between heats in the hope of preserving the engine. Moss led the first 11 laps of Heat 2 until a broken timing gear deranged the valve gear – but not before he had set a new lap record. Innes Ireland and Jo Bonnier continued their race-long tussle from Heat 1, now for second place, the decision going once again to the Porsche, with Ireland third. The winner of Heat 2, Belgian Willy Mairesse in a 'Sharknose' Ferrari 156 V6, continued on to win a processional Heat 3, ahead of Bonnier and Ireland once again. On aggregate Ireland finished third, the only 18 to finish.

The first British Formula 1 race of 1962 was the Lombank Trophy at Snetterton, where, this time, Moss snatched pole position from Clark by 0.2sec. Rob Walker had loaned the Lotus 18/21 V8 Special to UDT-Laystall for this and Easter Goodwood, where Stirling would race in the British 'grazing green' colours of the team. Masten Gregory and Innes Ireland were in their regular UDT 18/21s, lining up fifth and sixth fastest respectively. In addition, there were two brand 'new' Lotus 18/21s on the grid. These had been assembled independent of the Lotus factory, by Tim Parnell's team, from new chassis and factory spare parts, their 4-cylinder Climax FPF engines mated to GSD type 32 5-speed transmissions. To differentiate them from factory 18s, they carried chassis numbers 'P1' and 'P2.' Chassis P1 was acquired by John Dalton for the experienced New Zealander Tony Shelly, over in Europe to try his luck in Formula 1, whilst 'P2' was retained and driven by Tim Parnell himself.

Graham Hill (BRM) chases Stirling Moss in the now UDT-Laystall-liveried V8 Special during the early laps at Snetterton. (LAT Photographic)

From the start, Graham Hill's V8 BRM accelerated into the lead, pursued by Moss and Clark. On lap 5, Moss closed right up on the BRM, snatching the lead on the following lap. Gregory and Ireland, in fifth and sixth, collided when the former had a 'moment' on lap 5

TECHNICAL UPDATE: COVENTRY CLIMAX FWMV V8

The Coventry Climax FWMV V8 Mk I engine in the Rob Walker Racing Team Lotus 18/21 Special of Stirling Moss was producing around 181bhp at 8500rpm, with a wide spread of power, particularly strong from 6000rpm upwards, and 119lb/ft of torque at 7500rpm.

The FWMV was designed to be straightforward and simple, with many features carried over from previous Climax race engines. The bore and stroke dimensions of 63mm by 60mm were arrived at after a detailed analysis of the performance of the FPF series engines and a desire to achieve the best relationship between power and torque. The cylinder block was a one-piece aluminium casting, extending down well below the main bearing caps, and completed by a shallow sump. As in the 2½-litre FPF and the Mk II 1½-litre FPF, there were five steel main bearing caps; the centre and intermediate ones being side bolted to the crankcase walls for increased rigidity. Wet cylinder liners were of the compression type, with the top and bottom flanges compressed by cylinder head tightening.

A single roller chain drove twin overhead camshafts on each cylinder bank, operating two valves per cylinder disposed at a 60° included angle, to provide a more compact, hemispherical combustion chamber than on previous engines. The inlet valve was 1.30in in diameter with a 1.237in exhaust. Emphasising the conservative approach taken, the engine was designed from the outset to breathe through four twin choke Weber DCNL-4 type 38 carburettors with 32mm choke tubes. By contrast, the single plug per cylinder was sparked by a Lucas transistorised ignition system, an innovative step in 1961.

A distinctive feature of the FWMV was the complex exhaust system. With a two-plane crankshaft, firing sequences are unequal in each cylinder bank and evenly-spaced gas flow pulses, and higher power over a wide rev band, was achieved by linking the exhausts of the inner cylinders of one bank with the outer ones of the other, and vice versa. This necessitated the complex crossover 'spaghetti' type system, each set of four pipes combining in a single, slightly megaphoned tail pipe above the car's transmission.

Power was initially disappointing, when the first engine ran in May 1961. Once the crossover exhaust system had been adopted, it was soon developing 174bhp, and the engine first raced in this form at the German Grand Prix. By late August, power was up to 181bhp at 8500rpm, with a good spread from 6000rpm upwards, and a second V8 was supplied to the Rob Walker Racing Team, for installation in the specially modified Lotus 18/21 (906) in time for the Italian Grand Prix. The engine suffered overheating in practice in both Italy and the United States, and Stirling Moss declined to risk the engine in the races.

Despite modifications to the cooling system, nothing seemed to cure the water loss and overheating, but strenuous investigation over the winter of 1961/62 revealed that combustion gases were leaking into the cooling system, pressurising it and causing water to blow out of the header tank, due to differential expansion of the cast iron cylinder liners and the alloy block. The cure was to support the liners in alloy slip-fit type sleeves of the same co-efficient of expansion as the block. The sleeves would thus expand in unison with the block, maintaining the seal against leakage. The overheating problems solved, production could commence.

and both retired to the pits, where a quick check confirmed the end of their races. Tim Parnell pitted with an acute water shortage, losing a lap in the process. Moss pulled out a useful lead, but Clark in the Lotus 24 was now pressing forward, passing Hill on lap 16, then Moss two laps later. Moss hung on, until pitting on lap 23 with a throttle linkage problem. When he rejoined 58sec later, he had lost a lap on Clark and was fourth on the road. A lap later, he was back in the pits for a further 45sec stop, leaving him now two laps in arrears. Just when he seemed determined to win back some of the lost time, he came back in for a third time, remaining stationary for over 4mins whilst more drastic work was carried out. This dropped him back to seventh, five laps behind, leaving him with only the lap record to attack. This he duly set about achieving, finally lapping 0.6sec quicker than his pole time. Other than Moss, Tony Shelly was the only other 18 driver to finish, after a steady run into fifth, three laps in arrears.

In exchange for lending his 18/21 V8 Special to UDT-Laystall, Rob Walker borrowed a 4-cylinder 18/21 (918) in its place, for Maurice Trintignant to drive in the Pau Grand Prix on Easter Monday. Two other 18s were present, the Scuderia SSS Republica di Venezia

8: 1962 Formula 1 Season – Second Division

Maurice Trintignant (918) on his way to his third victory in the Pau Grand Prix, all three driving Rob Walker-entered cars. (LAT Photographic)

GRAND PRIX DE PAU

Located in the shadow of the Pyrénées in south western France, Pau hosted the 1930 French Grand Prix on a road circuit just out of town. A new circuit was devised in 1933 around the streets of the town, and the first Pau Grand Prix was held that year. It was a pure 'street circuit' in the style of Monte Carlo, with all the associated hazards of kerb stones, lamp posts, railings and stone walls, etc. The demanding 1.74-mile circuit led uphill between two hairpins, wound its way through public gardens, then swerved back downhill to the finish. Following World War II, it hosted mainly non-Championship Formula 1 events; then Formula 2 from 1958-60.

With the advent of the 1½-litre Regulations in 1961, the Pau Grand Prix reverted to Formula 1. The handling qualities of the Lotus 18 proved ideal for street circuits, allowing Jim Clark to score the first Formula 1 win of his career at Pau that year. Then, in 1962, the Lotus 18 scored its second successive Pau victory when Maurice Trintignant proved a popular event winner for the third time in his career.

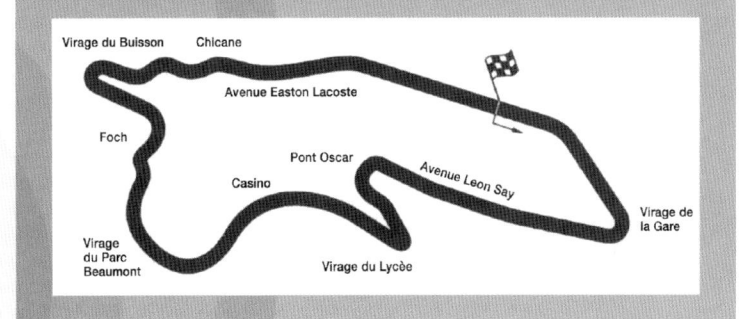

18/21 for Nino Vaccarella and an ex-Scuderia Colonia 18 (914), now running in the name of Autosport Team Wolfgang Seidel for German 500cc Formula 3 and Formula Junior exponent Kurt Kuhnke, who was too slow to qualify. Despite a clash with Easter Goodwood, there was a healthy entry, including the Lotus 24 Climax V8 of Jim Clark, and two Ferraris for Ricardo Rodriguez and Lorenzo Bandini. Trintignant started from fifth on the grid to run fourth, moving ahead of Bonnier's Porsche into third by lap 11. The following lap, he passed Rodriguez' Ferrari into second and began to close on Clark's Lotus in the lead.

On lap 16, Trintignant was ahead of Clark, who was having some difficulty changing gear, and would shortly retire. Driving comfortably and looking remarkably at ease, Maurice completed the distance unchallenged, 34sec ahead of Rodriguez, despite some gear selection problems. Vaccarella had been left on the line, unable to select first gear, but drove steadily throughout the afternoon without it to finish sixth, two laps in arrears. Significantly, this would be the last of the Lotus 18's 20 victories in its racing career.

Meanwhile, at Goodwood, the BARC decided to run a 4-cylinder-only Formula 1 race for the Lavant Cup, in addition to the feature 100-mile Glover Trophy. Four 18s appeared for the former, of which Tony Shelly was fastest, his 18/21 (P1) third on the grid. The former California Lotus dealer Jay Chamberlain was having his first Formula 1 drive in the ex-Camoradi 18 (905) with more streamlined nosecone, running in the name of Ecurie Excelsior. Gerry Ashmore had his 18/21 (919) and Günther Seiffert the second

Lotus 18 – Colin Chapman's U-turn

MAURICE TRINTIGNANT
(b 30 October 1917, d 12 February 2005)

Maurice Trintignant made his race debut in 1938 at Pau, driving a Bugatti T35 previously owned by his brother, who had been killed racing in 1933. When the first postwar race was held in the Bois de Boulogne in Paris in 1945, he dusted off the Bugatti to find it suffering from fuel starvation. This was revealed to be due to rat droppings (les petoules) in the fuel tank, causing much hilarity and earning him the lifelong nickname 'Le Petoulet.' He earned a place in the Gordini team from 1948-53, winning a number of minor races, yet never finishing better than fifth in Championship Grands Prix.

In 1954 he joined Ferrari, co-driving the winning 4.9-litre tipo 375 at Le Mans with Froilan Gonzalez, and profited from the failures of Mercedes and Lancia to win the 1955 Monaco Grand Prix. Maurice scored a brilliant win with a Rob Walker-entered Cooper in the 1958 Monaco Grand Prix, and had a highly successful season with the team in 1959. He had gained a reputation as a master of street circuits, as, in addition to his Monaco wins, he had victories in the Pau Grand Prix in 1958 and 1959 driving Walker Coopers. Then, in 1962, Maurice proved a popular winner of the event for the third time in his career, this time with a Walker Lotus 18/21.

Trintignant retired from Formula 1 at the end of the 1964 season at the age of 47, to concentrate on his vineyards and his role as long serving mayor of the small town of Vergèze in southern France. As one of a select band of French drivers of the 1940/50s, Maurice was utterly reliable, dependable and safe, with a mechanical sympathy that enabled him to nurse many an unreliable car through to the finish.

Maurice Trintignant – capable veteran. (LAT Photographic)

ex-Scuderia Colonia 18 (373) entered by Autosport Team Wolfgang Seidel. The race deteriorated into a procession once John Surtees (Lola Mk 4) had eliminated himself and Seiffert (who was already being lapped), in a lap 3 collision at the Chicane. Bruce McLaren (Cooper T55) ran out the winner, with Shelly third and Chamberlain fifth.

The same 18s appeared for the Glover Trophy, less Seiffert's damaged car but plus the UDT-Laystall 18/21s of Ireland (916) and Gregory (917) and Stirling Moss in the UDT-liveried 18/21 V8 Special. For the first time there were four V8-engined cars on the grid – two powered by BRM and two by Coventry Climax. In a wet practice session, Moss put the V8 Special on pole, 2sec quicker than Graham Hill's BRM with the 18/21s of Ireland, Shelly and Gregory fourth, seventh and eighth respectively. Bruce McLaren made the better start in his Cooper, but Hill soon established himself in the lead, Moss was fourth, ahead of Ireland with Gregory and

Shelly seventh and eighth. Moss began looking unhappy, despite momentarily taking Surtees' Lola Climax V8 for third, calling into the pits on lap 9 to have the gearchange linkage worked on. Rejoining over a lap later down in 12th, he now began driving really quickly, putting in a series of record-breaking laps and working his way back up to eighth by lap 29. Then on lap 36, Moss had a horrific accident. Catching Hill's BRM to unlap himself, he drew alongside at St Mary's, but shot straight off the circuit hitting the earth embankment hard. Hill went on to score the first win for the BRM P578, with McLaren second and Ireland third. The remaining 18/21s of Gregory and Shelly finished fifth and sixth respectively.

Why Stirling Moss went off the road and ploughed into the embankment at St Mary's has never been satisfactorily explained. The space frame chassis of the Lotus collapsed around him, trapping him in the remains of the cockpit for 40 minutes before he could be extricated and rushed to hospital semi-conscious. He suffered deep facial wounds and breaks to his nose, left arm and his left leg at the knee and ankle. Worse than breakages, the right side of his brain was severely bruised, leaving him in a coma for a month and paralysed down his left side for six months. Stirling had had other accidents, but Goodwood was the most serious; this time there would be no quick recovery. Having regained consciousness, he gradually began to mend, but he was powerless to speed recovery of his brain, and all the time both the public and the press eagerly awaited the answer to the question: would Moss race again?

Despite the loss of Stirling Moss, the season rolled onwards to the next non-Championship race, the BARC 200 at Aintree. Each of the five 18/21s and two 18s entered had already been seen at least once this season. Innes Ireland was fastest 18/21 driver in practice and fastest of the 4-cylinder cars, tying with Ginther's BRM P578 V8 for fourth place on the grid. Masten Gregory was seventh, quicker than both the Ferrari Dino 156s of Phil Hill and Giancarlo Baghetti. The increasingly impressive Shelly was 3sec slower in 13th, ahead of the other 18/21s, with Seiffert bringing up the rear, 15sec slower than Ireland.

The race proved to be rather dull, as Jim Clark dominated all 50 laps in the Lotus 24. The only excitement was provided by a furious battle between Baghetti's Ferrari and the UDT-Laystall duo of Ireland and Gregory for seventh place. Ireland led Gregory until Baghetti managed to split the UDT pair on lap 11, although Gregory's pale green car hung on for several laps not giving the Ferrari any peace. Baghetti managed to pass Ireland around the back of the circuit on lap 18, but the Lotus kept right with the Ferrari

Moss speeds through Woodcote Corner in the V8 Special, at Goodwood on Easter Monday. (LAT Photographic)

and the two cars passed the pits side by side, with Gregory only inches behind. The tremendous battle continued, with the UDT cars hounding Baghetti, who was not about to be flustered into making a mistake. Ireland managed to nose ahead briefly, before the pace told and the Lotus began to drop back, pulling in to the pits on lap 25 with a dropped valve. Baghetti was now clear of Gregory, whose engine suffered the same malady as his teammate on lap 34. Tony Shelly drove smoothly and capably once again to finish two laps in arrears, in seventh, with Tim Parnell in ninth, the only 18s to be classified as finishers.

The final non-Championship British Formula 1 event was the Silverstone International Trophy, for which six Lotus 18s were entered. Notable by their absence were the UDT-Laystall 18/21s, the team having taken delivery of its first Lotus 24 with Coventry Climax V8 that would be handled by Masten Gregory. Innes Ireland by contrast was entered to drive a Ferrari Dino 156 V6. This was purported to be the car that Stirling Moss would have driven

Lotus 18 – Colin Chapman's U-turn

UDT-Laystall team-mates – Masten Gregory (917) leads Innes Ireland (916) during the Aintree 200, prior to their retirement with engine failure. (LAT Photographic)

126 | Lotus 18

8: 1962 Formula 1 Season – Second Division

Innes Ireland and Masten Gregory make a UDT-Laystall sandwich of Giancarlo Baghetti's Ferrari 156 in the Aintree 200. (LAT Photographic)

Lotus 18 | 127

Lotus 18 – Colin Chapman's U-turn

for Rob Walker during 1962, yet why it was entered by UDT and not Walker is unknown. Maurice Trintignant in the Walker Pau-winning 18/21 chassis (918) and Nino Vaccarella in the ex-Walker example (912), supplemented the usual 18s of Shelly, Chamberlain, Parnell and Ashmore, the latter (919) driven for the first time by David Piper. Without a front line driver, all the 18s were in the second half of the grid, Trintignant fastest in 16th, 7sec away from the all-V8 front row on this faster circuit.

Jim Clark out-accelerated everyone to lead on a wet but drying track. Trintignant spun on to the grass at Abbey on the opening lap, taking Shelly with him, but, whilst the Frenchman regained the circuit, the New Zealander was out. Around lap 17, it started to rain again, although it was of little help to the 18s, of which Trintignant and Vaccarella were running 15th and 16th at half distance. Engine failures would ensure that they did not last, the only classified finisher being Jay Chamberlain, who had spun off four times on his way to 16th place, having completed only 46 of the 52 laps. The race was notable for the last minute charge by Graham Hill, who slid wildly past Jim Clark at Woodcote on the last lap, to claim victory for BRM by a matter of inches.

Grote Prijs van Nederland, Zandvoort, 20 May 1962

The 1962 Grand Prix season began in Holland, rather than the traditional opener at Monte Carlo. The 20 entries comprised a wealth of technical interest, including two new factory Porsche 804s with the long awaited flat-8 air-cooled engines. By far the most outstanding new arrival, however, was the revolutionary monocoque chassis Lotus 25. This new concept would change the face of chassis design for ever, and its appearance explained why Colin Chapman had been so happy to supply replicas of the space-framed Lotus 24 to all and sundry.

All the major British teams were now running two V8-engined cars per team, with the exception of UDT-Laystall and Cooper. UDT still only had a single Lotus 24, to be driven by Innes Ireland, whilst Gregory himself was back in his usual 18/21 (917). This was the only 18-type chassis in the race, and marked the last time that one would be fielded by a professional team in a Championship Grand Prix. Gregory was the fastest of the 4-cylinder brigade in Friday's first practice session, but had barely started the afternoon session before a piston broke. In the absence of a spare, UDT-Laystall had to have a new engine sent over from England, leaving Gregory to miss the remaining practice sessions and sink down the grid to 16th.

Jim Clark took off into the lead of the race in the new Lotus, pursued by eventual winner Graham Hill's BRM, whilst Gregory completed the opening lap in 12th. By lap 10, Gregory was in ninth, just ahead of Tony Maggs' works Cooper T55, which managed to slip past on lap 21, only to lose the place on the following lap. Now in sixth, Gregory pulled away from Maggs in

---

TECHNICAL UPDATE: LOTUS 18 CHASSIS UPGRADED TO 18/21 SPECIFICATION

- **371** Team Lotus – upgraded prior to sale to Jim Hall for US GP 8.10.61.
- **372** Team Lotus – upgraded prior to sale to J Wheeler Autosport for US GP 8.10.61.
- **904** Tim Parnell – upgraded prior to acquisition by Phillip Robinson for 1962 season.
- **906** RRC Walker Racing Team – total rebuild June/August 1961 as 18/21 V8 'Special' for Stirling Moss.
- **912** RRC Walker Racing Team regular car for Stirling Moss – upgraded prior to Belgian GP 18.6.61.
- **915** Ex-UDT-Laystall Team chassis upgraded by Tim Parnell winter 1962/63.
- **916** UDT-Laystall Racing Team – upgraded prior to French GP 2.7.61.
- **917** UDT-Laystall Racing Team – upgraded from new, debuted at Brands Hatch 3.6.61.
- **918** UDT-Laystall Racing Team – upgraded from new, debuted at Brands Hatch 3.6.61.
- **919** Gerry Ashmore – upgraded for 1962 season.
- **P1** } Two 18/21s built up by Tim Parnell around new chassis and Lotus spare parts over the winter of 1961/62,
- **P2** } numbered P1 and P2 to differentiate them from official Lotus products.

8: 1962 Formula 1 Season – Second Division

pursuit of Baghetti's Ferrari. On lap 31, he was lapped by leader Hill and took the opportunity to tuck in behind him for a number of laps to draw him closer to the Ferrari. He would never get close enough to challenge the Italian, as his gearbox broke on lap 55 and he took to the grass behind the pits, to retire after a good drive in an increasingly-obsolete Grand Prix car.

On the same day as the Dutch Grand Prix, a second division Formula 1 race was held, the Naples Grand Prix, on the Posillipo circuit. Of the ten cars permitted to start, two were works Ferraris and four were Lotus 18s. Tony Shelly was outpaced to bring his 18/21 (P1) home sixth, lapped twice by the winning Ferraris, with Tim Parnell (P2) five laps down in seventh. Gaetano Starrabba made his sole 1962 appearance in his Maserati-engined 18 (902), suffering transmission failure on the opening lap, and David Piper (919) was unclassified.

Grand Prix de Monaco, Monte Carlo, 3 June 1962

There was only one 18 on the entry list at Monte Carlo, that being

Lucien Bianchi, in the Rob Walker chassis (918) hired by Equipe National Belge for the Belgian Grand Prix – the Belgian driver finished ninth. Jo Siffert (Lotus 21) follows. (Sutton Images)

Lotus 18 | 129

Lotus 18 – Colin Chapman's U-turn

the 1961 winning chassis, the ex-Walker 18/21 (912) of Scuderia SSS Republica di Venezia for Nino Vaccarella. Unfortunately Vaccarella spun during the second, wet, practice session and bent the Lotus badly enough not to be able to take any further part in qualifying.

Vaccarella's car was back in action eight days later, however, for the '2000 Guineas' at Mallory Park, the first ever Formula 1 race on this tight 1.35-mile circuit. Driven by the Italian-domiciled Englishman Colin Davis, it qualified 12th out of 13 starters. In the absence of BRM, Graham Hill took a one-off drive in Rob Walker's UDT 18/21 (918), qualifying third. Having appeared at Monaco in a new BRM-engined Lotus 24, Masten Gregory was back in his faithful 4-cylinder 18/21 for this race. Also present was Tony Shelly in the John Dalton-entered 18/21 (P1), whilst John Dalton himself deputised for an unwell Tim Parnell in his 18/21 (P2). John Surtees took his Lola Mk 4 Climax V8 into an immediate lead and remained unchallenged for the duration of the race. Hill established the Walker 18/21 in third place, whilst Gregory fell back to fifth in the UDT car. After a good start, Shelly faded to eighth behind Davis.

Meanwhile, in the London suburbs yet another Formula 1 race was taking place, on the 1.4-mile Crystal Palace circuit for the Crystal Palace Trophy. The proliferation of Formula 1 races reflected the lack of a secondary single-seater formula to fill the role of a feature race. The 12 starters included the Gerry Ashmore 18/21 (919) driven by David Piper, and standard 18s for Seiffert, Chamberlain and Graham Eden. In a race dominated by the UDT-Laystall Lotus 24 BRM V8 of Innes Ireland, Piper's 18/21 struggled around to finish seventh, two laps behind, the only 18 to finish.

Grand Prix de Belgique, Spa-Francorchamps, 17 June 1962

The Lotus 18 made a return to the premier category for the Belgian Grand Prix. Keen to maintain its annual presence in its home event, Equipe National Belge had hired the Pau-winning 18/21 from Rob Walker for Belgian driver Lucien Bianchi. The car appeared in the usual Walker dark blue, rather than any attempt at Belgian racing yellow. Bianchi qualified only 18th fastest, 10sec slower than Stirling Moss in a similar car in 1961. A last minute additional 18 materialised, after John Campbell-Jones had the gearbox break on his 4-cylinder Emeryson Climax and arranged to borrow the Autosport Team Wolfgang Seidel 18 (373), usually driven by Günther Seiffert. Campbell-Jones was unable to drive the car any quicker than Seiffert, qualifying slowest of the 19 starters, with a time 30sec away from pole position. He would make the first of a number of

pit stops after the opening lap, eventually completing 16 of the scheduled 32 laps. Bianchi at least finished, three laps down in ninth, having trailed around at the tail of the field for the duration.

Denied the organisation of the French Grand Prix this year (it had been awarded to Rouen), the Automobile Club du Champagne organised its own Grand Prix de Reims. Held over a full Grand Prix distance, it attracted most major teams, including the Lotus 18/21s of Tony Shelly and Scuderia SSS Republica de Venezia, the latter to be driven by Carlo Abate on this occasion. Neither Shelly nor Abate had good practice sessions, both cars experiencing engine trouble and filling the back row of the grid, 20sec slower than the next row up and 30sec away from the front row. Shelly's bodged-up Climax engine allowed him to complete only the opening lap and at least claim the start money. Abate stopped twice in the first dozen laps, changed plugs and continued, until spinning out of the race into the long grass on the roadside on lap 22.

The Solitude Grand Prix suffered a lack of entries from being scheduled on the weekend between the French and British Grands Prix. Only two standard 18s appeared, both from Wolfgang Seidel's team, to be driven by Seiffert (373) and Kuhnke (914). To the delight

John Campbell-Jones borrowed the Autosport Team Wolfgang Seidel chassis (373) for the Belgian Grand Prix. (LAT Photographic)

130 | Lotus 18

of the partisan crowd, Dan Gurney and Jo Bonnier finished first and second in the works Porsche 804s. Kuhnke proved to be 30sec off the pace – his 18 lasted four laps before expiring with engine failure – whilst the even slower Seiffert finished unclassified, seven laps down on the winning Porsche.

RAC British Grand Prix, Aintree, 21 July 1962

The British Grand Prix was held at Aintree for a second consecutive year, much to the annoyance of the BRDC at Silverstone, with which the event normally alternated. In fact this would be the last occasion on which the Grand Prix would be hosted at the Liverpool circuit, and Brands Hatch would enter the equation in future. Only two 18s filed entries for this race, these being the usual cars of Tony Shelly and Jay Chamberlain. In practice, Shelly lapped 0.4sec slower than he had managed on this circuit back in April, whilst Chamberlain improved by 2sec, to fill 18th and 20th places on the grid. Shelly's black 18/21 lasted only five laps before expiring with overheating, but Chamberlain completed 64 of the 75 lap distance, insufficient to be classified as a finisher.

Großer Preis von Deutschland, Nürburgring, 5 August 1962

Two weeks later, Shelly and Chamberlain were the only 18 drivers to travel to the Nürburgring for the German Grand Prix. Shelly failed to set a time during Friday practice, but recorded a lap in the wet on Saturday morning good enough for 23rd on the grid. Chamberlain, meanwhile, had never lapped below 11min and the organisers decided that neither driver had completed sufficient laps in practice to qualify and they were both excluded.

Another seven days later, Chamberlain's Ecurie Excelsior 18 was entered for the Kanonloppet race at Karlskoga in Sweden, for local man Olle Nygren. Better known on the Speedway tracks of Europe, he was to make his Formula 1 debut – though quite why he chose this car is not recorded. Slowest in practice by nearly 7sec, he lasted only six laps before his gearbox failed.

Chamberlain's car was also entered for the next non-Championship Formula 1 race, the Mediterranean Grand Prix at Pergusa in Sicily, yet failed to materialise. There were two other 18s, however, the Scuderia SSS Republica di Venezia (912), back in the hands of Nino Vaccarella, plus Günther Seiffert's Autosport Team Wolfgang Seidel well-used 18 (373). Vaccarella had a dismal time – firstly his engine failed after he had set sixth best time in practice (albeit 5sec off the pace), and then suffered an electrical failure on the warm-up lap to leave him a non-starter. Seiffert completed only 26 of the 50 lap distance.

The regular non-Championship Danish Grand Prix was run on the short Roskildering circuit, for 11 starters, including two Lotus 18s. Driving Tim Parnell's 18/21 (P2) was the reigning 350 and 500cc Motorcycle Champion Gary Hocking, who impressed with a fourth place finish on aggregate, and looked set to follow the example of John Surtees into a successful career on four wheels. Jay Chamberlain was unclassified, after spinning off in the first heat and missing the second.

The Oulton Park Gold Cup was the last British Formula 1 event of the season, for which Stirling Moss made a very welcome appearance in the role of a spectator. By no means recovered from his Goodwood accident back in April, he was looking suitably fit and tanned after a recuperation period in Nassau. The field of 23 starters included six Lotus 18s, the best turn out since the Naples Grand Prix in May. Gerry Ashmore emerged with an 18/21 for himself (919) and the ex-Tony Marsh 18 for Graham Eden (909), Günther Seiffert had the Seidel 18, Philip Robinson his ex-Parnell 18/21 (904), Tony Shelly the John Dalton 18/21 and, finally, Gary Hocking the Parnell 18/21 that he had now purchased and was running in his own name. Parnell himself had not raced since May

Jay Chamberlain (46) has been lapped by the BRM of Ritchie Ginther (14), whilst John Surtees' Bowmaker Lola closes on them both, during the British Grand Prix at Aintree. (LAT Photographic)

Lotus 18 – Colin Chapman's U-turn

Tony Shelly (P1) hustles around the Karussel at the Nürburgring, but would fail to qualify for the German Grand Prix. (Sutton Images)

due to illness, but was recovering quickly, and appeared as a spectator looking very fit and considerably slimmer. Hocking was easily the fastest 4-cylinder runner in 11th spot on the grid, 2.4sec quicker than Shelly. He settled into ninth place in the early stages, on the tail of the V8-engined cars, not losing ground on them, until forced to pit on lap 10 with overheating. He made a splendid recovery, charging back up to sixth by lap 45, before his engine began misfiring. Then it began smoking, and he stopped out on the circuit to investigate, finally motoring slowly into the pits to retire on lap 62 with a broken oil line. Shelly was having a good race, moving up the order as the V8s floundered, to finish fifth, four laps down on Jim Clark, who had won as he pleased in a race of little excitement. Gerry Ashmore was the only other Lotus 18 finisher, in eighth place, having completed 67 of the 73 laps.

Gran Premio d'Italia, Monza, 16 September 1962

The final European event of the season was the Italian Grand Prix, entries for which included Gerry Ashmore with his 18/21, plus standard 18s from Ecurie Excelsior for Jay Chamberlain and Ernesto Prinoth in his former Scuderia Dolomiti chassis (913), now supported by Scuderia Jolly Club. With a 30-car entry and a starting grid limited to 22, all of which had to lap within 10% of the second fastest time overall, the likelihood of an 18 qualifying was remote. So it proved. Ashmore was the fastest, but 3.8sec away from the grid, whilst Prinoth disappeared into the paddock with water pouring from his Climax exhaust pipe, and Chamberlain had his engine in pieces: neither of the latter recording any times in the second, Saturday afternoon practice session.

8: 1962 Formula 1 Season – Second Division

The European season now over, Jay Chamberlain took his 18 home to the USA and entered it for the inaugural, non-Championship Mexican Grand Prix, held as a precursor to obtaining World Championship status for 1963. Several works teams travelled down to Mexico directly after the United States Grand Prix at Watkins Glen and, besides Chamberlain, US sports car champion Walt Hansgen had acquired the 18/21 (372) driven by Peter Ryan in 1961 for J Wheeler Autosport. Jim Hall entered the 18/21 (371) he had driven at Watkins Glen in 1961, for a certain Homer Rader, who actually achieved the sole finish for an 18, three laps behind in eighth place.

SOUTH AFRICAN FORMULA 1 SERIES

The South African season opened with two 'warm-up' races prior to the South African Grand Prix on 29 December, that would be the decider for the 1962 World Championship between Jim Clark and eventual winner Graham Hill. Gary Hocking had recently won the Rhodesian Grand Prix and the Rand Spring Trophy with his ex-Parnell 18/21 (P2), and also entered the Rand Grand Prix. In the event, Rob Walker offered him a drive in his Lotus 24 Climax V8 and thus the 18/21 was not seen. Tragically, this obviously talented young driver was killed in practice for the Natal Grand Prix a week later. The only 18 to appear, apart from a couple of up-engined Formula Junior

TIM PARNELL
(b. 25 June 1932)

As the son of Reg Parnell, who raced at Brooklands prewar and drove for BRM, Aston Martin, and ran his own Ferraris postwar, Tim might have been expected to have a smooth path into racing. In fact, despite a passion for the sport, he was actively discouraged from taking part. He persisted, however, on his own account, until some success in Club racing earned him support from his father.

After a couple of seasons in Formula 2 with a Cooper, he switched to Formula Junior, in 1960, with a Lotus 18, also running a couple of Formula 2 races in an 18 owned by his father. In 1961, Tim ran the 18 in the new 1½-litre Formula 1 in his own name. He was not overly successful, scoring only one third, together with three fifth places.

In 1962, he built up two 18/21s from new chassis and factory spares, one of which he retained for his own use, the other he sold. His season was curtailed by illness, but he returned in 1963 and graduated to a BRM V8-engined Lotus 24. A number of used single-seaters passed through his hands, including three ex-UDT-Laystall 18/21 chassis that he sold-on.

In 1964, Tim's father died suddenly of peritonitis and he gave up driving to run the Reg Parnell (Racing) team. He continued as a team manager for the remainder of his career, using his down-to-earth approach, organisational skills inherited from his father and experience as a driver, eventually managing the BRM team, from 1969 until it began to fade away in 1974. He retired to the family pig farm, whilst remaining involved in the sport in an administrative role with the BRDC.

Tim was typical of the private entrant of the 1960s, 'trailering' his car around Europe, taking in the vast number of non-Championship Formula 1 races held at the time, and living off start money and hopefully prize money. His claim to fame in the Lotus 18 story is the 24 starts he made in just over three years, a total beaten only by Innes Ireland (36) and Stirling Moss (27).

Men on the move: Tim Parnell (on the left) listens attentively to Stirling Moss making a point to Innes Ireland and Jim Clark. (LAT Photographic)

cars, was the Borgward-engined car previously driven by Helmut Menzler (911), now in the hands of Vern McWilliams. He failed to qualify for the Rand Grand Prix and retired from the first heat of the Natal Grand Prix.

SUMMARY

It was not anticipated that the Lotus 18 (or 18/21) would repeat the giant killing performances of 1961 and this proved to be the case. Before his untimely accident, Stirling Moss had enlivened the start of the season with some spectacular performances in the Rob Walker-entered 18/21 Climax V8 Special. The 18s could only hope for good placings in the early season non-Championship races before the new British V8s came on stream. Maurice Trintignant made the most of this short-term advantage to score an outstanding win at Pau and, in so doing, the final victory of the Lotus 18's career. For the remainder of the season, the 18s performed only a supporting role, as mid-field runners at best, but more often than not as tailenders.

Lotus 18 Performance Summary – 1962

	Starts	Finishes	1st	2nd	3rd	4th	5th	6th	PP	FL
Grands Prix	5	1	–	–	–	–	–	–	–	–
Other Formula 1	64	25	1	–	4	2	5	3	2	3
Total	69	26	1	–	4	2	5	3	2	3

Chassis Summary – 1962

Eighteen Lotus 18 chassis appeared in one or more Formula 1 events or Grands Prix during 1962, as follows:

371	18/21 retained by Jim Hall.
372	18/21 acquired by Walt Hansgen from J Wheeler Autosport.
373	Acquired from Scuderia Colonia by Autosport Team Wolfgang Seidel.
902	Retained by Prince Gaetano Starrabba.
904	Acquired by Phillip Robinson from Tim Parnell as 18/21.
905	Acquired by Ecurie Excelsior from Camoradi International.
906	RRC Walker Racing Team. The Lotus 18/21 V8 Special in which Stirling Moss ended his career – written-off 23.4.62.
909	Ex-Tony Marsh modified chassis acquired by Gerry Ashmore for Graham Eden.
911	South African domiciled, Borgward-engined chassis acquired by Vern McWilliams from Helmut Menzler.
912	Ex-RRC Walker/Stirling Moss 18/21 Monaco and Nürburgring winner from 1961 acquired by Count Volpi's Scuderia SSS Republica di Venezia.
913	Retained by Ernesto Prinoth supported by Scuderia Jolly Club.
914	Acquired from Scuderia Colonia by Autosport Team Wolfgang Seidel.
916 / 917	} 18/21s retained by UDT-Laystall Racing Team pending delivery of V8-engined Lotus 24s.
918	18/21 loaned by UDT-Laystall Racing Team to RRC Walker Racing Team. Winner of Pau GP.
919	Retained by Gerry Ashmore and converted to 18/21.
P1	New 18/21 chassis built up from spares by Tim Parnell – to John Dalton for Tony Shelly.
P2	New 18/21 chassis built up from spares retained by Tim Parnell. Sold to Gary Hocking in September.

Motorcyclist Gary Hocking had shown considerable talent behind the wheel of Tim Parnell's 18/21 (P2) before his tragic death in South Africa in December. (Sutton Images)

8: 1962 Formula 1 Season – Second Division

LOTUS 18 – FORMULA 1 RACING RECORD – 1962
(* signifies chassis to 18/21 specification)

Position	Driver	Entrant	Chassis	Engine	No	Grid	Comments
Grand Prix de Bruxelles, Brussels (B), 1.4.62, Aggregate of 3 Heats 186.78 miles (300.43km)							
3rd	Innes Ireland	UDT-Laystall Racing Team	*916	1.5 Climax FPF 4IL	2	Q7	
	Stirling Moss	RRC Walker Racing Team	*906	1.5 Climax FWMV V8	1	Q2	Valve gear Heat 2 (FL)
	Masten Gregory	UDT-Laystall Racing Team	*917	1.5 Climax FPF 4IL	3	Q9	Fr. suspension Heat 1
	Nino Vaccarella	Scud SSS Rep di Venezia	*912	1.5 Climax FPF 4IL	15		DNS accident in practice
Lombank Trophy, Snetterton (GB), 14.4.62, 135.50 miles (218.02km)							
5th	Tony Shelly	John Dalton	*P1	1.5 Climax FPF 4IL	15	Q12	47 laps/50
7th	Stirling Moss	UDT-Laystall Racing Team	*906	1.5 Climax FWMV V8	7	Q1	45 laps/50 (FL)
	Tim Parnell	RHH Parnell	*P2	1.5 Climax FPF 4IL	14	Q9	Overheating lap 10/50
	Masten Gregory	UDT-Laystall Racing Team	*917	1.5 Climax FPF 4IL	8	Q5	Accident lap 5/50
	Innes Ireland	UDT-Laystall Racing Team	*916	1.5 Climax FPF 4IL	6	Q6	Accident lap 5/50
Grand Prix de Pau, Pau (F), 23.4.62, 171.40 miles (275.85km)							
1st	Maurice Trintignant	RRC Walker Racing Team	*918	1.5 Climax FPF 4IL	12	Q5	
6th	Nino Vaccarella	Scud SSS Rep di Venezia	*912	1.5 Climax FPF 4IL	18	Q11	98 laps/100
	Kurt Kuhnke	Autosport Team W Seidel	914	1.5 Climax FPF 4IL	36		DNQ
Lavant Cup, Goodwood (GB), 23.4.62, 50.40 miles (81.09km)							
3rd	Tony Shelly	John Dalton	*P1	1.5 Climax FPF 4IL	17	Q3	
5th	Jay Chamberlain	Ecurie Excelsior	905	1.5 Climax FPF 4IL	16	Q7	19 laps/21
	Gerry Ashmore	G Ashmore	*919	1.5 Climax FPF 4IL	14	NT	Oil pipe lap 12/21
	Günther Seiffert	Autosport Team W Seidel	373	1.5 Climax FPF 4IL	12	Q11	Accident lap 3/21
Glover Trophy, Goodwood (GB), 23.4.62, 100.80 miles (162.18km)							
3rd	Innes Ireland	UDT-Laystall Racing Team	*916	1.5 Climax FPF 4IL	8	Q4	41 laps/42
5th	Masten Gregory	UDT-Laystall Racing Team	*917	1.5 Climax FPF 4IL	9	Q8	41 laps/42
6th	Tony Shelly	John Dalton	*P1	1.5 Climax FPF 4IL	17	Q7	40 laps/42
11th	Gerry Ashmore	G Ashmore	*919	1.5 Climax FPF 4IL	14	NT	37 laps/42
	Stirling Moss	UDT-Laystall Racing Team	*906	1.5 Climax FWMV V8	7	Q1	Accident lap 36/42 (=FL)
	Jay Chamberlain	Ecurie Excelsior	905	1.5 Climax FPF 4IL	16	Q12	Overheating lap 5/42
	Günther Seiffert	Autosport Team W Seidel	373	1.5 Climax FPF 4IL	12	Q16	DNS Accident in previous race
BARC 200, Aintree (GB), 29.4.62, 150.00 miles (241.35km)							
7th	Tony Shelly	John Dalton	*P1	1.5 Climax FPF 4IL	19	Q13	48 laps/50
9th	Tim Parnell	RHH Parnell	*P2	1.5 Climax FPF 4IL	21	Q16	46 laps/50
	David Piper	Speed Sport	*919	1.5 Climax FPF 4IL	22	Q17	N/C 38 laps/50
	Günther Seiffert	Autosport Team W Seidel	373	1.5 Climax FPF 4IL	27	Q22	N/C 37 laps/50
	Masten Gregory	UDT-Laystall Racing Team	*917	1.5 Climax FPF 4IL	9	Q7	Engine lap 34/50
	Innes Ireland	UDT-Laystall Racing Team	*916	1.5 Climax FPF 4IL	8	Q4	Engine lap 26/50
	Jay Chamberlain	Ecurie Excelsior	905	1.5 Climax FPF 4IL	20	Q18	DSQ Push-start lap 1/50
International Trophy, Silverstone (GB), 12.5.62, 152.20 miles (244.89km)							
16th	Jay Chamberlain	Ecurie Excelsior	905	1.5 Climax FPF 4IL	24	Q22	46 laps/52
	David Piper	G Ashmore	*919	1.5 Climax FPF 4IL	21	Q21	N/C 45 laps/52
	Maurice Trintignant	RRC Walker Racing Team	*918	1.5 Climax FPF 4IL	7	Q16	Engine lap 41/52
	Nino Vaccarella	Scud SSS Rep di Venezia	*912	1.5 Climax FPF 4IL	18	Q18	Engine lap 32/52
	Tim Parnell	RHH Parnell	*P2	1.5 Climax FPF 4IL	16	Q23	Oil pressure lap 5/52
	Tony Shelly	John Dalton	*P1	1.5 Climax FPF 4IL	22	Q20	Accident lap 1/52
GROTE PRIJS van NEDERLAND, Zandvoort (NL), 20.5.62, 208.43 miles (335.44km)							
	Masten Gregory	UDT-Laystall Racing Team	*917	1.5 Climax FPF 4IL	10	Q16	Gearbox lap 54/80
Gran Premio di Napoli, Posillipo (I), 20.5.62, 92.86 miles (149.41km)							
6th	Tony Shelly	John Dalton	*P1	1.5 Climax FPF 4IL	2	Q6	58 laps/60
7th	Tim Parnell	RHH Parnell	*P2	1.5 Climax FPF 4IL	14	Q4	55 laps/60
	David Piper	David Piper	*919	1.5 Climax FPF 4IL	46	Q9	N/C 51 laps/60
	Gaetano Starrabba	G Starrabba	902	1.5 Maserati 150S 4IL	26	Q10	Transmission lap 1/60
	Jay Chamberlain	Ecurie Excelsior	905	1.5 Climax FPF 4IL	8		DNQ
	Günther Seiffert	Autosport Team W Seidel	373	1.5 Climax FPF 4IL	48		DNQ
GRAND PRIX de MONACO, Monte Carlo (MC), 3.6.62, 195.42 miles (314.50km)							
	Nino Vaccarella	Scud SSS Rep di Venezia	*912	1.5 Climax FPF 4IL	42		DNQ Accident in practice
2000 Guineas, Mallory Park (GB), 11.6.62, 101.25 miles (162.91km)							
3rd	Graham Hill	RRC Walker Racing Team	*918	1.5 Climax FPF 4IL	12	Q3	
5th	Masten Gregory	UDT-Laystall Racing Team	*917	1.5 Climax FPF 4IL	7	Q7	74 laps/75
7th	Colin Davis	Scud SSS Rep di Venezia	*912	1.5 Climax FPF 4IL	11	Q12	73 laps/75
8th	Tony Shelly	John Dalton	*P1	1.5 Climax FPF 4IL	1	Q11	72 laps/75
	John Dalton	RHH Parnell	*P2	1.5 Climax FPF 4IL	3	Q13	Fuel starvation lap 32/75

Lotus 18 | 135

Lotus 18 – Colin Chapman's U-turn

Position	Driver	Entrant	Chassis	Engine	No	Grid	Comments
Crystal Palace Trophy, Crystal Palace (GB), 11.6.62, 50.04 miles (80.51km)							
7th	David Piper	Speed Sport	*919	1.5 Climax FPF 4IL	6	Q7	34 laps/36
	Günther Seiffert	Autosport Team W Seidel	373	1.5 Climax FPF 4IL	5	Q10	Gearbox lap 21/36
	Jay Chamberlain	Ecurie Excelsior	905	1.5 Climax FPF 4IL	7	NT	Connecting rod lap 1/36
	Graham Eden	G Ashmore	909	1.5 Climax FPF 4IL	12	Q9	Gearbox lap 1/36
GRAND PRIX de BELGIQUE, Spa (B), 17.6.62, 280.36 miles (451.20km)							
9th	Lucien Bianchi	Equipe Nationale Belge	*918	1.5 Climax FPF 4IL	19	Q18	29 laps/32
	J Campbell-Jones	Emeryson Cars	373	1.5 Climax FPF 4IL	4	Q19	N/C 16 laps/32
Grand Prix de Reims, Reims (F), 1.7.62, 257.90 miles (415.87km)							
	Carlo Abate	Scud SSS Rep di Venezia	*912	1.5 Climax FPF 4IL	38	Q20	Spun off lap 22/50
	Tony Shelly	John Dalton	*P1	1.5 Climax FPF 4IL	42	Q19	Head gasket lap 1/50
Großer Preis der Solitude, Solitude (D), 15.7.62, 177.23 miles (285.16km)							
	Günther Seiffert	Autosport Team W Seidel	373	1.5 Climax FPF 4IL	23	Q13	N/C 18 laps/25
	Kurt Kuhnke	Autosport Team W Seidel	914	1.5 Climax FPF 4IL	22	Q10	Engine lap 4/25
RAC BRITISH GRAND PRIX, Aintree (GB), 21.7.62, 225.00 miles (362.10km)							
	Jay Chamberlain	Ecurie Excelsior	905	1.5 Climax FPF 4IL	46	Q20	N/C 64 laps/75
	Tony Shelly	John Dalton	*P1	1.5 Climax FPF 4IL	48	Q18	Overheating lap 5/75
GROSSER PREIS von DEUTSCHLAND, Nürburgring (D), 5.8.62, 212.60 miles (342.15km)							
	Tony Shelly	John Dalton	*P1	1.5 Climax FPF 4IL	29		DNQ
	Jay Chamberlain	Ecurie Excelsior	905	1.5 Climax FPF 4IL	30		DNQ
Kanonloppet, Karlskoga (S), 12.8.62, 55.89 miles (89.88km)							
	Olle Nygren	Ecurie Excelsior	905	1.5 Climax FPF 4IL	15	Q10	Gearbox lap 6/30
Grand Premio del Mediterraneo, Pergusa (I), 19.8.62, 149.35 miles (240.30km)							
	Günther Seiffert	Autosport Team W Seidel	373	1.5 Climax FPF 4IL	6	Q12	N/C 26 laps/50
	Nino Vaccarella	Scud SSS Rep di Venezia	*912	1.5 Climax FPF 4IL	28	Q6	DNS Electrical
Danske Grand Prix, Roskildering (DK), 26.8.62, Aggregate of 3 Heats 59.20 miles (95.25km)							
4th	Gary Hocking	RHH Parnell	*P2	1.5 Climax FPF 4IL	22	Q7	
	Jay Chamberlain	Ecurie Excelsior	905	1.5 Climax FPF 4IL	20	Q10	N/C 46 laps/80
International Gold Cup, Oulton Park (GB), 1.9.62, 201.48 miles (324.18km)							
5th	Tony Shelly	John Dalton	*P1	1.5 Climax FPF 4IL	22	Q14	69 laps/73
8th	Gerry Ashmore	G Ashmore	*919	1.5 Climax FPF 4IL	5	Q19	67 laps/73
	Gary Hocking	G Hocking	*P2	1.5 Climax FPF 4IL	23	Q11	Engine lap 62/73
	Günther Seiffert	Autosport Team W Seidel	373	1.5 Climax FPF 4IL	12	Q22	N/C 50 laps/73
	Graham Eden	G Ashmore	909	1.5 Climax FPF 4IL	6	Q21	Engine lap 27/73
	Philip Robinson	Team Alexis	*904	1.5 Climax FPF 4IL	16	Q16	Engine lap 1/73
GRAN PREMIO d'ITALIA, Monza (I), 16.9.62, 307.28 miles (494.50km)							
	Jay Chamberlain	Ecurie Excelsior	905	1.5 Climax FPF 4IL	26		DNQ
	Gerry Ashmore	G Ashmore	*919	1.5 Climax FPF 4IL	52		DNQ
	Ernesto Prinoth	Scuderia Jolly Club	913	1.5 Climax FPF 4IL	54		DNQ
Gran Premio de Mexico, Mexico City (MEX), 4.11.62, 186.40 miles (299.92km)							
8th	Homer Rader	J Hall	*371	1.5 Climax FPF 4IL	24	Q14	57 laps/60
	Jay Chamberlain	Ecurie Excelsior	905	1.5 Climax FPF 4IL	52	Q16	N/C 53 laps/60
	Walt Hansgen	W Hansgen	372	1.5 Climax FPF 4IL	60	Q13	Ignition lap 45/60
Rand Grand Prix, Kyalami (ZA), 15.12.62, 127.25 miles (204.75km)							
	Vern McWilliams	V McWilliams	911	1.5 Borgward RS 4IL	30		DNQ
Natal Grand Prix, Westmead (ZA), 22.12.62, 2 Heats & Final 124.85miles (200.88km)							
	Vern McWilliams	V McWilliams	911	1.5 Borgward RS 4IL	30	Q13	DNF Heat 1

www.velocebooks.com / www.veloce.co.uk
Details of all current books • New book news • Special offers • Gift vouchers • Forum

1963-66 FORMULA 1 SEASONS – THE END OF THE ROAD ... AND BEYOND

9

1963 SEASON – ALMOST THE END OF THE ROAD

The 1963 season opened with the Lotus 18 now effectively obsolete: any self-respecting private entrant running either a Coventry Climax- or BRM V8-powered Lotus 24, the most readily available (though not necessarily competitive) chassis. Nevertheless, ten different Lotus 18 chassis made appearances, the only other 4-cylinder-engined Formula 1 cars still running being a Porsche 718/2, driven by the persistent Dutchman Carel Godin de Beaufort, and a few Maserati-powered Cooper or de Tomaso chassis appearing in Italian races only.

The Formula 1 season began on the 30 March, at a cold and wet Snetterton, with two 18/21s amongst ten starters that included World Champion Graham Hill's BRM and a Lotus 25 for Jim Clark. Jock Russell had acquired the ex-UDT-Laystall/Rob Walker chassis (918) that Maurice Trintignant had driven to victory in the 1962 Pau Grand Prix. Adam Wyllie drove the car to seventh on the road, six laps in arrears and hence unclassified. The second 18/21 was the Phillip Robinson chassis (904), run just once in 1962, that expired with ignition failure. Robinson was more fortunate at Goodwood on Easter Monday, when, in the only 18 and only 4-cylinder car entered for the Glover Trophy race, he finished eighth, lapped three times.

Now fully recovered from the illness that had sidelined him from the second half of 1962, Tim Parnell had purchased three chassis from UDT-Laystall, numbered 915 to 917. Chassis 916 and 917 were 18/21s whilst 915 was upgraded to that specification. Of these, Parnell entered two for the Pau Grand Prix to be driven by himself (917) and the Belgian André Pilette (916). Parnell lasted only 26 laps, whilst Pilette circulated at the tail of the field to complete 87 of the 100-lap distance. The four 18/21s seen so far were all entered for the BARC 200 at Aintree, none of them making it through to the finish. In fact, Pilette failed to make the start at either Aintree or the Silverstone International Trophy, where the 18/21s of Parnell (915) and Robinson were at least 12sec off the pace and succumbed to engine and transmission failures respectively.

Meanwhile, two Formula 1 races had taken place in Italy, at Imola and Syracuse. Prince Gaetano Starrabba dusted off his Maserati-engined 18 (902), as did Ernesto Prinoth his Climax-powered Jolly Club example (913). Prinoth contested only the Imola event, where he was plagued by a misfire, completing 41 of the 50 laps; whilst Starrabba suffered a broken throttle cable, then finished sixth on the road at Syracuse, although he completed

Tim Parnell (917) will have little opportunity to admire the scenic parkland during the Pau Grand Prix. (LAT Photographic)

Lotus 18 | 137

Philip Robinson (904) moves aside to let through Ian Raby (Gilby-BRM) during the Silverstone International Trophy. (LAT Photographic)

insufficient laps to be officially classified. Having appeared only once in 1962, it was a surprise to see Starrabba once again in the two-heat Rome Grand Prix at Vallelunga, where he finished four laps in arrears to be classified fifth: the highest placing for any 18 over the course of the year. Tim Parnell drove his Silverstone chassis into ninth place.

Autosport Team Wolfgang Seidel had folded towards the end of 1962; its two 18s (373 and 914) acquired by one of the team's former drivers, ex-Formula 3/Junior exponent Kurt Kuhnke. Operating from a base at Braunschweig near Hannover, Kuhnke had obtained four of the 4-cylinder, 16-valve, fuel-injected Borgward RS engines following the bankruptcy of the German motor manufacturer in 1961. This 165bhp engine had proved highly successful over the 1959 Formula 2 season, powering Cooper chassis in the hands of those such as Stirling Moss. The engines had not been seen in competition since – nor received any attention – and were not what they had been. Nevertheless, Kuhnke installed the engines in his 18s, though not without difficulty, necessitating the addition of a large hump on the engine cover. He had been making entries in various events for the two cars since August 1962, but always failing to show. They finally appeared in practice for the Rome Grand Prix, officially entered as 'BKLs,' as in 'Borgward-Kuhnke-Lotus.'

9: 1963-66 Formula 1 Seasons – the End of the Road ... and Beyond

The Borgward RS engine installed in the 'BKL' (373) of Ernst Maring at Solitude in 1963. Although not 'officially' an 18/21, the rear suspension clearly has an additional top link. (LAT Photographic)

Lotus 18 | 139

Lotus 18 – Colin Chapman's U-turn

If the engines were no longer competitive, then neither were the chassis, nor for that matter were the drivers – Kuhnke himself and Ernst Maring. Neither car qualified, being a good 16sec off the pace.

The 'BKL' 18s next appeared for the Solitude Grand Prix, where they at least started, yet failed to finish due to engine problems – Kuhnke's example on the opening lap. Solitude would see the largest gathering of 18s of the season, with five examples entered, although none would be classified as finishers. Tim Parnell turned up with his ex-UDT 18/21 (915) for Ron Carter, with Phillip Robinson's example (904) entered under the Parnell banner, to make it a two-car team. Parnell's third ex-UDT chassis (917) had been acquired by André Pilette, who would prove to be the most persistent 18/21 driver of the season, making nine entries in his own name, managing five starts yet recording only a single finish.

The ADAC organising the German Grand Prix accepted entries from all the works and private teams, plus an extra 11 entries from drivers or teams that had yet to prove themselves, or were of "dubious potential," as Denis Jenkinson put it in *Motor Sport*. This category included the two 18/21s of Tim Parnell and André Pilette, along with Kurt Kuhnke in a 'BKL,' none of which would prove quick enough to qualify. Pilette was the fastest of the trio, reducing his lap time to 10min 20sec over the practice sessions, 20sec slower than slowest actual starter.

9: 1963-66 Formula 1 Seasons – the End of the Road ... and Beyond

Opposite & above: Neither Kurt Kuhnke in the Borgward-engined 'BKL' (914), nor a bare-armed André Pilette (917) – both seen negotiating the Karussel at the Nürburgring during practice – would qualify for the German Grand Prix. (Sutton Images)

Seven days later, Pilette was in Sweden for the Kanonloppet race at Karlskoga, where he qualified 12th and was classified tenth on the aggregate of the two heats, having completed 37 of the 40 laps. Kurt Kuhnke's two Borgward-engined 18s turned up, Maring qualifying tenth then running off the road on lap 18 of Heat 1, damaging the chassis (373) badly enough for it not to be seen again in competition. Kuhnke survived 15 of the 20-lap first heat, only to expire on lap 7 of the second, with a fuel-injection problem. Ron Carter entered his 18/21, but suffered an engine failure in practice and failed to make the start.

Gaetano Starrabba entered his Maserati-engined 18 (902) for the Mediterranean Grand Prix at Pergusa in Sicily, only to fail to qualify, his best lap of 1min 31.6sec some 4sec too slow, and 15sec away from winner John Surtees' Ferrari on pole position. André Pilette was back in action for the Austrian Grand Prix on the Zeltweg airfield circuit, along with Ernesto Prinoth in his Jolly Club 18 (913). Pilette completed 64 of the scheduled 80 laps, whilst Prinoth fell foul of the uneven track surface to encounter suspension failure.

Starrabba and Pilette also optimistically entered their 18s for the Italian Grand Prix, for which all starters were required to lap within 10% of the second fastest practice time. Starrabba wisely decided not to show at Monza, whilst Pilette's best time over the two days of practice was 1min 53.7sec against what turned out to be the minimum qualifying time of 1min 47.2sec. He had better luck in the Oulton Park International Gold Cup, the final European Formula 1 race of 1963, for which there were no qualifying requirements. He

Lotus 18 – Colin Chapman's U-turn

Zeltweg's uneven runway surface will break the suspension of Ernesto Prinoth's Scuderia Jolly Club 18 (913), during the Austrian Grand Prix. (LAT Photographic)

André Pilette, driving the sole 18 (No 14) in the race, keeps out of the way of Innes Ireland's Lotus 24, during the Oulton Park Gold Cup. (LAT Photographic)

lined up 21st in a field of 22, 10sec away from the front of the grid. It made little difference, as he was not officially classified as a finisher having completed only 63 of the 73 lap race distance.

Attention now turned to South Africa and the Rand Grand Prix at Kyalami in December, the only preliminary event to the South African Grand Prix this season. Rhodesian-born Clive Puzey had acquired the Parnell built 18/21 chassis (P2) raced briefly the previous year by the late Gary Hocking. He started Heat 1 of the Rand Grand Prix from the back row of the grid, having missed practice. Gear selection problems forced his retirement after completing ten laps. He did not appear for the South African Grand Prix.

Lotus 18 Performance Summary – 1963

	Starts	Finishes	1st	2nd	3rd	4th	5th	6th	PP	FL
Grands Prix	–	–								
Other Formula 1	27	3	–	–	–	1	–	–	–	
Total	27	3	–	–	–	1	–	–	–	

Chassis Summary – 1963

Ten Lotus 18 chassis appeared in one or more Formula 1 events during 1963, as follows:

373	Acquired from Autosport Team Wolfgang Seidel by Kurt Kuhnke. Re-engined with 4-cylinder Borgward RS engine as 'BKL.'
902	Retained by Prince Gaetano Starrabba.
904	Retained by Phillip Robinson.
913	Retained by Ernesto Prinoth/Scuderia Jolly Club.
914	Acquired from Autosport Team Wolfgang Seidel by Kurt Kuhnke. Re-engined with 4-cylinder Borgward RS engine as 'BKL.'
915	Acquired from UDT-Laystall by Tim Parnell and converted to 18/21.
916	18/21 acquired from UDT-Laystall by Tim Parnell, driven by André Pilette until 11.5.63.
917	18/21 acquired from UDT-Laystall by Tim Parnell, passed to André Pilette from July.
918	18/21 acquired by Jock Russell from UDT-Laystall.
P2	Formerly Tim Parnell/Gary Hocking 18/21, acquired by Clive Puzey.

9: 1963-66 Formula 1 Seasons – the End of the Road ... and Beyond

LOTUS 18 – FORMULA 1 RACING RECORD – 1963

(* signifies chassis to 18/21 specification)

Position	Driver	Entrant	Chassis	Engine	No	Grid	Comments
Lombank Trophy, Snetterton (GB), 30.3.63, 135.50miles (218.02km)							
	Adam Wyllie	Jock Russell	*918	1.5 Climax FPF 4IL	12	Q6	N/C 44 laps/50
	Philip Robinson	A Robinson & Sons	*904	1.5 Climax FPF 4IL	14	Q7	Ignition lap 16/50
Grand Prix de Pau, Pau, 15.4.63, 171.40miles (275.85km)							
	André Pilette	RHH Parnell	*916	1.5 Climax FPF 4IL	28	Q15	N/C 87 laps/100
	Tim Parnell	RHH Parnell	*917	1.5 Climax FPF 4IL	26	Q12	Head gasket lap 26/100
Glover Trophy, Goodwood (GB), 15.4.63, 100.80 miles (162.18km)							
8th	Philip Robinson	A Robinson & Sons	*904	1.5 Climax FPF 4IL	9	Q10	39 laps/42
Gran Premio Citta di Imola, Imola (I), 21.4.63, 155.87 miles (250.79km)							
	Ernesto Prinoth	Scuderia Jolly Club	913	1.5 Climax FPF 4IL	38	Q10	Misfire 41 laps/50
	Gaetano Starrabba	G Starrabba	902	1.5 Maserati 150S 4IL	28	Q13	Throttle cable lap 5/50
Gran Premio di Siracusa, Syracuse (I), 25.4.63, 194.77 miles (313.38km)							
	Gaetano Starrabba	G Starrabba	902	1.5 Maserati 150S 4IL	28	Q10	N/C 49 laps/56
BARC 200, Aintree (GB), 27.4.63, 150.00 miles (241.35km)							
	Jock Russell	J Russell	*918	1.5 Climax FPF 4IL	20	Q15	Rear suspension lap 6/50
	Philip Robinson	A Robinson & Sons	*904	1.5 Climax FPF 4IL	18	Q12	Engine lap 2/50
	Tim Parnell	RHH Parnell	*917	1.5 Climax FPF 4IL	14	Q17	DSQ push start lap 8/50
	André Pilette	RHH Parnell	*916	1.5 Climax FPF 4IL	19	Q16	DNS
International Trophy, Silverstone (GB), 11.5.63, 152.20 miles (244.89km)							
	Tim Parnell	RHH Parnell	*915	1.5 Climax FPF 4IL	22	Q16	Engine lap 35/52
	Philip Robinson	A Robinson & Sons	*904	1.5 Climax FPF 4IL	26	Q19	Transmission lap 34/52
	André Pilette	RHH Parnell	*916	1.5 Climax FPF 4IL	23	Q20	DNS
Gran Premio di Roma, Vallelunga (I), 19.5.63, Aggregate of 2 Heats 159.04 miles (255.90km)							
5th	Gaetano Starrabba	G Starrabba	902	1.5 Maserati 150S 4IL	12	Q10	76 laps/80
	Tim Parnell	RHH Parnell	*915	1.5 Climax FPF 4IL	4	Q6	N/C 68 laps/80
	Kurt Kuhnke	K Kuhnke	914	1.5 Borgward RS 4IL	14		DNQ
	Ernst Maring	K Kuhnke	373	1.5 Borgward RS 4IL	16		DNQ
Großer Preis der Solitude, Solitude (D), 28.7.63, 177.23 miles (285.16km)							
	André Pilette	A Pilette	*917	1.5 Climax FPF 4IL	12	Q22	N/C 21 laps/25
	Philip Robinson	RHH Parnell	*904	1.5 Climax FPF 4IL	22	Q19	N/C 20 laps/25
	Ernst Maring	K Kuhnke	373	1.5 Borgward RS 4IL	11	Q25	Engine lap 17/25
	Ron Carter	RHH Parnell	*915	1.5 Climax FPF 4IL	21	Q26	Engine lap 2/25
	Kurt Kuhnke	K Kuhnke	914	1.5 Borgward RS 4IL	10	Q24	Engine lap 1/25
GROSSER PREIS von DEUTSCHLAND, Nürburgring (D), 4.8.63, 212.60 miles (342.15km)							
	Kurt Kuhnke	K Kuhnke	914	1.5 Borgward RS 4IL	27		DNQ
	André Pilette	A Pilette	*917	1.5 Climax FPF 4IL	29		DNQ
	Tim Parnell	RHH Parnell	*915	1.5 Climax FPF 4IL	30		DNQ
Kanonloppet, Karlskoga (S), 11.8.63, Aggregate of 2 Heats 74.52 miles (119.90km)							
10th	André Pilette	A Pilette	*917	1.5 Climax FPF 4IL	20	Q12	37 laps/40
	Kurt Kuhnke	K Kuhnke	914	1.5 Borgward RS 4IL	14	NT	Fuel injection Heat 2
	Ernst Maring	K Kuhnke	373	1.5 Borgward RS 4IL	15	Q10	Accident Heat 1
	Ron Carter	RHH Parnell	*915	1.5 Climax FPF 4IL	19	NT	DNS Engine in practice
Gran Premio del Mediterraneo, Pergusa (I), 18.8.63, 178.80 miles (287.69km)							
	Gaetano Starrabba	G Starrabba	902	1.5 Maserati 150S 4IL	32		DNQ
Großer Preis von Österreich, Zeltweg (A), 1.9.63, 159.07 miles (255.94km)							
	André Pilette	A Pilette	*917	1.5 Climax FPF 4IL	16	Q15	N/C 64 laps/80
	Ernesto Prinoth	Scuderia Jolly Club	913	1.5 Climax FPF 4IL	18	Q9	Suspension lap 13/80
GRAN PREMIO d'ITALIA, Monza (I), 8.9.63, 307.28 miles (494.50km)							
	André Pilette	A Pilette	*917	1.5 Climax FPF 4IL	46		DNQ
International Gold Cup, Oulton Park (GB), 21.9.63, 201.55 miles (324.29km)							
	André Pilette	A Pilette	*917	1.5 Climax FPF 4IL	14	Q21	N/C 63 laps/73
Rand Grand Prix, Kyalami (ZA), 14.12.63, Aggregate of 2 Heats 127.25 miles (204.75km)							
	Clive Puzey	CR Puzey	*P2	1.5 Climax FPF 4IL	15	NT	Gear selector Heat 1

Lotus 18 | 143

1964-65 SEASONS – THE END OF THE ROAD

1964 SEASON

The experienced observer could be forgiven for assuming that the Lotus 18 had run its last Formula 1 race by the end of 1963. It had completed four years of competition and was never going to achieve anything in the way of results with a 4-cylinder engine against the BRM and Coventry Climax V8-engined privateers with more up-to-date Brabham, Cooper or Lotus chassis. Nevertheless, four different chassis made one appearance each over the 1964 season, of which Jock Russell was first out with his ex-UDT-Laystall/Rob Walker 18/21 (918), at the traditionally damp and cold British season opener at Snetterton in March. In 1964, the weather was worse than ever, featuring heavy rain mixed with sleet, wind and a thick mist over the circuit, all of which persuaded the organisers to shorten the race distance from 50 to 35 laps. This was of little benefit to Russell, who lasted only six laps before experiencing an engine problem.

The next appearance by an 18 came some four months later, when the Solitude Grand Prix attracted entries from Kurt Kuhnke's two Borgward-engined 'BKL' chassis once again. A German team and drivers could be sure of gaining entries in this 'home' event, free of the threat of qualification. Kuhnke had acquired the 18/21 raced by Gerry Ashmore in 1962 (919), to replace chassis 373 damaged at Karlskoga in 1963, into which had been installed the once-competitive German fuel-injected engine. *Autosport* reported, on 14 February 1964, that, as the engines had not been producing their former power outputs, Kuhnke had enlisted the assistance of Dr Ing Kurt Löhner, who was engaged in piston engine development at the Institut für Verbrennungskraftmaschinen at Braunschweig in Germany. One of the engines run up on the test bed had, not unexpectedly, developed barely 120bhp. Dr Löhner put in hand a development programme, reportedly attaining 170bhp at 7300rpm. Nevertheless, the 'BKLs' remained uncompetitive. Ernst Maring drove the 'newer' chassis to survive 16 of the 20 laps as tenth man home, yet unclassified. The second car (914) was driven by Joachim Diel, a German helicopter pilot racing under the pseudonym 'Parker,' who had the misfortune to be eliminated in a multiple pile-up on a soaking wet track on the opening lap. Both 'BKLs' had started from the back row of the grid, 'Parker' 12sec faster than Maring yet nearly 30sec off the pace.

As the now-usual preliminary to the South African Grand Prix, the Rand Grand Prix was held at Kyalami, on 12 December. Clive Puzey entered his ex-Gary Hocking 18/21 (P2), with which he qualified 15th in a field of 22 and achieved a seventh place finish on aggregate in the two-heat event. The South African Grand Prix was rescheduled from the end of December to the 1 January to become the first Championship round of the 1965 season, rather than the final one of 1964. Fresh from Kyalami, Clive Puzey entered his 18/21 once again, as one of ten local drivers required to lap the East London circuit in less than 1min 37sec in order to pre-qualify for official practice. Unable to achieve this time, he returned home early.

1965 SEASON

Into the 1965 European season, the Solitude Grand Prix was held as a Formula 2 event under the 1.0-litre, 4-cylinder regulations introduced in 1964. Amongst the contemporary Brabham, Lotus, Lola and Cooper chassis powered by 4-cylinder Cosworth SCA or BRM engines, it was something of a surprise to find a five-year-old Lotus 18/21 chassis. Ernst Maring had taken over the 'BKL' (919) he had driven for Kurt Kuhnke in 1964, to run in his own name, having reduced the capacity of its basically Borgward RS engine to 1000cc. He managed to qualify 20th in a field of 25, 33sec off the pace. The car lasted seven of the 18 laps, before succumbing to clutch failure.

Only a solitary appearance would be made by an 18 during the 1965 Formula 1 season, when Colin Davis was entered for the non-Championship Mediterranean Grand Prix at Pergusa in Sicily. Driving the ex-Ernesto Prinoth, Jolly Club 18 (913), now running under the banner of Scuderia Nord-Ouest, he not unexpectedly failed to qualify for one of the 15 places on the grid.

This marked the end of the career of the Lotus 18 in Europe, and yet its story was not quite over.

Lotus 18 Performance Summary – 1964-65

	Starts	Finishes	1st	2nd	3rd	4th	5th	6th	PP	FL
1964 Formula 1	4	1	–	–	–	–	–	–	–	–
1965 Formula 2	1	–	–	–	–	–	–	–	–	–

Chassis Summary – 1964-65

Five Lotus 18 chassis appeared in one or more Formula 1 events over the 1964/65 seasons, as follows:

913	Ex-Ernesto Prinoth now run by Scuderia Nord-Ouest.
914	Borgward-engined 'BKL' retained by Kurt Kuhnke.
918	Retained by Jock Russell.
919	18/21 acquired by Kurt Kuhnke from Gerry Ashmore and fitted with Borgward RS engine as a 'BKL' for 1964. Converted to 1.0-litre F2 by Ernst Maring for 1965.
P2	18/21 retained by Clive Puzey.

9: 1963-66 Formula 1 Seasons – the End of the Road ... and Beyond

LOTUS 18 – FORMULA 1 RACING RECORD – 1964-65
(* signifies chassis to 18/21 specification)

Year	Position	Driver	Entrant	Chassis	Engine	No	Grid	Comments
1964	Daily Mirror Trophy, Snetterton (GB), 14.3.64, 94.85 miles (151.76km)							
		Jock Russell	J Russell	*918	1.5 Climax FPF 4IL	23	Q15	Engine lap 6/35
	Großer Preis der Solitude, Solitude (D), 19.7.64, 141.78 miles (228.13km)							
		"Parker"	K Kuhnke	914	1.5 Borgward RS 4IL	18	Q17	Accident Lap 1/20
		Ernst Maring	K Kuhnke	*919	1.5 Borgward RS 4IL	19	Q18	N/C 16 laps/20
	Rand Grand Prix, Kyalami, 12.12.64, Aggregate of 2 Heats 127.25 miles (204.75km)							
	7th	Clive Puzey	Clive Puzey (Motors)	*P2	1.5 Climax FPF 4IL	15	Q15	48 laps/50
1965	SOUTH AFRICAN GRAND PRIX, East London (ZA), 1.1.65, 206.98 miles (333.03km)							
		Clive Puzey	Clive Puzey (Motors)	*P2	1.5 Climax FPF 4IL	24	DNPQ	
	Großer Preis der Solitude (Formula 2), Solitude (D), 18.7.65, 127.71 miles (205.48km)							
		Ernst Maring	E Maring	*919	1.0 Borgward RS 4IL	16	Q19	Clutch lap 7/18
	Gran Premio del Mediterraneo, Pergusa, 15.8.65, 178.80 miles (287.69km)							
		Colin Davis	Scuderia Nord-Ouest	913	1.5 Climax FPF 4IL	18	DNQ	

1966 SOUTH AFRICAN FORMULA 1 SEASON – LIFE AFTER DEATH

The 1½-litre Formula 1 Regulations expired on 31 December 1965, after a five-year life. They had never been universally popular, due to the perception that the cars were under-powered and hence unspectacular. Under-powered they may have been, yet never unspectacular, having provided some excellent racing. More significantly, great strides had been made in chassis and tyre technology, to the extent that levels of grip far outstripped engine power outputs, leaving drivers needing more power at their disposal to tax their skills. A consensus of opinion favoured an increase in engine capacity to 3-litre for Formula 1 and, when put to the CSI in November 1963, the proposal was approved remarkably easily and would come into effect from 1 January 1966.

South African single-seater racing had traditionally been run to 1½-litre 4-cylinder engine regulations, but for 1966 it was decided to go with the 3-litre Formula 1 regulations, despite the dearth of suitable capacity engines in that part of the world, let alone Europe. The solution was to fall back on the ubiquitous 2½-litre, 4-cylinder Coventry Climax FPF engine of 1959/60 vintage. In late 1962, Coventry Climax had reluctantly put a 2.75-litre FPF into modest production for mainly sports car use. This was based on the engine developed for Cooper's challenge in the 1961 Indianapolis 500 and represented the physical limit of capacity enlargement of the FPF. The bore and stroke were increased by 2mm and 5mm respectively to 96mm by 94.9mm, giving a capacity of 2751cc, and these engines were said to produce 250bhp at a reduced rev limit of 6200rpm. A number of 2.75-litre FPF engines appeared in European Grand Prix racing during 1966, notably powering Dan Gurney's Anglo-American Racers Eagle. Similarly, a few engines found their way to the South African Formula 1 series where the top runners installed them in redundant Formula 1/Tasman chassis from Cooper or Brabham or the locally built LDS.

Not to be outdone, Clive Puzey entered into the spirit of the new era by installing such an engine in his Lotus 18/21 chassis (P2), at his Bulawayo-based garage premises, and continued to campaign it, having reportedly updated it by fitting smaller diameter 13in Lotus type 33 wheels that would have required modifications to the suspension. The car was finished in a shade of dark green with a central yellow stripe, not unlike Team Lotus colours.

The organisers of the Rand Grand Prix in December 1965 decided to anticipate the engine capacity change by a month and hold their race to the new 3-litre regulations. Puzey entered his 18/21 to finish ninth, four laps in arrears. The South African Grand Prix opened the 1966 season on 1 January, but, despite attracting an overseas entry, was not classified as a World Championship qualifier, being deemed to be too early in the life of the new regulations for the major competitors to be ready. Clive Puzey rolled up with his 18/21 to qualify 18th, 10sec off the pace, and finish seventh, lapped four times.

A further 12 South African Formula 1 Series races were held over the course of 1966, contested by around a dozen local drivers, including Puzey. Generally 5sec or more slower in practice than the three or four front runners, he finished in the top six on seven occasions, with a best placing of second on aggregate in the two-heat Pat Fairfield Trophy at Pietermaritzburg. He also accumulated third place finishes in the Rand Autumn Trophy at Kyalami, the Bulawayo 100 and the Rhodesian Grand Prix, the latter two both on the Kumalo circuit in Southern Rhodesia. Puzey's results

CLIVE PUZEY
(b. 11 July 1941)

Rhodesian-born Clive Puzey has the distinction of being the last driver to actively and successfully campaign a Lotus 18 in Formula 1. He had raced a Formula Junior Yimkin in Britain during 1960, before returning home and building his own rear-engined Junior chassis for the 1962 season, with a BMC engine and Volkswagen transmission.

For the 1963 season, he upgraded himself to the South African Gold Star series, having acquired the Lotus 18/21 (P2) raced briefly by fellow Rhodesian Gary Hocking, before his untimely death in December 1962. He had little success with the car in the Springbok Series that had by now declined to only the Rand Grand Prix and the Championship qualifying South African Grand Prix.

The arrival of the 3-litre Formula 1 regulations for 1966, saw the four-year-old Lotus 18 attain a new lease of life when re-engined with a 4-cylinder, initially 2.5- then 2.75-litre Coventry Climax FPF engine. Though never fast enough to mix it with the more modern Cooper or Brabham chassis, the 18/21 achieved a high degree of reliability, sufficient to place him fourth in the South African Formula 1 season. Puzey recorded the final race in the Formula 1 competition career of the Lotus 18, when he finished third in the Rhodesian Grand Prix, at Bulawayo on 4 December 1966.

Puzey did not race his Lotus 18/21 again, preferring to upgrade to a locally-built LDS chassis for 1967, before retiring from racing in 1969. As a critic of the Mugabe regime, his Bulawayo garage premises were attacked in 2000, prompting him to quit Zimbabwe and move to Australia.

Clive Puzey, in his 18/21 (P2), finished in very Team Lotus-like colours of green with a central yellow stripe. (www.motoprint.co.za)

reflected both the reliability of his 18/21, but also the shortage of competition in this premier South African series, allowing him to accumulate sufficient points to be classified fourth behind two Coopers and an LDS in the 1966 Championship, although with less than a third of the score of winner John Love.

Significantly, the six-year 11-month Formula 1 competition career of the Lotus 18 finally drew to a close in the Rhodesian Grand Prix at Kumalo on 4 December 1966.

Lotus 18 Performance Summary – 1966

	Starts	Finishes	1st	2nd	3rd	4th	5th	6th	PP	FL
S African Formula 1	14	9	–	1	3	1	1	1	–	–

9: 1963-66 Formula 1 Seasons – the End of the Road ... and Beyond

Puzey at Kyalami, in the ex-Gary Hocking/ Tim Parnell 18/21 (P2), now with a 2½-litre Climax FPF, 13in diameter wheels and wider tyres. (www.motoprint.co.za)

Clive Puzey (P2) is sandwiched between the Cooper of Tony Jefferies (No 2) and the LDS of Doug Serrurier, at Kyalami during 1966. (www.motoprint.co.za)

Lotus 18 | 147

LOTUS 18 – FORMULA 1 RACING RECORD – 1966

(* signifies chassis to 18/21 specification)

Position	Driver	Entrant	Chassis	Engine	No	Grid	Comments
Rand Grand Prix, Kyalami (ZA), 4.12.65, 127.20 miles (204.66km)							
9th	Clive Puzey	Clive Puzey (Motors)	*P2	2.5 Climax FPF 4IL	17	Q11	46 laps/50
South African Grand Prix, East London (ZA), 1.1.66, 145.98 miles (234.88km)							
7th	Clive Puzey	Clive Puzey (Motors)	*P2	2.7 Climax FPF 4IL	17	Q18	56 laps/60
Cape South Easter Trophy, Killarney (ZA), 8.1.66, Aggregate of 2 Heats 102.89 miles (165.55km)							
5th	Clive Puzey	Clive Puzey (Motors)	*P2	2.7 Climax FPF 4IL	17	N/A	
Rand Autumn Trophy, Kyalami (ZA), 5.3.66, 101.76 miles (163.73km)							
3rd	Clive Puzey	Clive Puzey (Motors)	*P2	2.7 Climax FPF 4IL	5	Q6	39 laps/40
Coronation 100, Pietermaritzburg (ZA), 11.4.66, Aggregate of 2 Heats 118.80 miles (191.15km)							
	Clive Puzey	Clive Puzey (Motors)	*P2	2.7 Climax FPF 4IL	9	N/A	Engine Heat 2
Bulawayo 100, Kumalo (RSR), 4.5.66, 103.00 miles (165.73km)							
3rd	Clive Puzey	Clive Puzey (Motors)	*P2	2.7 Climax FPF 4IL	5	N/A	
South African Republic Festival Trophy, Kyalami (ZA), 28.5.66, 101.76 miles (163.73km)							
	Clive Puzey	Clive Puzey (Motors)	*P2	2.7 Climax FPF 4IL	5	Q6	Overheating lap 19/40
Natal Winter Trophy, Pietermaritzburg (ZA), 26.6.66, Aggregate of 2 Heats 118.80 miles (191.15km)							
6th	Clive Puzey	Clive Puzey (Motors)	*P2	2.7 Climax FPF 4IL	5	N/A	
Border 100, East London (ZA), 11.7.66, Aggregate of 2 Heats 121.65 miles (195.73km)							
4th	Clive Puzey	Clive Puzey (Motors)	*P2	2.7 Climax FPF 4IL	5	N/A	
Taca Governador Génerale de Mocambique, Lourenco Marques (MOC), 24.7.66, 62.77 miles (101.00km)							
	Clive Puzey	Clive Puzey (Motors)	*P2	2.7 Climax FPF 4IL	25	N/A	Placing unknown
Rand Winter Trophy, Kyalami (ZA), 6.8.66, 101.76 miles (163.73km)							
	Clive Puzey	Clive Puzey (Motors)	*P2	2.7 Climax FPF 4IL	5	Q6	Gearlever lap 14/40
Pat Fairfield Trophy, Pietermaritzburg (ZA), 21.8.66, Aggregate of two Heats, 95.40 miles (153.50km)							
2nd	Clive Puzey	Clive Puzey (Motors)	*P2	2.7 Climax FPF 4IL	5	Q3	
Van Riebeek Trophy, Killarney (ZA), 3.9.66, Aggregate of two Heats 102.89 miles 165.55km)							
	Clive Puzey	Clive Puzey (Motors)	*P2	2.7 Climax FPF 4IL	5	N/A	Fire Heat 1
Rhodesian Grand Prix, Kumalo (RSR), 4.12.66, 103.00 miles (165.73km)							
3rd	Clive Puzey	Clive Puzey (Motors)	*P2	2.7 Climax FPF 4IL	5	Q6	48 laps/50

www.velocebooks.com / www.veloce.co.uk
Details of all current books • New book news • Special offers • Gift vouchers • Forum

ANALYSIS AND STATISTICS 10

The success, or otherwise, of any racing car is relative to the quality of the opposition that it has to face and the length of time it remains in front line service. Opposition to the Lotus 18 comprised the resident Constructors' Championship title holder, Cooper in 1960, and a resurgent Ferrari in 1961, both of which proved to be ahead of the game in their respective seasons and tough nuts to crack. The purpose of this section is to consider the question 'how successful was the Lotus 18 in the two years of its front line service?'

Throughout 1960, the Lotus 18 was campaigned extensively in Formula 1 by Team Lotus and the RRC Walker Racing Team. A straightforward statistical analysis reveals that the 18 won two (25%) of the eight Grands Prix in which it competed, although, significantly, neither of those wins were achieved by Team Lotus, rather by the customer-entered Walker chassis driven by Stirling Moss. Two wins in a season does not compare favourably with the six wins (75%) achieved by Cooper.

Lotus 18 – Comparison with Rivals in 1960 Grands Prix

1960	GPs	Wins	Rate (per cent)	PP	FL
BRM	8	–		–	1
Cooper	8	6	(75%)	4	5
Ferrari	8	1	(13%)	1	2
Lotus 18	8	2	(25%)	4	3

Yet the 1960 season had started so well for the Lotus 18, Innes Ireland demonstrating its potential by setting new performance standards in a brace of early season wins in both non-Championship Formula 1 and Formula 2 races. Then, come the Monaco Grand Prix, just when it appeared that Team Lotus could dominate the Grand Prix season, its advantage ebbed away. So what went wrong?

Strategically, Colin Chapman's introduction of the Lotus 18 in Argentina, though understandable, proved to be a tactical error. Cooper immediately recognised the potential the Lotus demonstrated in Argentina and had three months in which to

Early season promise – a win for the Lotus 18 (371) and Innes Ireland in the 1960 Silverstone International Trophy. (Ferret Fotographics)

respond before the European Grand Prix season opened. That they were able to do so successfully reflected the capabilities of the Cooper design process that included Jack Brabham as an essential contributor aside from his role as driver and engineer. His ability to set up a chassis exactly how he wanted it, and his hands-on approach to achieving that aim, generated results.

Cooper husbanded its resources more effectively by running only a two-car Formula 1 team, whereas Team Lotus was consistently running three cars in both Formulae 1 and 2, and, significantly, using the same chassis for both categories. The Lotus chassis undoubtedly tired as the season progressed, if for no other reason than the race mileage each accumulated. By comparison, the Rob Walker-entered car competed almost exclusively in Grands Prix. This goes some way to explaining why Team Lotus seemed unable to attain the Grand Prix distance reliability necessary to prevent Cooper from winning five consecutive Grands Prix, and why it began to lack the pace to make the front row of the grid.

Technically, the Lotus 18 was much more sophisticated than the ruggedly-built Cooper and, although more robust than the previous Type 16, an element of fragility began to emerge. Engine mounting failures arose at Monaco, front suspension breakages in France and Britain, transmission problems in Monaco and Holland, and the frightening rear hub failures in Belgium. The hub failures raised the spectre of the sacrifice of strength and safety in the pursuit of lightness. Chapman was a skilled innovator, yet was prepared to trim components down to the bone, without necessarily leaving a sufficient margin for reliability or safety.

Aerodynamically, the slab-sided Lotus was inferior to the Cooper in terms of straight line speed, Innes Ireland finding that he was losing 800rpm when running in clean air on the flat out sections at Spa. Adoption of a high penetration nosecone at Reims failed to provide an improvement.

As Team Lotus fortunes declined, so Stirling Moss and the Rob Walker Lotus 18 assumed the role of lead Lotus driver. Had the accident at Spa not put him out of action for eight weeks, it is certain that he would have consistently taken the fight to Cooper and even challenged for the World Championship itself. During his enforced absence, Lotus lacked a 'star' driver; Innes Ireland, though highly competent and able to match him on a good day, was the first to admit that he was not in the same league as the 'maestro.'

Nevertheless, the Lotus marque enjoyed its best-ever season in Grand Prix racing, the two wins contributing to a second place finish in the 1960 Manufacturers' Championship, 14 points behind Cooper. In non-Championship events by comparison, the Lotus 18 was almost totally dominant, winning four times against a single win for Cooper, significantly each of less than a Grand Prix distance. Conversely, Team Lotus failed to make a significant impact in Formula 2, with only five wins (31%) from 16 events contested – once again the wins were generally in 'sprint' type events of up to 100 miles. Meanwhile, Porsche (six wins) and Ferrari (two) won the more prestigious, longer distance events.

Into 1961, the Lotus 18 was now history as far as Colin Chapman was concerned, as he concentrated on the Lotus 21, the state-of-the-art 4-cylinder Formula 1 car of the 1½-litre Formula 1. In the event, the 21 failed to deliver its full potential until the latter part of the season, leaving the Lotus 18 to defend the honour of the marque and, indeed, all the British constructors. The Lotus 18 had no right to be competitive, and indeed it was not, other than in the hands of Stirling Moss, the only driver of an 18 able to finish a Grand Prix in the points. That he should overcome the might of Ferrari against the odds at both Monaco and the Nürburgring, demonstrated both the sheer brilliance of Moss and his ability to exploit the superior handling qualities of the 18. Those two wins enabled the Lotus marque to finish second in the Manufacturers' Championship once again, something it would not have achieved without the contribution of the Lotus 18.

In the absence of a Formula 2 category, the number of non-Championship Formula 1 events expanded from five in 1960 to 21 in 1961, of which the Lotus 18 won six (29%), mostly courtesy of Stirling Moss, compared to five each for Cooper and the Lotus 21. The competitiveness of the Lotus 18 drew to a close in South Africa, when Moss was beaten twice by Jim Clark in a Lotus 21, prompting him to remark that henceforth he needed at least an equal car to better the Scotsman.

Lotus 18 – Comparison with Rivals in 1961
(a) Grands Prix

1961	GPs	Wins	Rate (per cent)	PP	FL
Ferrari	7	5	(71%)	6	5
Lotus 18	**8**	**2**	**(25%)**	**1**	**1**
Lotus 21	8	1	(13%)	–	1
Cooper	8	–		1	1
Porsche	8	–		–	–

(b) Non-Championship Formula 1

1961	Non-Champ F1	Wins	Rate (per cent)	PP	FL
Cooper	21	5	(24%)	5	6
Ferrari	2	2	(100%)	–	1
Lotus 18	**21**	**6**	**(29%)**	**6**	**7**
Lotus 21	9	5	(56%)	5	2
Porsche	11	1	(9%)	3	3
Others	8	2	–	2	2

10: Analysis and Statistics

Rob Walker provided an interesting solution to the shortage of competitive chassis by installing a Coventry Climax V8 engine in his spare Lotus 18/21 chassis, creating perhaps the ultimate version of the car. Stirling Moss made it more competitive than it would otherwise have been, before it was written-off on Easter Monday 1962, in his career-ending accident. That apart, the dawning of the V8 era from Coventry Climax and BRM brought an end to all serious competition from the 4-cylinder-powered Lotus 18. The 18/21 scored its final race win early in the 1962 season, before the V8s came on stream in numbers, Maurice Trintignant driving Rob Walker's car to victory in the Pau Grand Prix. The Lotus 18 made its final Grand Prix start in the British Grand Prix at Silverstone on 21 July 1962, yet raced on in non-Championship events until 1966.

In 1960, the Lotus 18 was certainly superior technically to its rivals, yet not strong enough to be way ahead of them. In terms of the achievement of purpose, it must be evaluated as the first step on the road to change for Colin Chapman and Lotus. Sometimes under-rated, this chassis turned Lotus from an also-ran into a force to be reckoned with in Grand Prix racing. It led to a wave of innovations over succeeding years, the first being the monocoque chassis Lotus 25, introduced in 1962.

Nevertheless, the combination of the chassis and suspension technology skills of Colin Chapman and the supreme driving talent of Stirling Moss, ensured that the Lotus 18 has earned a place in the history books. Yet in the spring of 1960, it had seemed to promise so much more.

Lotus 18 Record in Grand Prix Racing

Year	Starts	Finishes	1st	2nd	3rd	4th	5th	6th	PP	FL
1960	25	15	2	3	2	1	2	3	4	3
1961	40	18	2	–	–	1	–	–	1	1
1962	5	1	–	–	–	–	–	–	–	–
Total	70	34	4	3	2	2	2	3	5	4

Lotus 18 Record in Non-Championship Formula 1 Racing

Year	Starts	Finishes	1st	2nd	3rd	4th	5th	6th	PP	FL
1960	19	8	4	1	–	1	–	1	2	4
1961	96	56	6	8	4	4	8	4	6	8
1962	64	25	1	–	4	2	5	3	2	3
1963	27	3	–	–	–	–	1	–	–	–
1964	4	1	–	–	–	–	–	–	–	–
1965	1	–	–	–	–	–	–	–	–	–
1966	14	9	–	1	3	1	1	1	–	–
Total	225	102	11	10	11	8	15	9	10	15

Lotus 18 Record in Formula 2 (1960) and Inter-Continental Formula (1961)

	Starts	Finishes	1st	2nd	3rd	4th	5th	6th	PP	FL
Formula 2	35	20	5	2	1	2	1	2	5	6
Inter-Continental	18	6	–	2	–	1	1	–	1	1

Lotus 18 Record – Total All Formulae

	Starts	Finishes	1st	2nd	3rd	4th	5th	6th	PP	FL
1960-1966	348	162	20	17	14	13	19	14	21	26

Lotus 18 – Record by Chassis

Chassis No	Starts	Finishes	1st	2nd	3rd	4th	5th	6th	PP	FL
369	6	3	1	–	–	1	–	1	–	1
370	7	2	1	–	–	1	–	–	1	1
371	27	16	3	1	1	1	–	2	–	3
372	14	9	3	2	–	–	2	–	1	1
373	36	10	–	3	–	–	3	2	1	1
374	16	7	–	1	2	–	–	2	3	5
376	4	3	2	–	–	1	–	–	3	1
901	–	–	–	–	–	–	–	–	–	–
902	9	1	–	–	–	–	1	–	–	–
903	7	6	–	–	–	–	1	–	1	1
904	28	9	–	–	1	–	3	–	–	–
905	13	6	–	–	–	1	1	–	–	–
906	8	6	2	–	–	1	–	–	4	4
907	2	1	–	–	–	–	–	–	–	–
908	3	1	–	–	–	–	–	–	–	–
909	15	11	1	–	2	1	1	2	1	1
911	5	2	–	–	–	–	–	–	–	–
912	14	8	3	–	–	2	–	1	3	2
913	6	2	–	1	1	–	–	–	–	–
914	10	2	–	–	1	–	–	–	–	–
915	11	6	–	1	–	–	1	–	–	–
916	18	9	1	2	2	–	–	1	1	2
917	25	6	–	–	–	2	3	–	–	–
918	16	10	3	2	1	–	–	–	1	3
919	15	6	–	–	–	–	–	–	1	–
P1	10	7	–	–	1	–	2	2	–	–
P2	23	13	–	1	3	2	1	1	–	–
Total	348	162	20	17	14	13	19	14	21	26

Lotus 18 | 151

11 VARIATIONS ON A THEME 1960-65

LOTUS 18 FORMULA JUNIOR – 1960

Colin Chapman showed little interest in the Formula Junior category, until he received several enquiries at the London Motor Show in October 1959. When rival constructors Cooper, Elva and Lola announced their intention to build suitable cars, he began to appreciate the customer sales potential of the new Formula.

The category had been devised by Count Giovanni Lurani in Italy, as a cheaper way of enabling beginners to make a start in single-seater racing and to encourage new driver talent, in which that country was sadly lacking, following the deaths of Eugenio Castellotti and Luigi Musso in the 1950s. To limit costs, the formula was governed by relatively simple rules. The engine and transmission had to come from a recognised touring car with a maximum engine capacity of 1100cc. There was a minimum weight limit of 400kg (882lb), reduced to 360kg (794lb) for cars with engines of under 1000cc. The braking system had to remain the same as that on the car from which the engine was taken, which, in 1960, meant drum brakes. Initially an Italian National formula in 1958, it became Internationally recognised in 1959, but did not take off in the UK until 1960.

Design and Construction

Chapman adapted his multi-purpose rear-engined Lotus 18 chassis to comply with the Junior regulations. The space frame chassis was as described in Chapter 2, the only exception being that the rear bulkhead was of tubular construction rather than of the perforated hoop type of the Formula 1/2 car. Suspension was identical, but braking was by outboard-mounted Lockheed drums of 9in diameter by 1.75in width. Operated by separate master cylinders with a balance bar from the pedal, the shoes acted on transversely-ribbed Alfin drums. Lotus cast magnesium 'wobbly web' wheels of 15in diameter carried 4.50 section front tyres and 5.00 rears. The battery for the self-starter, mounted behind the radiator, helped to provide a 48% front, 52% rear weight distribution, with the 15-gallon scuttle-mounted fuel tank half full. The wheelbase was identical to the Formula 1/2 car, whereas the track was narrower by 3in at the front and 6in at the rear.

Although a variety of engine types could be installed, the chosen engine for Team Lotus was the 997cc 4-cylinder Ford 105E, introduced in the autumn of 1959 for the new Ford Anglia saloon. This was a modern engine of 80.96mm bore and short, 48.4mm

Lotus 18 debut – Alan Stacey, in the unpainted Formula Junior prototype, during the 1959 Boxing Day Brands Hatch meeting. (LAT Photographic)

11: Variations on a Theme 1960-65

Jim Clark leads John Surtees (Cooper) to win the first Formula Junior event of the season, in March 1960 at Goodwood. (LAT Photographic)

Lotus 18 | 153

Lotus 18 – Colin Chapman's U-turn

stroke with pushrod-operated valves (overhead camshafts were banned by the regulations) developing 39bhp in standard form. It was tuned by Cosworth Engineering, the company set up by former Lotus employee Keith Duckworth and current Lotus chief development engineer Mike Costin. By the end of the 1960 season, Duckworth was able to extract a genuine 88bhp out of the engine at 7250rpm on 40DCOE9 Weber carburettors.

A Lotus-produced bell-housing, containing the hydraulically-operated 7.25in diameter dry plate Borg & Beck clutch, mated the engine with the transmission sourced from the Renault Dauphine saloon. In the Renault, the engine and transmission were overhung behind the rear axle and facing in the wrong direction. By rotating the transmission through 180° and mounting it upside down in the Lotus chassis, the rotation of the input shaft was brought into line with that of the Ford engine and the input shaft passed beneath the differential, enabling the engine to be mounted much lower in the chassis. The standard Dauphine gearbox provided 4-speed with synchromesh on the upper three ratios, but a 5-speed conversion marketed by the French company Redele was available as an alternative.

In excess of 120 Formula Junior 18s were built, at a cost (subject to specification) of £1250, in component form – thus avoiding purchase tax.

Performance – 1960

The prototype Formula Junior chassis was produced from the drawing board in just five weeks and was the first Lotus 18 to make a public appearance. It was hurriedly prepared for the 1959 Boxing Day Brands Hatch meeting – so hurried that it did not feature a regulation roll-over bar. Its unpainted, slab-sided, functional-rather-than-attractive body panels prompted *Autosport* to comment that "it wore an extremely ugly – and we hope temporary – tank-like body." Alan Stacey qualified on the fourth row of the grid with a standard engine and on springs that were much too soft. With a tuned engine installed for the race, he moved up to seventh from the start, before spinning off at Druids. He resumed working his way gingerly back up to seventh by the finish, having lapped within 0.6sec of the fastest lap. Not an auspicious debut, but it was early days.

The Junior chassis next appeared at the first annual London Racing Car Show in January 1960, complete with the regulation roll-over bar and a smart green, yet nonetheless slab-sided, set of glass-fibre body panels, although *Autosport* continued to hope that "perhaps a more pleasing bodyshell will eventually be evolved." Nevertheless some 12 orders for chassis were taken. Early testing was suitably encouraging, after alterations to the suspension set-up, harder springs and the addition of an anti-roll bar in the rear suspension.

Team Lotus entered a three-car team in all the major British Formula Junior races throughout the 1960 season. The team comprised Jim Clark, Trevor Taylor and Peter Arundel – none of them exactly 'Junior,' each having had extensive sports racing car and/or 500cc Formula 3 experience. From the very beginning, these three set the pace, Clark scoring six wins, Taylor five and Arundel four. Every race of note fell to the Lotus 18, totalling 20 wins, 17 second places and 18 thirds, with ten 1-2-3 finishes. Taylor won the BARC Formula Junior Championship and shared the *Motor Racing* magazine National Championship with Clark, who won the John Davy Trophy series at Brands Hatch.

Despite having a two-year start, the Italian constructors raced

Syd van der Vyver built his successful Alfa Romeo-engined Lotus 18 from a kit of factory-supplied parts. (www.motoprint.co.za)

11: Variations on a Theme 1960-65

front-engined designs with relatively crude chassis and FIAT engines. It was thought that the British constructors would have a certain amount of catching up to do, but the Italians had failed to grasp rear-engined technology. In the event, the two disciplines never really competed against one another, except in the prestigious support event to the Monaco Grand Prix, where Taylor finished third behind a Cooper and a Lola. The Italian constructors tended to race on their home circuits, whilst Team Lotus journeyed to the continent on only two other occasions, finishing first and second in the Coupe de Vitesse at Reims and 1-2-3 at Solitude in West Germany.

In the highly competitive world of Formula Junior, technology never stood still and, when Colin Chapman produced the lower and sleeker Lotus 20 for 1961, such was its impact that the Lotus 18 became instant history. It lingered on in British Club racing, but was never a force to be reckoned with in subsequent years.

LOTUS 18 CHASSIS IN SOUTH AFRICAN RACING 1961-67

Due to its relative isolation from the European motorsport scene, South Africa, Rhodesia and neighbouring countries developed their own form of racing. The South African Gold Star Championship catered for single-seaters with 1½-litre, 4-cylinder engines, on a par with European Formula 2 yet with a more relaxed interpretation of the regulations. Many of the competing drivers acquired mainly secondhand British chassis, into which they fitted a variety of engines, popular choices including the Coventry Climax FPF and the Alfa Romeo Guilietta.

In December 1960, a number of Formula 2 drivers, including Stirling Moss in a factory Porsche, were invited to compete in a 'winter' series of races in South Africa. The success of this initiative prompted the RAC of South Africa to organise a series of four races over December 1961/January 1962, comprising the Rand, Natal, South African and Cape Grands Prix. This 'Springbok' series attracted entries from Team Lotus, Porsche, UDT-Laystall and Yeoman Credit, to compete against drivers from the local South African series that was now theoretically operating to the current European 1½-litre Formula 1 regulations.

Local driver Helmut Menzler purchased a new Formula 2 Lotus 18 chassis (911) from the factory in the latter part of 1960 and fitted it with an ex-works 1959 Borgward 4-cylinder, fuel-injected sports car engine. As a 'genuine' Formula 1/2 chassis, this is detailed in Chapter 6.

The most competitive local driver in the series was Syd van der Vyver, the 40-year-old 1960 and 1961 South African National Champion. He had purchased a Formula 2 Lotus 18 chassis from the factory during 1960, as a kit of parts and, as such, it was never allocated an appropriate factory chassis number. A talented engineer in his own right, van der Vyver installed a self-tuned Alfa Romeo Guilietta engine, developing around 140bhp in the chassis for its debut in the 1960 Cape Grand Prix. With the car fully developed, he was consistently the fastest local driver in the 1961 Springbok series. Nevertheless, he was between 2 and 4sec away from the front of the grid dominated by the Team Lotus 21s, and not as quick as Masten Gregory in the UDT-Laystall Lotus 18/21. His 18 was 100% reliable, however, giving him four finishes from as many starts, with a fifth, a sixth and two sevenths, albeit a lap or two in arrears. Van der Vyver's mechanical skills earned him a place in Rob Walker's team for 1961, on the recommendation of Stirling Moss. This proved to be a short-lived position after a clash of personalities with resident chief mechanic Alf Francis.

A number of Lotus 18 Formula Junior chassis were sold to South Africa during 1960 and, perhaps inevitably, some of these found their way into the Gold Star Series, either retaining their Ford 105E engines, or adapted to take Climax or Alfa Guilietta 4-cylinder engines. Five of these Formula Junior chassis appeared for the 1961 'Springbok' Series. A chassis number was observed on only one of these chassis, that being 'FJ-720' on the Climax-engined version of Jack Holme. He spun out of the Rand Grand Prix and was not seen again until 1962. Three other Junior 18s retained their Ford engines, driven by Bob van Niekirk, Bernard Podmore and Neville Lederle, amassing nine starts between them and four finishes, all in the lower half of the field.

The 1962 Series comprised the Rand and Natal Grands Prix, whilst the South African Grand Prix itself had been promoted to a round of the Formula 1 World Championship, for which none of the Junior 18 owners had entries accepted. Jack Holme reappeared with FJ-720 to finish 14th in Natal, having failed to qualify for the Rand Grand Prix. Peter van Niekirk also failed to qualify in the Rand and was a non-finisher in Natal, as was Bill Scheepers with his Alfa-engined ex-van der Vyver chassis. Into 1963, Jack Holme once more ran FJ-720, to finish 13th in the Rand Grand Prix, whilst Bob Hay, with a similar Climax-engined chassis, failed to make the start.

By now, many local drivers had been able to upgrade to more up-to-date Lotus or Cooper chassis, or the locally-built LDS. Nevertheless, the Junior 18s, after an absence of two years, suddenly reappeared in 1966, when the Series began running to the European 3-litre Formula 1 regulations. Peter Gaylard entered

Lotus 18 – Colin Chapman's U-turn

the Natal Winter Trophy in June 1966 with a Junior 18, powered by the Lotus 'LF' twin-cam/Ford 116E-based engine, developed for the Lotus Elan sports car introduced for 1962. He failed to finish, but survived the 1967 Cape South Easter Trophy, six months later, to finish unclassified eight laps behind the winner. Meanwhile, Bob Hay, not seen since 1963, had run the former Jack Holme chassis 'FJ-720' at Lourenco Marques, in July 1966, to be rewarded with a non-finish. Finally, Alex Kirstein appeared with a Lotus LF-engined Junior (the Peter Gaylard chassis?) for the 1967 Rand Spring Trophy, but failed to make the start.

The Lotus 18 Junior chassis had finally passed into South African Formula 1 history.

Lotus 18 – Chassis Racing Record in South Africa 1961-67

Year	Position	Driver	Entrant	Chassis	Engine	No	Grid	Comments
1961	Rand Grand Prix, Kyalami (ZA), 9.12.61, 190.88 miles (307.03km)							
	7th	Syd van der Vyver	S van der Vyver	F2	1.5 Alfa Romeo 4IL	3	Q6	72 laps/75
	9th	Bob van Niekerk	Equipe Judette	FJ	1.0 Ford 105E 4IL	22	Q13	70 laps/75
		Jack Holme	J Holme	FJ-720	1.5 Climax FPF 4IL	17	Q22	Accident lap 25/75
		Bernard Podmore	B Podmore	FJ	1.0 Ford 105E 4IL	23	Q21	Spun off lap 5/75
	Natal Grand Prix, Westmead (ZA), 17.12.61, 200.21 miles (322.14km)							
	5th	Syd van der Vyver	S van der Vyver	F2	1.5 Alfa Romeo 4IL	1	Q7	86 laps/89
		Bob van Niekerk	Equipe Judette	FJ	1.0 Ford 105E 4IL	27	Q16	Engine
		Neville Lederle	NA Lederle	FJ	1.0 Ford 105E 4IL	29	Q15	DNF
	South African Grand Prix, East London (ZA), 26.12.61, 194.80 miles (313.43km)							
	6th	Syd van der Vyver	S van der Vyver	F2	1.5 Alfa Romeo 4IL	3	Q8	77 laps/80
	9th	Bob van Niekerk	Equipe Judette	FJ	1.0 Ford 105E 4IL	22	Q16	76 laps/80
		Bernard Podmore	B Podmore	FJ	1.0 Ford 105E 4IL	26	Q18	Engine lap 5/80
1962	Cape Grand Prix, Killarney (ZA), 2.1.62, 123.47 miles (198.66km)							
	7th	Syd van der Vyver	S van der Vyver	F2	1.5 Alfa Romeo 4IL	3	Q8	58 laps/60
	11th	Bob van Niekerk	Equipe Judette	FJ	1.0 Ford 105E 4IL	22	Q12	56 laps/60
	13th	Bernard Podmore	B Podmore	FJ	1.0 Ford 105E 4IL	24	Q17	54 laps/60
		Neville Lederle	NA Lederle	FJ	1.0 Ford 105E 4IL	10	Q16	N/C 48 laps/60
	Rand Grand Prix, Kyalami (ZA), 15.12.62, 127.25 miles (204.75km)							
		Peter van Niekerk	Ted Lanfear	FJ	1.0 Ford 105E 4IL	31		DNQ
		Jack Holme	J Holme	FJ-720	1.5 Climax FPF 4IL	39		DNQ
	Natal Grand Prix, Westmead (ZA), 22.12.62, 2 Heats & Final 125.85 miles (200.88km)							
	14th	Jack Holme	J Holme	FJ-720	1.5 Climax FPF 4IL	39	Q14	Heat 1 8th
		Bill Scheepers	H Muller	FJ	1.5 Alfa Romeo 4IL	5	Q14	DNF Heat 2
		Peter van Niekerk	Ted Lanfear	FJ	1.5 Climax FPF 4IL	31	Q11	DNF Final
1963	Rand Grand Prix, Kyalami (ZA), 14.12.63, Aggregate of 2 Heats 127.25 miles (204.75km)							
	13th	Jack Holme	J Holme	FJ-720	1.5 Climax FPF 4IL	25	Q17	46 laps/50
		Bob Hay	R Hay	FJ	1.5 Climax FPF 4IL	24		DNS
1966	Natal Winter Trophy, Pietermaritzburg (ZA), 26.6.66, Aggregate of 2 Heats 118.80 miles (191.15km)							
		Peter Gaylard	George Harvey Motors	FJ	1.6 Lotus-Ford LF 4IL	18	N/A	DNF Heat 1
	Taca Governador Génerale de Mocambique, Lourenco Marques (MOC), 24.7.66, 62.77 miles (101.00km)							
		Bob Hay	RL Hay	FJ-720	1.5 Climax FPF 4IL	21	N/A	DNF
1967	Cape South Easter Trophy, Killarney (ZA), 7.1.67, Aggregate of 2 Heats 102.89 miles (165.55km)							
		Peter Gaylard	PH Gaylard	FJ	1.6 Lotus-Ford LF 4IL	19	Q12	N/C 42 laps/50
	Rand Winter Trophy, Kyalami (ZA), 7.10.67, 101.76 miles (163.73km)							
		Alex Kirstein	A Kirstein	FJ	1.6 Lotus-Ford LF 4IL	24		DNS

Lotus 18 Chassis in South African F1 – Performance 1961-67

Engine	Starts	Finishes	1st	2nd	3rd	4th	5th	6th	PP	FL
Alfa Romeo	5	4	–	–	–	1	1	–	–	–
Coventry Climax	5	2								
Ford	9	4								
Lotus-Ford	2	–								
Total	21	10	–	–	–	1	1	–	–	–

11: Variations on a Theme 1960-65

LOTUS 19 – THE SPORTS RACING 18

Having designed and produced a successful rear-engined chassis for Formulae 1 and 2, it was inevitable that Colin Chapman would extend the principle to a new sports racing car to replace the Lotus 15. This was the Type 19, nicknamed the 'Monte Carlo' early on – a jibe against the Cooper sports racing car known as the 'Monaco' in celebration of the Cooper works team's first Grand Prix win. Why should Lotus not celebrate its first Grand Prix win, coincidentally, achieved around the streets of the Principality?

Design and Construction

The Lotus 19 was based around the three-bay space frame of the 18, widened out in the central cockpit bay to provide two seats, in accordance with contemporary Appendix C regulations of the International Sporting Code. As many Formula 1 components were utilised as possible, including the front and rear bulkheads, suspension, steering, disc brakes, wheels and tyres. The wheelbase and track dimensions were also identical, all furthering the accusation that the 19 was little more than a two-seat Formula 1 car. Chassis stiffness was enhanced by a full width stressed aluminium undertray and weighed in at approximately 70lbs.

The standard power unit was the Formula 1 2½-litre 4-cylinder Coventry Climax FPF, developing 243bhp at 6750rpm, that, for sports car use, had Lucas coil ignition, dynamo and an electric starter. Smaller capacity Climax engines could also be fitted, and a couple of American-owned chassis would be fitted with the all-aluminium Buick V8 engine, very similar in weight to the Climax FPF.

Other requirements of Appendix C included a spare wheel, located above the driver's legs, in the space occupied by the main fuel tank of the 18, with a battery below it in the passenger footwell. Fuel was carried in a 12-gallon fabricated aluminium tank outside the frame, on the left side ahead of the scuttle, with a further 10-gallon auxiliary tank behind and partly alongside the driver. The standard 5-speed Lotus 'queerbox' was modified to include the regulation reverse gear, operated through first gear and engaged, with the gearlever in neutral, by a spring that pushed it into mesh with that gear. A Bowden cable ensured positive disengagement. A central gear change necessitated a more complex gear selector linkage that reversed the direction of the gear change movement – forward for up-changes, backwards for down-changes.

Full width body panels were of glass-fibre, comprising a forward-hinged front section and rearward-hinged engine cover with horizontally-hinged drop down doors of aluminium. Lighting equipment included two 7in Lucas Le Mans headlamps mounted behind clear plastic fairings, together with side, tail and brake lights.

Performance 1960-63

The prototype Lotus 19 (chassis 950) was entrusted to the British Racing Partnership and tested by Stirling Moss, on 25 July 1960, at Silverstone. This was his first outing in a racing car since his heavy accident at Spa during practice for the Belgian Grand Prix and he lapped in 1min 41.4sec for a new unofficial sports car lap record, proving that he was back in the groove. Moss found the 19 to be much quicker than a Cooper Monaco and very much in the Lotus 18 mould, being "taut, highly strung, very much an extension of the driver fitted into it, never as easy to drive as any contemporary Cooper, but potentially superior." After a further test session on 30 July at Brands Hatch, he gave the unpainted, aluminium-bodied 19 its race debut on 7 August, winning a 50-mile event at Karlskoga in Sweden.

The second chassis (951) was ordered by the Arciero brothers, Frank and Phil of Montebello California, long time sponsors of Dan Gurney. Gurney had been really impressed by the Lotus 18 he had driven in Formula 2 for Louise Bryden-Brown and was quick to persuade Frank Arciero to put in an order for a 19. Gurney: "I just had enormous faith in that car before it even ran. I convinced Frank he ought to buy it, and it turned out to be a fabulous car. A giant-killer kind of a car." Gurney spent time at Cheshunt assisting its build, to ensure it was completed in time for the Riverside and Laguna Seca 'fall' series of West Coast professional sports car races in California during October. Arriving barely in time for qualifying at Riverside, he completed just three laps to claim pole position, over 4sec quicker than the existing lap record. Alongside him on the grid was Moss in the BRP 19, some 3sec slower, his car featuring a somewhat makeshift roll-over bar behind the driver to comply with local regulations. Neither car would finish the race, Moss out after 10 laps with transmission failure and Gurney after 17, when an engine cylinder lost compression.

A week later, at Laguna Seca, Moss set a new course record in qualifying, then went on to win both 102-mile heats of the $20,000 Pacific Grand Prix. Gurney failed to start after all eight flywheel retaining screws sheered in practice. In the six weeks before the Nassau Speed Week in December, the Arciero team had time to race prepare the 19 to its high standards, allowing Gurney to win the feature Nassau Trophy easily, whilst on this occasion it was Moss that retired.

Stirling Moss has just tested the prototype, unpainted, alloy-bodied Lotus 19 (chassis 950) at Silverstone in July 1960. (LAT Photographic)

11: Variations on a Theme 1960-65

Bahamas Speedweek 1961: Le Mans start for the Nassau Trophy. Stirling Moss is off and away in his Lotus 19, whilst the similar cars of Jack Nethercutt (102) and eventual winner Dan Gurney (1) have yet to move. (LAT Photographic)

The potential shown by the 19 to unseat the dominance of the 'Birdcage' Maserati tipo 61 in the healthy US sports car racing market began to generate orders for replicas from North America, where it was priced at $15,650 (c £5600) POE East Coast. In Europe, by contrast, sports car racing was in decline. Nevertheless the BRP-run UDT-Laystall Racing Team acquired a further two examples for the 1961 season. Moss scored three of UDT-Laystall's four wins in British sprint races, but enjoyed more significant wins in the Players 200 at Mosport in Canada and a second consecutive Pacific Grand Prix at Laguna Seca, ahead of Dan Gurney. Gurney repeated his 1960 win in the Nassau Trophy, whilst Peter Ryan won the Canadian Grand Prix at Mosport for the Canadian Comstock team.

Into 1962, Dan Gurney drove the Arciero Brothers 19 to wins in the Daytona 3 Hours (coasting across the line with a broken connecting rod) and the World Fair Grand Prix at Seattle. Six British sprint races were won by UDT-Laystall 19s over the season, and there was also an isolated Continental win at Innsbruck in Austria. Of the

Lotus 18 | 159

more significant events, Masten Gregory won both the Players 200 and the Canadian Grand Prix at Mosport for UDT-Laystall. Six 19s appeared on the entry list for the Los Angeles Times Grand Prix at Riverside, although they were rewarded only with a third place finish. Dan Gurney won Heat 1 of the Pacific Grand Prix at Laguna Seca, with Lloyd Ruby taking Heat 2 in J Frank Harrison's 19 to finish second on aggregate, with Gurney fourth. Innes Ireland made it three in a row for the Lotus 19, in the Nassau Trophy, driving the ex-Moss UDT-Laystall chassis now owned by Team Rosebud of Texas.

Despite their successes, the 19s suffered the usual Lotus maladies of fragility in the chassis, suspension and transmission. The Arciero brothers' mechanic Bill Fowler was convinced that "the Achilles heel of that car was the Lotus transmission. We had gearbox failures, just one after the other. Other than that it would have won a lot more races than it did." In addition, Climax engine parts were in short supply and the disc brakes, whilst adequate for the lighter Lotus 18, were reportedly prone to fade with high rates of wear.

By 1963, the Lotus 19 was beginning to be outpaced by the new breed of American V8-engined sports racing cars or by the Lotus 23, introduced in 1962 for lower capacity categories. Chuck Daigh become the last driver to win a major race in a Climax-engined 19, taking the Arciero brothers chassis to victory in the Players 200 at Mosport. Jim Clark had never driven a 19 until offered a drive in the Arciero brothers' car for the 1963 Times Grand Prix at Riverside and the Pacific Grand Prix at Laguna Seca. The car never made the start at Riverside, due to a lack of oil pressure in its 2.7-litre Climax engine, but he qualified second at Laguna Seca and led ten laps of the race, before running over a course marker and rupturing his oil cooler.

The 19 lived on in larger-engined form, when J Frank Harrison had his chassis considerably reworked to take a small block 289cu.in (4.7-litres) Ford V8 engine with Colotti 4-speed transmission. Brakes were increased to 12in diameter front and 11in rear and the chassis was clothed in new lower, wider aluminium body panels. Lloyd Ruby raced the car as the 'Harrison Special' and was competitive enough to win the 1963 Northwest Grand Prix at Seattle. Meanwhile, Team Rosebud in Texas went a different route and reworked its 19 to take a 3.0-litre Ferrari V12 engine. This combination, with Innes Ireland at the wheel, was not far off the pace initially but, following an accident, it was never quite the same, and failed to live up to its promise.

LOTUS 19B

During 1963, Dan Gurney commissioned Colin Chapman to design him a new 19 chassis, specifically to take a Ford V8 engine. Chapman passed the project to Len Terry who had recently rejoined Lotus as chief designer. Although outwardly similar to the Lotus 19 and designated the '19B,' Terry drew a completely new space frame chassis with exterior triangulation to the cockpit area, to provide a much stiffer structure. The frame was clothed in 19 body panels, widened by 4in to accommodate the latest generation of wide tyres.

The 19B would prove fast yet unreliable, breaking its suspension on its debut at Nassau, in December 1963. Dan scored the 19B's only outright win in a short race at Riverside in October 1964, before finishing second at Laguna Seca the same month. In February 1965, Gurney and co-driver Jerry Grant were set up as the 'hare' in the Ford v Ferrari battle for the Daytona 2000 kilometres. Gurney's All American Racers Inc 19B was powered by a special 342cu.in (5.4-litre) Ford V8 and featured a revised nose section, with low mounted radiator inlet and top ducted hot air outlet to help reduce front end lift. After seven hours, having completed 809 miles (65% distance) of racing, and with a five-lap lead, the 19B retired with a holed piston. The car was also entered for the Sebring 12 Hours in March, but was eliminated after a couple of hours by a fractured fuel pump drive.

This was the final noteworthy performance by a 19 and, in 1964, Colin Chapman introduced the Lotus 30 with a backbone chassis frame to take large capacity American V8s. Nevertheless, neither the 30, nor its successor, the 40, would prove a match for the Lotus 19 in terms of international success.

www.velocebooks.com / www.veloce.co.uk
Details of all current books • New book news • Special offers • Gift vouchers • Forum

APPENDIX I
SUMMARY OF INDIVIDUAL CHASSIS HISTORIES

NOTE RE CHASSIS NUMBERS
In the 1960s, it was a complex task to travel outside the UK with a single seat racing car. It was necessary to register the car with the Board of Trade and the RAC (the UK motorsport authority) to obtain a Customs carnet, a special document identifying the car and spare parts. This exempted the owner of the car from paying import duty whenever it crossed international borders. These were expensive and time-consuming items to obtain. As chassis/parts numbers had to be stated on the carnets, it was considerably cheaper and less complicated to switch chassis number identification plates, and the relative Customs carnets, from crashed or damaged chassis to replacement chassis, when in actual fact the replacement required new registration and certification. Such practices can make the accurate tracking of chassis numbers somewhat difficult and those quoted in the Appendices have to be viewed against this background and the likelihood that in some cases the chassis number quoted may not necessarily refer to the actual chassis raced.

Chassis built by Team Lotus

369 Team Lotus, 1960 – 2½-litre Coventry Climax engine. The prototype 18 with alloy body panels debuted by Innes Ireland in the Argentine Grand Prix on 6.2.60. Three Formula 2 events with 1½-litre Climax engine, including a win for Innes Ireland in Oulton Park Spring Trophy (**first Formula 2 win** for Lotus). Re-engined back to Formula 1 for Alan Stacey to drive at Easter Goodwood Glover Trophy 18.4.60 – last race for Team Lotus.

Sold to Taylor & Crawley Ltd – first Formula 1 Lotus 18 in private hands. Driven by Mike Taylor in the Silverstone International Trophy on 14.5.60, then in practice for the Belgian Grand Prix, where it was written-off in an accident on 18.6.60 after the steering column sheared.

370 Team Lotus, 1960 – 1½-litre Coventry Climax engine. Race debut in the Formula 2 Brussels Grand Prix on 8.4.60, driven by Alan Stacey. Driven by Innes Ireland to beat Stirling Moss to win the Easter Goodwood Formula 2 Lavant Cup. Re-engined with 2½-litre Climax for the Silverstone International Trophy for Alan Stacey, then became his regular chassis, until written-off in his fatal accident during the Belgian Grand Prix at Spa on 19.6.60.

'370:' Innes Ireland in the Goodwood Lavant Cup winner. This chassis would be written-off in Alan Stacey's tragic Spa accident. (Ferret Fotographics)

Lotus 18 | 161

'371:' The winner at Goodwood and Silverstone in 1960 and at Pau in 1961. Here, at Reims in 1960, it shows off trunking to duct cool air to the carburettors, and a smaller, high-penetration radiator inlet. (LAT Photographic)

371 Team Lotus, 1960 – 2½-litre Coventry Climax engine. Race debut: Goodwood, Easter Monday 18.4.60, driven by Innes Ireland to beat Stirling Moss and win the Glover Trophy (**first Formula 1 win** for Lotus). A second win followed in the Silverstone International Trophy. His regular Grand Prix chassis, until driven by Jim Clark in the United States Grand Prix. Also raced, with 1½-litre Climax engine, in Formula 2 by Trevor Taylor in the Solitude Grand Prix and by Ireland in the German Grand Prix. Driven by Jim Clark in the 1961 Tasman Formule Libre series.

1961 – retained by Team Lotus. Driven in early season non-Championship Formula 1 races by Jim Clark, including his first career Formula 1 win in the Pau Grand Prix. Thereafter, it was utilised by Innes Ireland for non-Championship Formula 1 and Inter-Continental formula events. Driven by Trevor Taylor in the Dutch Grand Prix. Stand-in for the Lotus 21 in various non-Championship Formula 1 races.

Up-graded to 18/21 specification, prior to sale to Jim Hall for the United States Grand Prix.

1962 – retained by Jim Hall. Single Formula 1 (and last recorded) appearance on 4.11.62, in the non-Championship Mexico Grand Prix, driven by Homer Rader.

372 Team Lotus, 1960 – 1½-litre Coventry Climax engine. Race debut: Formula 2 Brussels Grand Prix 8.4.60, driven by Jim Clark. Formula 2 race wins for Trevor Taylor in the Crystal Palace Trophy and Jim Clark in the Kentish 100 at Brands Hatch. Re-engined to Formula 1 for Innes Ireland, to win the Lombank Trophy at Snetterton and finish second in the United States Grand Prix. Driven by Ireland in the 1961 Tasman Formule Libre series.

1961 – retained by Team Lotus. Mainly driven by Jim Clark in the early season non-Championship Formula 1 races, then re-engined for the Inter-Continental British Empire Trophy, Silverstone and the Guards Trophy, Brands Hatch.

Upgraded to 18/21 specification, with 1½-litre Coventry Climax engine, prior to sale to J Wheeler Autosport for Peter Ryan to drive in the United States Grand Prix.

1962 – acquired by Walt Hansgen. Last recorded Formula 1 race: Mexican Grand Prix 4.11.62.

373 Team Lotus, 1960 – 2½-litre Coventry Climax engine. Race debut: Silverstone International Trophy on 14.5.60, for John Surtees to make his Formula 1 debut. Grand Prix debuts for Surtees at Monaco, then Jim Clark in the Dutch Grand Prix. Driven by Surtees into second place in the British Grand Prix. Re-engined for three mid-season Formula 2 events for Innes Ireland, then back to Formula 1 for Surtees for the Portuguese Grand Prix and the remainder of the Formula 1 season. Driven by Surtees in the 1961 Tasman Formule Libre series.

1961 – acquired by Scuderia Colonia. Driven by Wolfgang Seidel in ten non-Championship Formula 1 races plus the British, German and Italian Grands Prix. Loaned to Equipe Nationale Belge for Lucien Bianchi to drive in the Belgian Grand Prix.

1962 – acquired by Autosport Team Wolfgang Seidel. Driven by Günther Seiffert in eight non-Championship Formula 1 races. Loaned to Emeryson Cars for John Campbell-Jones in the Belgian Grand Prix.

1963 – acquired by Kurt Kuhnke from the defunct Seidel team and re-engined with a 4-cylinder, 1.5-litre Borgward RS engine.

Appendix I: Summary of Individual Chassis Histories

'373:' A suitably stylish Jim Clark at Reims in 1960. This chassis made 36 race starts in period, the highest number for any Lotus 18 chassis. (LAT Photographic)

Entered as a 'BKL' (Borgward-Kuhnke-Lotus) for Ernst Maring in the non-Championship Solitude Grand Prix. Accident in its last recorded race, at Karlskoga on 11.8.63.

Lotus 18 chassis with **highest number of recorded race starts** at 36 between 1960 and 1963.

374 Team Lotus, 1960 – 2½-litre Coventry Climax engine. Unique chassis with the engine canted 17½° to the right to bring the carburettor inlets out of turbulent air ahead of rear wheel. Race debut in the French Grand Prix on 3.7.60 driven by Ron Flockhart. Driven by Jim Clark in the British Grand Prix then re-engined to Formula 2 for the Solitude Grand Prix. Back to Formula 1 specification for the Brands Hatch Silver City Trophy and the Portuguese Grand Prix where Clark extensively bent the chassis in a practice accident yet repaired overnight enabling him to finish third. Back to Formula 2 for John Surtees to drive in the Kentish 100, Brands Hatch then the Danish Grand Prix at Roskilde for Graham Hill on a one-off return to

'374:' The 17½° cant of the engine towards the right side can be made out here, as the car receives attention in the pits from mechanic Jim Endruweit, with Colin Chapman looking on attentively. (LAT Photographic)

Team Lotus. Converted back to Formula 1 for Jim Clark to drive in the end of season non-Championship races.

1961 – retained by Team Lotus. Driven in early season non-Championship Formula 1 races by Trevor Taylor/Jim Clark then re-engined for the Inter-Continental Silverstone International Trophy.

Acquired by Jim Diggory for Bruce Halford to drive in the Inter-Continental Guards Trophy at Brands Hatch.

Driven by Ron Flockhart in the 1962 Tasman Formule Libre series. Last recorded race appearance: Warwick Farm, Australia on 4.2.62.

375 No record of this chassis in Team Lotus files – certainly never raced in period.

Lotus 18 | 163

Lotus 18 – Colin Chapman's U-turn

376 RRC Walker Racing Team, 1960, for Stirling Moss – 2½-litre Coventry Climax engine. Winner of the Monaco Grand Prix on its race debut on 29.5.60 – **first Grand Prix win** for Lotus. Extensively damaged in practice accident for the Belgian Grand Prix at Spa on 18.6.60. Rebuilt around a new chassis frame (906 – see below) with modifications to the front anti-roll bar mountings, relocation of the rear brakes outboard and installation of Colotti type 21 transmission. Reappeared on Moss' return from injury at the Portuguese Grand Prix. Winner of the Watkins Glen Formule Libre Grand Prix and then the United States Grand Prix – **second Grand Prix win** for Lotus.

Driven by Moss in the 1961 Tasman Formule Libre series, including a win in the Warwick Farm International, Australia on 28.1.61, the last recorded race under this chassis number.

'376:' the 1960 Monaco and United States Grands Prix winning chassis. Here, Stirling Moss is on his come-back drive, following a puncture in the Dutch Grand Prix – note the 'borrowed' replacement front wheel. (Sutton Images)

Production chassis built by Lotus Components Ltd

901 Vandervell Products Ltd, 1960. Extensively modified to accept the 4-cylinder Vanwall V254 2½-litre engine as a test bed for a rear-engined Vanwall project. Entered for the Lombank Trophy at Snetterton on 17.9.60 to be driven by Tony Brooks but it was withdrawn following practice due to engine damage. Not raced again in period.

1964 – Sold to Chris Ashmore ex-engine but not seen in Formula 1/2.

902 Scuderia Centro Sud, 1960 – race debut on 24.9.60 with a 4-cylinder 2½-litre Maserati 250S engine for the Oulton Park Gold Cup in the hands of Ian Burgess. Re-engined with a 1½-litre Maserati 150S engine for the Formula 2 Modena Grand Prix.

1961 – acquired by Prince Gaetano Starrabba with the 1½-litre Maserati engine. Driven in the Modena Grand Prix by Giorgio Scarlatti, then by Starrabba in the Coppa Italia at Vallelunga, followed by the Italian Grand Prix.

1962 – retained by Gaetano Starrabba. Driven only in the non-Championship Naples Grand Prix.

1963 – retained by Gaetano Starrabba. Entered for four Italian non-Championship Formula 1 races, including a fifth place finish in the Rome Grand Prix. Last recorded Formula 1 appearance: in practice for the Mediterranean Grand Prix at Pergusa, on 18.8.63, where Starrabba failed to qualify.

903 Mrs Louise Bryden-Brown, 1960, for Dan Gurney – 1½-litre Coventry Climax engine. Race debut on 31.7.60 in the Formula 2 German Grand Prix. Pole position for Gurney in the Kentish 100 at Brands Hatch, recording the fastest lap in finishing runner-up to Jim Clark.

1961 – retained by Mrs Bryden-Brown. 2½-litre Coventry Climax engine installed for Inter-Continental events. Damaged by Dan Gurney, in an accident during the Lavant Cup at Goodwood on Easter Monday. Repaired, but damaged again in practice for the Silverstone International Trophy and did not start. Repaired and re-engined with 1½-litre Climax engine for the Formula 1 Brands Hatch Silver City Trophy. Driven by Tony Maggs in the British and German Grands Prix. Last recorded Formula 1 appearance: Nürburgring on 6.8.61.

1962 – acquired by the Arciero Brothers. Driven by Dan Gurney to win the 1962 Formule Libre Bossier Grand Prix, Louisiana. He failed to finish the 1962 Formule Libre Hoosier Grand Prix at Indianapolis, but won the 1963 event.

164 | Lotus 18

Appendix I: Summary of Individual Chassis Histories

'903:' the former Louise Bryden-Brown chassis now owned by the Arciero Brothers, with which Dan Gurney won a couple of US Formule Libre events in 1962/63. (LAT Photographic)

904 Reg Parnell (Racing) 1960 – 1½-litre Coventry Climax engine. Race debut on 1.8.60 in the Formula 2 Aintree Trophy. Four further Formula 2 starts for Geoff Duke and two for Tim Parnell, plus a single for Stirling Moss in the Modena Grand Prix. Driven by Roy Salvadori in the 1961 Tasman Formule Libre series.

1961 – retained, and driven by Tim Parnell in 11 non-Championship Formula 1 races, plus the British and Italian Grands Prix. Driven by André Pilette in the Brussels Grand Prix. Re-engined during the season for the Inter-Continental Silverstone International and British Empire Trophies.

1962 – acquired by Phillip Robinson and upgraded to 18/21 specification. A single outing only in the Oulton Park Gold Cup.

1963 – retained by Phillip Robinson and run in five non-Championship Formula 1 races. Last recorded appearance: Solitude Grand Prix 28.7.63.

Lotus 18 chassis with second highest number of recorded race starts at 28 between 1960 and 1963.

905 Ian Burgess, 1960 – 1½-litre Coventry Climax engine. Race debut on 28.8.60, in Formula 2 Kentish 100 at Brands Hatch, entered in the name of Scuderia Centro Sud.

1961 – acquired by Camoradi International via Burgess. Raced in the Naples Grand Prix, plus starts in the French and British Grands Prix.

'905:' Jay Chamberlain, in the Ecurie Excelsior 18, exits the paddock during practice at Crystal Palace. (Ferret Fotographics)

Lotus 18 | 165

1962 – acquired by Ecurie Excelsior/Jay Chamberlain, the former California Lotus dealer. Run in seven non-Championship Formula 1 events, plus the British Grand Prix. Driven by Swedish speedway star Olle Nygren in the Kanonloppet at Karlskoga. Chamberlain failed to qualify for the German and Italian Grands Prix. Last recorded appearance: non-Championship Mexico Grand Prix on 4.11.62.

906 RRC Walker Racing Team, 1960, for Stirling Moss – 2½-litre Coventry Climax engine. The rebuilt '376' for Customs carnet purposes – see above. Race debut as '906' on 24.9.60, to win the Oulton Park Gold Cup.

1961 – retained by Walker Team with 1½-litre Coventry Climax engine for Moss in early season non-Championship Formula 1 races, including win in Preis von Wien. Loaned to UDT-Laystall Racing Team and re-engined for the Inter-Continental Silverstone International Trophy.

Re-built at Ferguson Research to 18/21 specification around a Coventry Climax FWMV V8 and GSD type 32 transmission to create the Lotus 18/21 'V8 Special.' Run in practice only for the Italian and United States Grands Prix, due to overheating problems.

1962 – retained by Walker Team and run in the Brussels Grand Prix. Loaned to UDT-Laystall and run in team pale green colours for the Lombank Trophy, Snetterton and the Glover Trophy at Goodwood on Easter Monday 23.4.62, where it was written-off in Moss' career-ending accident.

907 Carroll Shelby/Jim Hall, 1960 – supplied with 2-litre Coventry Climax engine. Re-engined with 2½-litre Climax for race debut in United States Grand Prix on 20.11.60, driven by Jim Hall.

1961 – acquired by J Frank Harrison, with a 1½-litre Climax engine, for Lloyd Ruby to drive in the United States Grand Prix on 8.10.61, its last recorded Formula 1 appearance.

908 Camoradi International, new, 1961 – 1½-litre Coventry Climax engine. Race debut in the Pau Grand Prix on 3.4.61, for Ian Burgess. Driven by him in two further early season non-Championship races. Not seen again after Lloyd Casner failed to qualify for the Solitude Grand Prix on 23.7.61.

909 AE Marsh ('hill-climb' champion Tony Marsh), 1960, in kit form less engine. Race debut, with 1½-litre Coventry Climax engine on 28.8.60, in the Formula 2 Kentish 100 at Brands Hatch. Four further Formula 2 events, including a win for Marsh in the Lewis-Evans Trophy at Brands Hatch.

1961 – retained by Tony Marsh, with modifications to the front and rear suspensions, and replacement of the 'queerbox' with a Cooper transmission. Entered for five non-Championship Formula 1 races, plus the British and German Grands Prix. Loaned to Equipe National Belge for Willy Mairesse to drive in the Belgian Grand Prix.

'906:' The UDT-Laystall liveried 18/21 V8 Special in the paddock at Snetterton in April 1962. In its earlier life, Stirling Moss drove it to two non-Championship wins. (Ferret Fotographics)

'908:' Ian Burgess with the Camoradi International chassis during the 1961 Brussels Grand Prix. (Author)

Appendix I: Summary of Individual Chassis Histories

1962 – acquired by Gerry Ashmore for Graham Eden to drive in two British non-Championship Formula 1 races. Last recorded Formula 1 race: Oulton Park Gold Cup on 1.9.62.

910 Chris Summers 1960. No record of this chassis racing in Formula 1, F2 or Inter-Continental in period.

911 Ecurie Wolman, South Africa, December 1960, less engine, for Helmut Menzler. Fitted with a 1½-litre, 4-cylinder Borgward RS engine. Race debut in the non Championship South African Grand Prix on 27.12.60, then competed in the South African Gold Star Series.

1961 – retained by Ecurie Wolman and driven by Menzler in three Springbok series races, including the Cape Grand Prix on 2.1.62.

1962 – acquired by Vern McWilliams. Raced in the Springbok series Rand and Natal Grands Prix. Last recorded Formula 1 appearance: Natal Grand Prix, Westmead 22.12.62.

912 RRC Walker Racing Team, new, autumn 1960 for Stirling Moss – 2½-litre Coventry Climax engine. Used as spare in practice for the United States Grand Prix.

1961 – retained by Walker Team. Race debut: Glover Trophy, Goodwood on Easter Monday 3.4.61, with 1½-litre Coventry Climax

'912:' Stirling Moss at La Source Hairpin at Spa with the famous 1961 Monaco Grand Prix winner newly upgraded to 18/21 specification. (LAT Photographic)

Lotus 18 | 167

Lotus 18 – Colin Chapman's U-turn

engine and GSD type 32 transmission. Full Grand Prix season, plus the non-Championship Modena Grand Prix. The famous Stirling Moss/Rob Walker Monaco and the German Grands Prix winner – **third and fourth Grand Prix wins** for Lotus. Upgraded to 18/21 specification, May/June, for the Belgian Grand Prix. Driven by Innes Ireland in the Italian Grand Prix in a swap with his Team Lotus 21. Final race for the Walker Team in the United States Grand Prix, on 8.10.61.

1962 – acquired by Count Giovanni Volpi di Misurata for his Scuderia SSS Republica di Venezia and driven mainly by Nino Vaccarella. Entered for six non-Championship Formula 1 races, but Vaccarella failed to qualify for the Monaco Grand Prix. Last recorded Formula 1 appearance: Mediterranean Grand Prix, Pergusa on 19.8.61.

913 Scuderia Dolomiti, new, April 1961, for Ernesto Prinoth – 1½-litre Coventry Climax engine. Race debut the Preis von Wien on 16.4.61. Five non-Championship Formula 1 races in total.

1962 – retained by Ernesto Prinoth – now entered in name of Scuderia Jolly Club for the Italian Grand Prix, but failed to qualify.

1963 – retained by Prinoth/Jolly Club for two non-Championship Formula 1 races.

1965 – re-appeared, entered by Scuderia Nord-Ouest for Colin Davis, who failed to qualify for the Mediterranean Grand Prix at Pergusa on 15.8.65, its last recorded Formula 1 appearance.

914 Scuderia Colonia, new, November 1960 – 1½-litre Coventry Climax engine. Race debut at the Pau Grand Prix on 3.4.61, driven by Jo Bonnier. Driven by Maurice Trintignant in the Brussels Grand Prix, then by Michael May in three non-Championship Formula 1 races plus the Monaco and French Grands Prix. Failed to qualify for the German Grand Prix.

1962 – acquired for Autosport Team Wolfgang Seidel. Entered for two non-Championship Formula 1 races, driven by Kurt Kuhnke.

'913:' Ernesto Prinoth running during practice at Imola in 1963 minus the engine cover of the Jolly Club chassis (Ferret Fotographics)

'914:' Kurt Kuhnke leaves the Nürburgring pits in 1963 with the Borgward-engined 'BKL.' (Ferret Fotographics)

168 | Lotus 18

Appendix I: Summary of Individual Chassis Histories

1963 – acquired by Kurt Kuhnke and re-engined with 4-cylinder, 1½-litre Borgward RS engine. Entered as a 'BKL' (Borgward-Kuhnke-Lotus) – see also '373.' Started two non-Championship Formula 1 races, but failed to qualify for the German Grand Prix.

1964 – retained by Kurt Kuhnke and run in the Solitude Grand Prix for 'Parker' (Joachim Diel) on 19.7.64, its last recorded Formula 1 appearance.

915 UDT-Laystall Racing Team, delivered February 1961 – 2½-litre Coventry Climax engine. Race debut in Inter-Continental Lombank Trophy at Snetterton on 26.3.61, in hands of Cliff Allison. Re-engined to Formula 1 for Easter Goodwood and three other non-Championship Formula 1 races for Allison. Henry Taylor failed to qualify for the Monaco Grand Prix. Returned to Inter-Continental specification for the British Empire Trophy at Silverstone and the Guards Trophy at Brands Hatch, driven by Lucien Bianchi and Dan Gurney respectively.

1962 – not raced.

1963 – acquired by Tim Parnell and up-graded to 18/21 specification for four non-Championship Formula 1 races, driven by Parnell or Ron Carter. Parnell failed to qualify for the German Grand Prix. Last recorded Formula 1 appearance: Karlskoga on 11.8.63.

916 UDT-Laystall Racing Team, delivered February 1961 – 1½-litre Coventry Climax engine. Race debut in the Lombank Trophy at Snetterton on 26.3.61, in hands of Henry Taylor. Entered in a further five non-Championship Formula 1 races, plus the Monaco Grand Prix for Cliff Allison. Upgraded to 18/21 specification with Taylor for the French Grand Prix, then re-engined for the Inter-Continental British Empire Trophy at Silverstone. Returned to Formula 1 specification for the British Grand Prix. Returned to Inter-Continental specification for the Guards Trophy at Brands Hatch, driven by Masten Gregory. Finally, re-engined to Formula 1 specification for Stirling Moss to win the non-Championship Danish Grand Prix.

1962 – retained by UDT-Laystall for Innes Ireland to drive in four early season non-Championship Formula 1 races.

1963 – acquired by Tim Parnell and entered for André Pilette in the Pau Grand Prix. Entered by Pilette himself in both the Aintree 200 and the Silverstone International Trophy, for which he practised, but failed to start. Last recorded Formula 1 appearance: Silverstone on 11.5.63.

917 UDT-Laystall Racing Team, new, 1961, in 18/21 specification – 1½-litre Coventry Climax engine. Race debut at Silver City Trophy, Brands Hatch on 3.6.61, driven by Jo Bonnier. A further seven non-Championship Formula 1 events, including a single start for Stirling Moss. Driven in the French and British Grands Prix by Lucien Bianchi, then by Masten Gregory for the remainder of the season, including the Italian and United States Grands Prix.

1962 – retained by UDT-Laystall for Masten Gregory to drive in the early season non-Championship Formula 1 events, plus the Dutch Grand Prix.

1963 – acquired by Tim Parnell for two non-Championship Formula 1 races, then passed to André Pilette for a further four non-Championship races and the German and Italian Grands Prix, for which he failed to qualify. Last recorded appearance: Oulton Park Gold Cup on 21.9.63.

'917:' Stirling Moss in the UDT-Laystall 18/21 at Solitude in 1961, a chassis in which he never won a race. (LAT Photographic)

918 UDT-Laystall Racing Team, new, 1961, in 18/21 specification – 1½-litre Coventry Climax engine. Race debut, with win for Stirling Moss, in the Silver City Trophy, Brands Hatch on 3.6.61. Damaged in practice accident for the Belgian Grand Prix, ending career of Cliff Allison. Repaired, and driven by Stirling Moss to win the Kanonloppet at Karlskoga. Entered for three other non-Championship Formula 1 races, plus the Italian and United States Grands Prix, mainly for Henry Taylor. Driven by Stirling Moss in the South African Springbok series, to finish runner-up to Jim Clark twice.

1962 – retained by UDT-Laystall. Loaned to RRC Walker Racing Team for Maurice Trintignant to win the Pau Grand Prix. Two further non-Championship Formula 1 races, including the Mallory Park

Lotus 18 | 169

Lotus 18 – Colin Chapman's U-turn

'918:' Graham Hill leads Jim Clark (Lotus 25) at Mallory Park in 1962. This chassis was a three-time winner, including the 1962 Pau Grand Prix, the final win for a Lotus 18. (LAT Photographic)

2000 Guineas driven by Graham Hill. Loaned to Equipe Nationale Belge for Lucien Bianchi to drive in the Belgian Grand Prix.

1963 – acquired by Jock Russell for himself/Adam Wyllie to drive in two non-Championship Formula 1 races.

1964 – retained by Jock Russell for the Daily Mirror Trophy at Snetterton on 14.3.64, its last recorded Formula 1 appearance.

1967 – written-off in fire at Jock Russell's premises.

919 Tim Parnell, new, 1961, for Gerry Ashmore – 1½-litre Coventry Climax engine. Race debut at the Preis von Wien on 16.4.61. Two further non-Championship Formula 1 races (including second place in the Naples Grand Prix) and the British Grand Prix.

Acquired by Gerry Ashmore for the German and Italian Grands Prix.

1962 – retained by Gerry Ashmore and up-graded to 18/21 for three non-Championship Formula 1 races. Failed to qualify for the Italian Grand Prix. Also driven by David Piper in four mid-season non-Championship Formula 1 races.

1963 – not raced.

1964 – acquired by Kurt Kuhnke to replace '373' – see above.

Re-engined with 4-cylinder, 1½-litre Borgward RS engine. Driven by Ernst Maring as a 'BKL' in the Solitude Grand Prix only.

1965 – acquired by Ernst Maring. Borgward RS engine reduced to 1.0-litre, to comply with the new Formula 2 regulations. A single entry made for the Solitude Formula 2 Grand Prix on 18.7.65, its last recorded appearance.

Lotus 18/21 Chassis constructed outside Lotus factory by Tim Parnell

P1 John Dalton, 1962, for New Zealander Tony Shelly – 1½-litre Coventry Climax engine. Race debut at Lombank Trophy, Snetterton on 14.4.62. Season of nine non-Championship Formula 1 races plus the British Grand Prix. Failed to qualify for the German Grand Prix. Last recorded Formula 1 appearance: Oulton Park Gold Cup on 1.9.62.

1963 – shipped to New Zealand by Tony Shelly, for the 1963 and 1964 Tasman Formule Libre series, with 2½-litre Coventry Climax engine. Three top-six placings in 1963, plus six in 1964. Not run in 1965, but reappeared in 1966 series, for John Riley, at Teretonga on 29.1.66 – last recorded appearance.

P2 Tim Parnell, 1962 – 1½-litre Coventry Climax engine. Race debut at Lombank Trophy, Snetterton on 14.4.62. Three further non-Championship Formula 1 races for Parnell, plus a single race for John Dalton at Mallory Park 2000 Guineas. Entered for Gary Hocking in the Danish Grand Prix.

Acquired by Gary Hocking for the remainder of the season including the Oulton Park Gold Cup. Shipped to South Africa for Hocking to win the South African Gold Star series Rhodesian Grand Prix and the Rand Spring Trophy. Not raced following his fatal accident in Rob Walker Lotus 24 in Natal on 20.12.62

1963 – acquired by Clive Puzey. Competed in the South African Gold Star Series and the Rand Grand Prix.

1964 – retained by Clive Puzey for the Gold Star Series and the Rand Grand Prix.

1965 – retained by Clive Puzey for the Gold Star Series and the Rand Grand Prix. Failed to pre-qualify for the South African Grand Prix.

1966 – retained by Clive Puzey and re-engined with a 2.5/2.75-litre 4-cylinder, Coventry Climax FPF engine for the South African 3-litre Formula 1 Championship Series. A full season of 13 events, giving Puzey fourth place in the South African Championship. Last recorded Formula 1 appearance: Rhodesian Grand Prix, Kumalo on 4.12.66.

APPENDIX II
LOTUS 18 RACE RECORD – CHASSIS BY CHASSIS

All events shown are Formula 1 unless otherwise stated. Championship Grands Prix shown in bold/capital letters.

Chassis No. 369		Engine:	2.5 Coventry Climax FPF 4IL (1960 F1) / 1.5 Coventry Climax FPF 4IL (1960 F2)			
	Entrant	Date	Event	Driver	No	Grid	Result
1960	Team Lotus	6 Feb	**ARGENTINE Grand Prix**	Innes Ireland	20	Q2	6th
		19 Mar	Grand Premio di Siracusa (F2)	Innes Ireland	8	Q2	4th
		2 Apr	Oulton Park Trophy (F2)	Innes Ireland	20	Q4	1st (FL)
		8 Apr	Grand Prix de Bruxelles (F2)	Innes Ireland	4	Q11	Gear selector Heat 2 lap 10
		18 Apr	Glover Trophy, Goodwood	Alan Stacey	12	Q11	Engine lap 15/42
	Taylor & Crawley Ltd	14 May	International Trophy, Silverstone	Mike Taylor	19	Q24	N/C 32 laps/50
		19 Jun	**BELGIAN Grand Prix**	Mike Taylor	20		DNS – accident in practice. Chassis written-off

Chassis No 370		Engine:	2.5 Coventry Climax FPF 4IL (1960 F1) / 1.5 Coventry Climax FPF 4IL (1960 F2)			
	Entrant	Date	Event	Driver	No	Grid	Result
1960	Team Lotus	2 Apr	Oulton Park Trophy (F2)	Alan Stacey	19		DNS not ready
		8 Apr	Grand Prix de Bruxelles (F2)	Alan Stacey	8	Q8	Out of fuel Heat 2
		18 Apr	Lavant Cup, Goodwood (F2)	Innes Ireland	25	Q1	1st (FL)
		30 Apr	BARC 200, Aintree (F2)	Alan Stacey	2	Q4	Gear selector lap 10/50
		14 May	International Trophy, Silverstone	Alan Stacey	11	Q9	4th
		29 May	**MONACO Grand Prix**	Alan Stacey	24	Q13	Chassis lap 23/100
		6 Jun	**DUTCH Grand Prix**	Alan Stacey	5	Q8	Final drive lap 57/75
		19 Jun	**BELGIAN Grand Prix**	Alan Stacey	16	Q16	Fatal accident lap 24/36 Chassis written-off

Chassis No 371		Engine:	2.5 Coventry Climax FPF 4IL (1960 F1 & 1961 I/C) / 1.5 Coventry Climax FPF 4IL (1960 F2 & 1961-62 F1)			
	Entrant	Date	Event	Driver	No	Grid	Result
1960	Team Lotus	18 Apr	Glover Trophy, Goodwood	Innes Ireland	14	Q4	1st
		30 Apr	BARC 200, Aintree (F2)	Clark/Ireland	3	Q12	9th
		14 May	International Trophy, Silverstone	Innes Ireland	10	Q11	1st (FL)
		29 May	**MONACO Grand Prix**	Innes Ireland	22	Q7	Misfire lap 56/100
		6 Jun	**DUTCH Grand Prix**	Innes Ireland	4	Q3	2nd
		19 Jun	**BELGIAN Grand Prix**	Innes Ireland	14	Q7	Spin lap 13/36 (=FL)
		3 Jul	**FRENCH Grand Prix**	Innes Ireland	20	Q4	7th – 43 laps/50
		16 Jul	**BRITISH Grand Prix**	Innes Ireland	7	Q5	3rd
		24 Jul	Großer Preis der Solitude (F2)	Trevor Taylor	18	Q17	Engine lap 15/20
		31 Jul	Großer Preis von Deutschland (F2)	Innes Ireland	11	Q10	7th
		14 Aug	**PORTUGUESE Grand Prix**	Innes Ireland	16	Q7	6th – 48 laps/55
		20 Nov	**UNITED STATES Grand Prix**	Jim Clark	12	Q5	N/C 61 laps/75
1961	Team Lotus	26 Mar	Lombank Trophy, Snetterton	Jim Clark	7	Q3	4th
		3 Apr	Grand Prix de Pau	Jim Clark	6	Q2	1st (FL)
		9 Apr	Grand Prix de Bruxelles	Innes Ireland	20	Q13	6th
		22 Apr	BARC 200, Aintree	Innes Ireland	18	Q7	10th – 48 laps/50
		25 Apr	Grand Prix di Siracusa	Innes Ireland	38	Q9	Throttle lap 26/56
		6 May	Int Trophy, Silverstone (I/C)	Innes Ireland	7	Q5	N/C 60 laps/80
		22 May	**DUTCH Grand Prix**	Trevor Taylor	16	Q14	13th – 73 laps/75
		3 Jun	Silver City Trophy	Trevor Taylor	22	Q11	9th – 69 laps/76
		8 Jul	Brit Emp Trophy, Silverstone (I/C)	Innes Ireland	10	Q5	9th – 50 laps/52
		7 Aug	Guards Trophy, Brands Hatch (I/C)	Innes Ireland	14	Q6	Gearbox lap 34/76

Lotus 18 | 171

Lotus 18 – Colin Chapman's U-turn

Chassis No 371 continued		Engine:	2.5 Coventry Climax FPF 4IL (1960 F1 & 1961 I/C) / 1.5 Coventry Climax FPF 4IL (1960 F2 & 1961-62 F1)			
	Entrant	Date	Event	Driver	No	Grid	Result
		20 Aug	Kanonloppet, Karlskoga	Innes Ireland	9	Q5	Transmission lap 10/30
		27 Aug	Danske Grand Prix, Roskilde	Jim Clark	4	NT	N/C 60 laps/80
		23 Sep	Int Gold Cup, Oulton Park	Trevor Taylor	6	Q13	Exhaust lap 40/60
	Jim Hall	8 Oct	**UNITED STATES Grand Prix**	Jim Hall	17	Q18	Fuel pipe lap 76/100
1962	Jim Hall	4 Nov	Gran Premio de Mexico	Homer Rader	24	Q14	8th – 57 laps/60

Chassis No 372		Engine:	2.5 Coventry Climax FPF 4IL (1960 F1 & 1961 I/C) / 1.5 Coventry Climax FPF 4IL (1960 F2 & 1961-62 F1)			
	Entrant	Date	Event	Driver	No	Grid	Result
1960	Team Lotus	8 Apr	Grand Prix de Bruxelles (F2)	Jim Clark	6	Q5	Engine Heat 1
		30 Apr	BARC 200, Aintree (F2)	Innes Ireland	1	Q9	Carburettor lap 20/50
		6 Jun	Crystal Palace Trophy (F2)	Trevor Taylor	1	Q1	1st (=FL)
		1 Aug	Silver City Trophy, Brands Hatch	Innes Ireland	32	Q3	Oil pressure lap 6/50
		28 Aug	Kentish 100, Brands Hatch (F2)	Jim Clark	48	Q3	1st
		17 Sep	Lombank Trophy, Snetterton	Innes Ireland	6	Q1	1st
		24 Sep	Int Gold Cup, Oulton Park	Innes Ireland	4	Q6	Gearbox lap 30/60
		20 Nov	**UNITED STATES Grand Prix**	Innes Ireland	10	Q7	2nd
1961	Team Lotus	3 Apr	Glover Trophy, Goodwood	Innes Ireland	5	Q5	5th
		22 Apr	BARC 200, Aintree	Jim Clark	19	Q5	9th – 48 laps/50
		8 Jul	Brit Emp Trophy, Silverstone (I/C)	Jim Clark	9	Q10	5th – 50 laps/52
		7 Aug	Guards Trophy, Brands Hatch (I/C)	Jim Clark	16	Q7	2nd
	J Wheeler Autosport	8 Oct	**UNITED STATES Grand Prix**	Peter Ryan	16	Q13	9th – 96 laps/100
1962	W Hansgen	4 Nov	Gran Premio de Mexico	Walt Hansgen	60	Q13	Ignition lap 45/60

Chassis No 373		Engine:	2.5 Coventry Climax FPF 4IL (1960 F1) / 1.5 Coventry Climax FPF 4IL (1960 F2 & 1961-62 F1) / 1.5 Borgward RS 4IL (1963)			
	Entrant	Date	Event	Driver	No	Grid	Result
1960	Team Lotus	14 May	International Trophy, Silverstone	John Surtees	12	Q6	Oil leak lap 9/50
		29 May	**MONACO Grand Prix**	John Surtees	26	Q15	Gearbox lap 18/100
		6 Jun	**DUTCH Grand Prix**	Jim Clark	6	Q11	Final drive lap 42/75
		19 Jun	**BELGIAN Grand Prix**	Jim Clark	18	Q9	5th
		3 Jul	**FRENCH Grand Prix**	Jim Clark	24	Q12	5th
		16 Jul	**BRITISH Grand Prix**	John Surtees	9	Q11	2nd
		24 Jul	Großer Preis der Solitude (F2)	Innes Ireland	16	Q11	6th
		1 Aug	Silver City Trophy, Brands Hatch	John Surtees	36	Q6	6th
		14 Aug	**PORTUGUESE Grand Prix**	John Surtees	18	Q1	Radiator lap 37/55 (FL)
		28 Aug	Kentish 100, Brands Hatch (F2)	Innes Ireland	46	Q5	8th
		11 Sep	Danske Grand Prix, Roskilde (F2)	Innes Ireland	2	N/A	2nd
		17 Sep	Lombank Trophy, Snetterton	John Surtees	7	Q4	Engine lap 11/37
		24 Sep	Int Gold Cup, Oulton Park	John Surtees	6	Q7	Fuel pump lap 1/60
		20 Nov	**UNITED STATES Grand Prix**	John Surtees	11	Q6	Accident lap 3/75
1961	Scuderia Colonia	3 Apr	Grand Prix de Pau	W Seidel	20	Q15	Oil leak lap 40/100
		9 Apr	Grand Prix de Bruxelles	W Seidel	28	Q11	Gearbox Heat 1
		16 Apr	Preis von Wien	W Seidel	5	Q6	2nd
		25 Apr	Gran Premio di Siracusa	W Seidel	40	Q19	N/C 49 laps/56
		22 May	London Trophy, Crystal Palace	W Seidel	26	Q6	5th
		3 Jun	Silver City Trophy, Brands Hatch	W Seidel	48	Q16	Gearbox lap 12/76
	Equipe Nationale Belge	18 Jun	**BELGIAN Grand Prix**	Lucien Bianchi	12	NT	Oil pipe lap 9/30
	Scuderia Colonia	15 Jul	**BRITISH Grand Prix**	W Seidel	52	Q22	N/C 58 laps/75
		23 Jul	Großer Preis der Solitude	W Seidel	15	Q14	Steering 7/25
		6 Aug	**GERMAN Grand Prix**	W Seidel	26	Q23	Steering lap 3/15
		3 Sep	Gran Premio di Modena	W Seidel	24		DNQ
		10 Sep	**ITALIAN Grand Prix**	W Seidel	56	Q28	Engine lap 1/43
		17 Sep	Flugplatzrennen Zeltweg	W Seidel	16	Q6	Engine lap 36/80
		23 Sep	Int Gold Cup, Oulton Park	W Seidel	28	Q18	10th – 56 laps/60

Appendix II: Lotus 18 Race Record – Chassis by Chassis

Chassis No 373 continued
Engine: 2.5 Coventry Climax FPF 4IL (1960 F1) / 1.5 Coventry Climax FPF 4IL (1960 F2 & 1961-62 F1) / 1.5 Borgward RS 4IL (1963)

Year	Entrant	Date	Event	Driver	No	Grid	Result
1962	Autosport Team W Seidel	23 Apr	Lavant Cup, Goodwood	Günther Seifert	12	Q11	Accident lap 3/21
		23 Apr	Glover Trophy, Goodwood	Günther Seifert	12	Q16	DNS accident previous race
		29 Apr	BARC 200, Aintree	Günther Seifert	27	Q22	N/C 37 laps/50
		20 May	Gran Premio di Napoli	Günther Seifert	48		DNQ
		11 Jun	Crystal Palace Trophy	Günther Seifert	5	Q10	Gearbox lap 21/36
	Emeryson Cars	17 Jun	**BELGIAN Grand Prix**	J Camp' Jones	4	Q19	N/C 16 laps/32
	Autosport Team W Seidel	15 Jul	Großer Preis der Solitude	Günther Seifert	23	Q13	N/C 18 laps/25
		19 Aug	Grand Premio del Mediterraneo	Günther Seifert	6	Q12	N/C 26 laps/50
		1 Sep	Int Gold Cup, Oulton Park	Günther Seifert	12	Q22	N/C 50 laps/73
1963	Kurt Kuhnke	19 May	Gran Premio di Roma, Vallelunga	Ernst Maring	16		DNQ
		28 Jul	Großer Preis der Solitude	Ernst Maring	11	Q25	Engine lap 17/25
		11 Aug	Kanonloppet, Karlskoga	Ernst Maring	15	Q10	Accident Heat 1.

Chassis No 374
Engine: 2.5 Coventry Climax FPF 4IL (1960 F1 & 1961 I/C) / 1.5 Coventry Climax FPF 4IL (1961 F1)

Year	Entrant	Date	Event	Driver	No	Grid	Result
1960	Team Lotus	3 Jul	**FRENCH Grand Prix**	Ron Flockhart	22	Q8	6th
		16 Jul	**BRITISH Grand Prix**	Jim Clark	8	Q8	16th – 70 laps/77
		24 Jul	Großer Preis der Solitude (F2)	Jim Clark	17	Q1	8th
		1 Aug	Silver City Trophy, Brands Hatch	Jim Clark	34	Q1	Gearbox lap 21/50 (=FL)
		14 Aug	**PORTUGUESE Grand Prix**	Jim Clark	14	Q8	3rd
		28 Aug	Kentish 100, Brands Hatch (F2)	John Surtees	16	Q7	Accident lap 18/40
		11 Sep	Danske Grand Prix, Roskilde (F2)	Graham Hill	11	N/A	3rd (FL)
		17 Sep	Lombank Trophy, Snetterton	Jim Clark	8	Q2	2nd (FL)
		24 Sep	Int Gold Cup, Oulton Park	Jim Clark	5	Q2	Accident lap 13/60 (FL)
1961	Team Lotus	26 Mar	Lombank Trophy, Snetterton (I/C)	Innes Ireland	6	Q1	Gearbox lap 14/37 (FL)
		3 Apr	Grand Prix de Pau	Trevor Taylor	8	Q6	Transmission lap 41/100
		9 Apr	Grand Prix de Bruxelles	Jim Clark	22	Q6	Gearbox Heat 1
		22 Apr	BARC 200, Aintree	Trevor Taylor	20	Q14	N/C 41 laps/50
		25 Apr	Gran Premio di Siracusa	Jim Clark	20	Q12	6th – 53 laps/56
		6 May	Int Trophy, Silverstone (I/C)	Jim Clark	8	Q9	Clutch lap 55/80
	SJ Diggory	7 Aug	Guards Trophy, Brands Hatch (I/C)	Bruce Halford	22	Q14	Final drive lap 26/76

Chassis No 376
Engine: 2.5 Coventry Climax FPF 4IL (1960 F1)

Year	Entrant	Date	Event	Driver	No	Grid	Result
1960	RRC Walker Racing Team	29 May	**MONACO Grand Prix**	Stirling Moss	28	Q1	1st
		6 Jun	**DUTCH Grand Prix**	Stirling Moss	7	Q1	4th (FL)
		19 Jun	**BELGIAN Grand Prix**	Stirling Moss	12		DNS – accident in practice
		14 Aug	**PORTUGUESE Grand Prix**	Stirling Moss	12	Q4	DSQ lap 51/55
		20 Nov	**UNITED STATES Grand Prix**	Stirling Moss	5	Q1	1st

Chassis No 901
Engine: 2.5 Vanwall V254 4IL (1960 F1)

Year	Entrant	Date	Event	Driver	No	Grid	Result
1960	Vandervell Products Ltd.	17 Sep	Lombank Trophy, Snetterton	Tony Brooks	15		DNS Engine in practice

Chassis No 902
Engine: 2.5 Maserati 250S 4IL (1960 F1) / 1.5 Maserati 150S 4IL (1960 F2 & 1961-63 F1)

Year	Entrant	Date	Event	Driver	No	Grid	Result
1960	Scuderia Centro Sud	24 Sep	Int Gold Cup, Oulton Park	Ian Burgess	22	NT	Suspension lap 16/60
		2 Oct	Gran Premio di Modena (F2)	Ian Burgess	4	Q7	Engine lap 29/100
1961	Prince Gaetano Starrabba	3 Sep	Gran Premio di Modena	G Scarlatti	18	Q14	Engine lap 4/100
		10 Sep	**ITALIAN Grand Prix**	G Starrabba	72	Q30	Engine lap 19/43
		12 Oct	Coppa Italia, Vallelunga	G Starrabba	4	Q5	Engine Heat 2
1962	Prince Gaetano Starrabba	20 May	Gran Premio di Napoli	G Starrabba	26	Q10	Transmission lap1/60

Lotus 18 | 173

Lotus 18 – Colin Chapman's U-turn

Chassis No 902 continued — Engine: 2.5 Maserati 250S 4IL (1960 F1) / 1.5 Maserati 150S 4IL (1960 F2 & 1961–63 F1)

Entrant	Date	Event	Driver	No	Grid	Result
1963 Prince Gaetano Starrabba	21 Apr	Gran Premio Citta di Imola	G Starrabba	28	Q13	Throttle cable lap 5/50
	25 Apr	Gran Premio di Siracusa	G Starrabba	28	Q10	N/C 49 laps/56
	19 May	Gran Premio di Roma, Vallelunga	G Starrabba	12	Q10	5th – 76 laps/80
	18 Aug	Gran Premio del Mediterraneo	G Starrabba	32		DNQ

Chassis No 903 — Engine: 1.5 Coventry Climax FPF 4IL (1960 F2 & 1961 F1) / 2.5 Coventry Climax FPF 4IL (1961 I/C)

Entrant	Date	Event	Driver	No	Grid	Result
1960 Mrs L Bryden-Brown	31 Jul	Großer Preis von Deutschland (F2)	Dan Gurney	21	Q8	8th
	28 Aug	Kentish 100, Brands Hatch (F2)	Dan Gurney	50	Q1	2nd (FL)
1961 Mrs L Bryden-Brown	3 Apr	Lavant Cup, Goodwood (I/C)	Dan Gurney	18	Q5	Accident lap 20/21
	22 Apr	BARC 200, Aintree	Dan Gurney	23	Q15	14th – 47 laps/50
	6 May	Int Trophy, Silverstone (I/C)	Dan Gurney	21		DNS – accident in practice
	3 Jun	Silver City Trophy, Brands Hatch	Dan Gurney	32	Q12	5th – 74 laps/76
	15 Jul	**BRITISH Grand Prix**	Tony Maggs	50	Q24	13th – 69 laps/75
	6 Aug	**GERMAN Grand Prix**	Tony Maggs	33	Q22	11th

Chassis No 904 — Engine: 1.5 Coventry Climax FPF 4IL (1960 F2 & 1961–63 F1) / 2.5 Coventry Climax FPF 4IL (1961 I/C)

Entrant	Date	Event	Driver	No	Grid	Result
1960 Reg Parnell (Racing)	1 Aug	Aintree Trophy, Aintree (F2)	Geoff Duke	1	N/A	DNF Engine
	6 Aug	Vanwall Trophy, Snetterton (F2)	Geoff Duke	74	N/A	Engine lap 7/25
RHH Parnell	28 Aug	Kentish 100, Brands Hatch (F2)	Geoff Duke	52	Q20	Accident lap 18/40
	11 Sep	Danske Grand Prix, Roskilde (F2)	Geoff Duke	4	N/A	DNF
	18 Sep	Flugplatzrennen Zeltweg (F2)	Tim Parnell	11	Q7	DNF
	2 Oct	Gran Premio di Modena (F2)	Stirling Moss	16	Q2	Engine lap 21/100
	8 Oct	Preis von Tirol, Innsbruck (F2)	Tim Parnell	167	N/A	DNF
1961 RHH Parnell	26 Mar	Lombank Trophy, Snetterton	Tim Parnell	19	Q7	5th – 34 laps/36
	9 Apr	Grand Prix de Bruxelles	André Pilette	24	Q17	Gear selector Heat 1
	16 Apr	Preis von Wien	Tim Parnell	10	Q5	N/C 34 laps/55
	22 Apr	BARC 200, Aintree	Tim Parnell	25	NT	Engine lap 7/50
	6 May	Int Trophy, Silverstone (I/C)	Tim Parnell	22	Q18	Accident lap 8/80
(The Three Musketeers)	14 May	Gran Premio di Napoli	Tim Parnell	8	Q12	8th – 54 laps/60
	3 Jun	Silver City Trophy, Brands Hatch	Tim Parnell	38	Q19	7th – 71 laps/76
	8 Jul	Brit Emp Trophy, Silverstone (I/C)	Tim Parnell	23	Q15	Spin lap 10/52
	15 Jul	**BRITISH Grand Prix**	Tim Parnell	38	Q29	Clutch lap 12/75
	20 Aug	Kanonloppet, Karlskoga	Tim Parnell	12	Q7	5th – 28 laps/30
	27 Aug	Danske Grand Prix, Roskilde	Tim Parnell	10	Q7	5th
	3 Sep	Gran Premio di Modena	Tim Parnell	48		DNQ
	10 Sep	**ITALIAN Grand Prix**	Tim Parnell	16	Q27	10th – 40 laps/43
	17 Sep	Flugplatzrennen Zeltweg	Tim Parnell	15	Q12	7th – 74 laps/80
	23 Sep	Int Gold Cup, Oulton Park	Tim Parnell	18	Q21	Fuel pump lap 1/60
	1 Oct	Lewis-Evans Trophy, Brands Hatch	Tim Parnell	11	Q4	3rd
1962 Team Alexis	1 Sep	Int Gold Cup, Oulton Park	P Robinson	16	Q16	Engine lap 1/73
1963 A Robinson & Sons	30 Mar	Lombank Trophy, Snetterton	P Robinson	14	Q7	Engine lap 16/50
	15 Apr	Glover Trophy, Goodwood	P Robinson	9	Q10	8th – 39 laps/42
	27 Apr	BARC 200, Aintree	P Robinson	18	Q12	Engine lap 2/50
	11 May	International Trophy, Silverstone	P Robinson	26	Q19	Transmission lap 34/52
RHH Parnell	28 Jul	Großer Preis der Solitude	P Robinson	22	Q19	N/C 20 laps/25

Chassis No 905 — Engine: 1.5 Coventry Climax FPF 4IL (1960 F2 & 1961–62 F1)

Entrant	Date	Event	Driver	No	Grid	Result
1960 Scuderia Centro Sud	28 Aug	Kentish 100, Brands Hatch (F2)	Ian Burgess	44	Q21	13th – 36 laps/40
1961 Camoradi International	14 May	Gran Premio di Napoli	Ian Burgess	30	Q5	4th – 58 laps/60
	22 May	**DUTCH Grand Prix**	Ian Burgess	18		DNS Reserve entry
	18 Jun	**BELGIAN Grand Prix**	Ian Burgess	50		DNQ
	2 Jul	**FRENCH Grand Prix**	Ian Burgess	38	Q24	14th – 42 laps/52
	15 Jul	**BRITISH Grand Prix**	Ian Burgess	44	Q25	14th – 69 laps/75

Appendix II: Lotus 18 Race Record – Chassis by Chassis

Chassis No 905 continued
Engine: 1.5 Coventry Climax FPF 4IL (1960 F2 & 1961-62 F1)

	Entrant	Date	Event	Driver	No	Grid	Result
1962	Ecurie Excelsior	23 Apr	Lavant Cup, Goodwood	J Chamberlain	16	Q7	5th – 19 laps/21
		23 Apr	Glover Trophy, Goodwood	J Chamberlain	16	Q12	Overheating lap 5/42
		29 Apr	BARC 200, Aintree	J Chamberlain	20	Q18	DSQ push-start lap 1/50
		12 May	International Trophy, Silverstone	J Chamberlain	24	Q22	16th – 46 laps/52
		20 May	Gran Premio di Napoli	J Chamberlain	8		DNQ
		11 Jun	Crystal Palace Trophy	J Chamberlain	7	NT	Engine lap 1/36
		21 Jul	**BRITISH Grand Prix**	J Chamberlain	46	Q20	N/C 64 laps/75
		5 Aug	**GERMAN Grand Prix**	J Chamberlain	30		DNQ
		12 Aug	Kanonloppet, Karlskoga	Olle Nygren	15	Q10	Gearbox lap 6/30
		26 Aug	Danske Grand Prix	J Chamberlain	20	Q10	N/C 46 laps/80
		16 Sep	**ITALIAN Grand Prix**	J Chamberlain	26		DNQ
		4 Nov	Gran Premio de Mexico	J Chamberlain	52	Q16	N/C 53 laps/60

Chassis No 906
Engine: 2.5 Coventry Climax FPF 4IL (1960 F1 & 1961 I/C) / 1.5 Coventry Climax FPF 4IL (1961 F1 to 4/61) / 1.5 Coventry Climax FWMV V8 (1961 F1 from 09/61)

	Entrant	Date	Event	Driver	No	Grid	Result
1960	RRC Walker Racing Team	24 Sep	Int Gold Cup, Oulton Park	Stirling Moss	7	Q1	1st
1961	RRC Walker Racing Team	9 Apr	Grand Prix de Bruxelles, Brussels	Stirling Moss	18	Q9	7th
		16 Apr	Preis von Wien	Stirling Moss	7	Q1	1st (FL)
		25 Apr	Gran Premio di Siracusa	Stirling Moss	18	Q7	8th – Engine lap 52/56
	UDT Laystall Racing Team	6 May	Int Trophy, Silverstone (I/C)	Henry Taylor	14	Q17	4th
	RRC Walker Racing Team	10 Sep	**ITALIAN Grand Prix**	Stirling Moss	28		DNS – overheating in practice
		8 Oct	**UNITED STATES Grand Prix**	Stirling Moss	7		DNS – overheating in practice
1962	RRC Walker Racing Team	1 Apr	Grand Prix de Bruxelles, Brussels	Stirling Moss	1	Q2	Engine Heat 2 (FL)
	UDT Laystall Racing Team	14 Apr	Lombank Trophy, Snetterton	Stirling Moss	7	Q1	7th – 47 laps/50 (FL)
		23 Apr	Glover Trophy, Goodwood	Stirling Moss	7	Q1	Accident lap 36/42 (=FL) Chassis written-off

Chassis No 907
Engine: 2.5 Coventry Climax FPF 4IL (1960 F1) / 1.5 Coventry Climax FPF 4IL (1961 F1)

	Entrant	Date	Event	Driver	No	Grid	Result
1960	Jim Hall	20 Nov	**UNITED STATES Grand Prix**	Jim Hall	24	Q12	7th – 73 laps/75
1961	J Frank Harrison	8 Oct	**UNITED STATES Grand Prix**	Lloyd Ruby	26	Q19	Magneto drive lap 76/100

Chassis No 908
Engine: 1.5 Coventry Climax FPF 4IL (1961 F1)

	Entrant	Date	Event	Driver	No	Grid	Result
1961	Camoradi International	3 Apr	Grand Prix de Pau	Ian Burgess	16	Q16	Gearbox lap 25/100
		9 Apr	Grand Prix de Bruxelles	Ian Burgess	12	Q18	8th
		22 Apr	BARC 200, Aintree	Ian Burgess	14	Q25	DSQ lap 34/50
		23 July	Großer Preis der Solitude	Lloyd Casner	14		DNS – engine in practice

Chassis No 909
Engine: 1.5 Coventry Climax FPF 4IL (1960 F2 & 1961-62 F1)

	Entrant	Date	Event	Driver	No	Grid	Result
1960	AE Marsh	28 Aug	Kentish 100, Brands Hatch (F2)	Tony Marsh	28	Q16	6th
		18 Sep	Flugplatzrennen Zeltweg (F2)	Tony Marsh	10	Q3	5th – 57 laps/59
		2 Oct	Gran Premio di Modena (F2)	Tony Marsh	22	Q10	7th – 94 laps/100
		8 Oct	Preis von Tirol, Innsbruck (F2)	Tony Marsh	162	N/A	4th
		16 Oct	Lewis-Evans Trophy, B/Hatch (F2)	Tony Marsh	40	Q1	1st (FL)
1961	AE Marsh	3 April	Glover Trophy, Goodwood	Tony Marsh	29	Q9	7th
		9 Apr	Grand Prix de Bruxelles	Tony Marsh	26	Q8	3rd
		22 Apr	BARC 200, Aintree	Tony Marsh	27	Q8	7th
		22 May	London Trophy, Crystal Palace	Tony Marsh	24	Q5	3rd
		3 Jun	Silver City Trophy, Brands Hatch	Tony Marsh	34	Q13	6th – 71 laps/76
	(Equipe Nationale Belge)	18 Jun	**BELGIAN Grand Prix**	W Mairesse	10	NT	Engine lap 7/30
		15 Jul	**BRITISH Grand Prix**	Tony Marsh	48	Q27	Ignition lap 25/75
		6 Aug	**GERMAN Grand Prix**	Tony Marsh	37	Q20	16th
1962	G Ashmore	11 Jun	Crystal Palace Trophy	Graham Eden	12	Q9	Gearbox lap 1/36
		1 Sep	Int Gold Cup, Oulton Park	Graham Eden	6	Q21	Engine lap 27/73

Lotus 18 | 175

Lotus 18 – Colin Chapman's U-turn

Chassis No 911 — Engine: 1.5 Borgward RS 4IL (1961-62 F1)

Year	Entrant	Date	Event	Driver	No	Grid	Result
1961	Ecurie Wolman	9 Dec	Rand Grand Prix, Kyalami	H Menzler	16	Q10	Overheating lap 24/75
		17 Dec	Natal Grand Prix, Westmead	H Menzler	16	Q14	DNF Suspension
		26 Dec	South African Grand Prix	H Menzler	16	Q14	10th – 75 laps/80
1962	Ecurie Wolman	2 Jan	Cape Grand Prix, Killarney	H Menzler	16	Q11	10th – 57 laps/60
	V McWilliams	15 Dec	Rand Grand Prix, Kyalami	V McWilliams	30		DNQ
		22 Dec	Natal Grand Prix, Westmead	V McWilliams	30	Q13	DNF

Chassis No 912 — Engine: 1.5 Coventry Climax FPF 4IL (1961-62 F1)

Year	Entrant	Date	Event	Driver	No	Grid	Result
1961	RRC Walker Racing Team	3 Apr	Glover Trophy, Goodwood	Stirling Moss	7	Q1	4th
		14 May	**MONACO Grand Prix**	Stirling Moss	20	Q1	1st (FL)
		22 May	**DUTCH Grand Prix**	Stirling Moss	14	Q4	4th
		18 Jun	**BELGIAN Grand Prix**	Stirling Moss	14	Q8	8th
		2 Jul	**FRENCH Grand Prix**	Stirling Moss	26	Q4	Brake pipe lap 31/52
		15 Jul	**BRITISH Grand Prix**	Stirling Moss	28	Q5	Brake pipe lap 44/75
		6 Aug	**GERMAN Grand Prix**	Stirling Moss	7	Q3	1st
		3 Sep	Gran Premio di Modena	Stirling Moss	26	Q1	1st (FL)
	(Team Lotus)	10 Sep	**ITALIAN Grand Prix**	Innes Ireland	38	Q9	Chassis lap 5/43
		8 Oct	**UNITED STATES Grand Prix**	Stirling Moss	7	Q3	Engine lap 58/100
1962	Scud SSS Rep di Venezia	1 Apr	Grand Prix de Bruxelles, Brussels	N Vaccarella	15		DNS accident in practice
		23 Apr	Grand Prix de Pau	N Vaccarella	18	Q11	6th – 98 laps/100
		12 May	International Trophy, Silverstone	N Vaccarella	18	Q18	Engine lap 32/52
		3 Jun	**MONACO Grand Prix**	N Vaccarella	42		DNQ accident in practice
		11 Jun	2000 Guineas, Mallory Park	Colin Davis	11	Q12	7th – 73 laps/75
		1 Jul	Grand Prix de Reims	Carlo Abate	38	Q20	Spun off lap 22/50
		19 Aug	Gran Premio del Mediterraneo	N Vaccarella	28	Q6	DNS electrical fault

Chassis No 913 — Engine: 1.5 Coventry Climax FPF 4IL (1961-65 F1)

Year	Entrant	Date	Event	Driver	No	Grid	Result
1961	Scuderia Dolomiti	16 Apr	Preis von Wien	Ernesto Prinoth	8	Q7	3rd
		25 Apr	Gran Premio di Siracusa, Sicily	Ernesto Prinoth	4		DNS Gasket in practice
		14 May	Gran Premio di Napoli	Ernesto Prinoth	40	Q6	N/C 34 laps/60
		17 Sep	Flugplatzrennen Zeltweg	Ernesto Prinoth	18	Q9	Accident lap 6/80
		12 Oct	Coppa Italia, Vallelunga	Ernesto Prinoth	2	Q3	2nd
1962	Scuderia Jolly Club	16 Sep	**ITALIAN Grand Prix**	Ernesto Prinoth	54		DNQ
1963	Scuderia Jolly Club	21 Apr	Gran Premio Citta di Imola	Ernesto Prinoth	38	Q10	Misfire lap 41/50
		1 Sep	Gross Preis von Österreich, Zeltweg	Ernesto Prinoth	18	Q9	Suspension lap 13/80
1965	Scuderia Nord-Ouest	15 Aug	Gran Premio del Mediterraneo	Colin Davis	18		DNQ

Chassis No 914 — Engine: 1.5 Coventry Climax FPF 4IL (1961-62 F1) / 1.5 Borgward RS 4IL (1963-64 F1)

Year	Entrant	Date	Event	Driver	No	Grid	Result
1961	Scuderia Colonia	3 Apr	Grand Prix de Pau	Jo Bonnier	18	Q10	2nd
		9 Apr	Grand Prix de Bruxelles	M Trintignant	10		DNS Final drive in practice
		22 Apr	BARC 200, Aintree	Michael May	24	Q21	Engine lap 7/50
		14 May	**MONACO Grand Prix**	Michael May	8	Q13	Oil leak lap 42/100
		3 Jun	Silver City Trophy, Brands Hatch	Michael May	52	Q14	Overheating lap 16/76
		2 Jul	**FRENCH Grand Prix**	Michael May	46	Q22	11th – 48 laps/52
		23 Jul	Großer Preis der Solitude	Michael May	16	Q12	Accident lap1/25
		6 Aug	**GERMAN Grand Prix**	Michael May	25		DNQ Accident in practice
1962	Autosport Team W Seidel	23 Apr	Grand Prix de Pau	Kurt Kuhnke	36		DNQ
		15 Jul	Großer Preis der Solitude	Kurt Kuhnke	22	Q10	Engine lap 4/25
1963	Kurt Kuhnke	19 May	Gran Premio di Roma, Vallelunga	Kurt Kuhnke	14		DNQ
		28 Jul	Großer Preis der Solitude	Kurt Kuhnke	10	Q24	Engine lap 1/25
		4 Aug	**GERMAN Grand Prix**	Kurt Kuhnke	27		DNQ
		11 Aug	Kanonloppet, Karlskoga	Kurt Kuhnke	14	NT	Fuel injection Heat 2

Appendix II: Lotus 18 Race Record – Chassis by Chassis

Chassis No 914 continued — Engine: 1.5 Coventry Climax FPF 4IL (1961-62 F1) / 1.5 Borgward RS 4IL (1963-64 F1)

Year	Entrant	Date	Event	Driver	No	Grid	Result
1964	Kurt Kuhnke	19 Jul	Großer Preis der Solitude	"Parker"	18	Q17	Accident lap 1/20

Chassis No 915 — Engine: 2.5 Coventry Climax FPF 4IL (1961 I/C) / 1.5 Coventry Climax FPF 4IL (1961-63 F1)

Year	Entrant	Date	Event	Driver	No	Grid	Result
1961	UDT Laystall Racing Team	26 Mar	Lombank Trophy, Snetterton (I/C)	Cliff Allison	4	Q3	2nd
		3 Apr	Glover Trophy, Goodwood	Cliff Allison	15	Q8	8th – 40 laps/42
		9 Apr	Grand Prix de Bruxelles	Cliff Allison	14	Q12	5th
		22 Apr	BARC 200, Aintree	Cliff Allison	21	Q11	15th – 46 laps/50
		6 May	Int Trophy, Silverstone (I/C)	Cliff Allison	12	Q11	Spun off lap 68/80
		14 May	**MONACO Grand Prix**	Henry Taylor	34		DNQ
		22 May	London Trophy, Crystal Palace	Cliff Allison	20	Q4	8th – 35 laps/37
		8 Jul	Brit Emp Trophy, Silverstone (I/C)	Lucien Bianchi	3	Q16	10th (with H Taylor)
		7 Aug	Guards Trophy, Brands Hatch (I/C)	Dan Gurney	20	Q9	Gearbox lap 26/76
1963	RHH Parnell	11 May	International Trophy, Silverstone	Tim Parnell	22	Q16	Engine lap 35/52
		19 May	Gran Premio di Roma, Vallelunga	Tim Parnell	4	Q6	N/C 68 laps/80
		28 Jul	Großer Preis der Solitude	Ron Carter	21	Q26	Engine lap 2/25
		4 Aug	**GERMAN Grand Prix**	Tim Parnell	30		DNQ
		11 Aug	Kanonloppet, Karlskoga	Ron Carter	19		DNS Engine in practice

Chassis No 916 — Engine: 2.5 Coventry Climax FPF 4IL (1961 I/C) / 1.5 Coventry Climax FPF 4IL (1962-63 F1)

Year	Entrant	Date	Event	Driver	No	Grid	Result
1961	UDT Laystall Racing Team	26 Mar	Lombank Trophy, Snetterton	Henry Taylor	5	Q4	2nd
		3 Apr	Glover Trophy, Goodwood	Henry Taylor	17	Q7	6th
		9 Apr	Grand Prix de Bruxelles	Henry Taylor	16	Q10	Front suspension Heat 1
		22 Apr	BARC 200, Aintree	Henry Taylor	22	Q17	Gearbox lap 26/50
		14 May	**MONACO Grand Prix**	Cliff Allison	32	Q14	8th – 93 laps/100
		22 May	London Trophy, Crystal Palace	Henry Taylor	22	Q2	2nd (=FL)
		3 Jun	Silver City Trophy	Henry Taylor	28	Q10	8th – 69 laps/76
		2 Jul	**FRENCH Grand Prix**	Henry Taylor	30	Q25	10th 49 laps/52
		8 Jul	Br Emp Trophy, Silverstone (I/C)	Henry Taylor	4	Q9	Transmission lap 3/52
		15 Jul	**BRITISH Grand Prix**	Henry Taylor	30	Q17	Accident lap 5/75
		7 Aug	Guards Trophy, Brands Hatch (I/C)	M Gregory	18	Q11	Accident lap 5/76
		27 Aug	Danske Grand Prix, Roskilde	Stirling Moss	7	Q1	1st (FL)
		26 Dec	South African Grand Prix	M Gregory	6	Q5	Brake pipe lap 9/80
1962	UDT Laystall Racing Team	1 Apr	Grand Prix de Bruxelles, Brussels	Innes Ireland	2	Q7	3rd
		14 Apr	Lombank Trophy, Snetterton	Innes Ireland	6	Q6	Accident lap 5/50
		23 Apr	Glover Trophy, Goodwood	Innes Ireland	8	Q4	3rd
		29 Apr	BARC 200, Aintree	Innes Ireland	8	Q4	Engine lap 26/50
1963	RHH Parnell	15 Apr	Grand Prix de Pau	André Pilette	28	Q15	N/C 87 laps/100
	A Pilette	27 Apr	BARC 200, Aintree	André Pilette	19	Q16	DNS
		11 May	International Trophy, Silverstone	André Pilette	23	Q20	DNS

Chassis No 917 — Engine: 1.5 Coventry Climax FPF 4IL (1961-63 F1)

Year	Entrant	Date	Event	Driver	No	Grid	Result
1961	UDT Laystall Racing Team	3 Jun	Silver City Trophy	Jo Bonnier	30	Q15	N/C 57 laps/76
		2 Jul	**FRENCH Grand Prix**	Lucien Bianchi	28	Q19	Clutch lap 21/52
		15 Jul	**BRITISH Grand Prix**	Lucien Bianchi	32	Q30	Gearbox lap 45/75
		23 Jul	Großer Preis der Solitude	Stirling Moss	17	Q5	Gearbox lap 22/25
		20 Aug	Kanonloppet, Karlskoga	C Hammarlund	6	Q8	Spin lap 4/30
		27 Aug	Danske Grand Prix, Roskilde	Henry Taylor	9	Q4	4th
		3 Sep	Gran Premio di Modena	M Gregory	32	Q7	N/C 71 laps/100
		10 Sep	**ITALIAN Grand Prix**	M Gregory	22	Q17	Rear wishbone lap 11/43
		23 Sep	Int. Gold Cup, Oulton Park	M Gregory	14	Q8	5th – 58 laps/60
		8 Oct	**UNITED STATES Grand Prix**	M Gregory	22	Q11	Gear selector lap 23/100
		9 Dec	Rand Grand Prix, Kyalami	M Gregory	6	Q3	Overheating lap 42/75
		17 Dec	Natal Grand Prix, Westmead	M Gregory	6	Q4	Engine lap 14/89

Lotus 18 | 177

Lotus 18 – Colin Chapman's U-turn

Chassis No 917 continued		Engine:	1.5 Coventry Climax FPF 4IL (1961-63 F1)				
	Entrant	Date	Event	Driver	No	Grid	Result
1962	UDT Laystall Racing Team	2 Jan	Cape Grand Prix, Killarney	M Gregory	6	Q4	4th
		1 Apr	Grand Prix de Bruxelles, Brussels	M Gregory	3	Q9	Front suspension Heat 1
		14 Apr	Lombank Trophy, Snetterton	M Gregory	8	Q5	Accident lap 5/50
		23 Apr	Glover Trophy, Goodwood	M Gregory	9	Q8	5th
		29 Apr	BARC 200, Aintree	M Gregory	9	Q7	Engine lap 34/50
		20 May	**DUTCH Grand Prix**	M Gregory	10	Q16	Gearbox lap 54/80
		11 Jun	2000 Guineas, Mallory Park	M Gregory	7	Q7	5th
1963	RHH Parnell	15 Apr	Grand Prix de Pau	Tim Parnell	26	Q12	Engine lap 26/100
		27 Apr	BARC 200, Aintree	Tim Parnell	14	Q17	DSQ push start lap 8/50
	A Pilette	28 Jul	Großer Preis der Solitude	André Pilette	12	Q22	N/C 21 laps/25
		4 Aug	**GERMAN Grand Prix**	André Pilette	29		DNQ
		11 Aug	Kanonloppet, Karlskoga	André Pilette	20	Q12	10th – 37 laps/40
		1 Sep	Gross Preis von Österreich, Zeltweg	André Pilette	16	Q15	N/C 64 laps/80
		8 Sep	**ITALIAN Grand Prix**	André Pilette	46		DNQ
		21 Sep	Int. Gold Cup, Oulton Park	André Pilette	14	Q21	N/C 63 laps/73

Chassis No 918		Engine:	1.5 Coventry Climax FPF 4IL (1961 64 F1)				
	Entrant	Date	Event	Driver	No	Grid	Result
1961	UDT Laystall Racing Team	3 Jun	Silver City Trophy	Stirling Moss	26	Q1	1st (FL)
		18 Jun	**BELGIAN Grand Prix**	Cliff Allison	16		DNS – accident in practice
		20 Aug	Kanonloppet, Karlskoga	Stirling Moss	1	NT	1st (FL)
		27 Aug	Danske Grand Prix, Roskilde	M Gregory	8	Q8	Gearbox Heat 2
		3 Sep	Gran Premio di Modena	Henry Taylor	30	Q11	Engine lap 42/100
		10 Sep	**ITALIAN Grand Prix**	Henry Taylor	20	Q23	11th – 39 laps/43
		23 Sep	Int. Gold Cup, Oulton Park	Henry Taylor	15	Q12	8th – 56 laps/60
		8 Oct	**UNITED STATES Grand Prix**	O Gendebien	21	Q15	11th – 92 laps/100
		17 Dec	Natal Grand Prix, Westmead	Stirling Moss	7	NT	2nd (FL)
		26 Dec	South African Grand Prix	Stirling Moss	7	Q2	2nd
1962	RRC Walker Racing Team	23 Apr	Grand Prix de Pau	M Trintignant	12	Q5	1st
		12 May	International Trophy, Silverstone	M Trintignant	7	Q16	Engine lap 41/52
		11 Jun	2000 Guineas, Mallory Park	Graham Hill	12	Q3	3rd
	Equipe Nationale Belge	17 Jun	**BELGIAN Grand Prix**	Lucien Bianchi	19	Q18	9th – 29 laps/32
1963	Jock Russell	30 Mar	Lombank Trophy, Snetterton	Adam Wyllie	12	Q6	N/C 44 laps/50
		27 Apr	BARC 200, Aintree	Jock Russell	20	Q15	Rear suspension lap 6/50
1964	Jock Russell	14 Mar	Daily Mirror Trophy, Snetterton	Jock Russell	23	Q15	Engine lap 6/35

Chassis No 919		Engine:	1.5 Coventry Climax FPF 4IL (1961-62 F1) / 1.5 Borgward RS 4IL (1963-64 F1) / 1.0 Borgward RS 4IL (1965 F2)				
	Entrant	Date	Event	Driver	No	Grid	Result
1961	RHH Parnell	16 Apr	Preis von Wien	Gerry Ashmore	11	Q3	Brakes lap 5/55
		22 Apr	BARC 200, Aintree	Gerry Ashmore	26	Q12	11th – 48 laps/50
	(The Three Musketeers)	14 May	Gran Premio di Napoli	Gerry Ashmore	10	Q1	2nd
		15 Jul	**BRITISH Grand Prix**	Gerry Ashmore	40	Q26	Ignition lap 7/75
	G Ashmore	6 Aug	**GERMAN Grand Prix**	Gerry Ashmore	27	Q25	17th
		10 Sep	**ITALIAN Grand Prix**	Gerry Ashmore	18	Q25	Accident lap 1/43
1962	G Ashmore	23 Apr	Lavant Cup, Goodwood	Gerry Ashmore	14	NT	Oil pipe lap 12/21
		23 Apr	Glover Trophy, Goodwood	Gerry Ashmore	14	NT	11th – 37 laps/42
	Speed Sport	29 Apr	BARC 200, Aintree	David Piper	22	Q17	N/C 38 laps/50
	G Ashmore	12 May	International Trophy, Silverstone	David Piper	21	Q21	N/C 45 laps/52
	David Piper	20 May	Gran Premio di Napoli	David Piper	46	Q9	N/C 51 laps/60
	Speed Sport	11 Jun	Crystal Palace Trophy	David Piper	6	Q7	7th – 34 laps/36
	G Ashmore	1 Sep	Int. Gold Cup, Oulton Park	Gerry Ashmore	5	Q19	8th – 69 laps/73
		16 Sep	**ITALIAN Grand Prix**	Gerry Ashmore	52		DNQ
1964	K Kuhnke	19 Jul	Großer Preis der Solitude	Ernst Maring	19	Q18	N/C 16 laps/20
1965	E Maring	18 Jul	Großer Preis der Solitude (F2)	Ernst Maring	16	Q19	Clutch lap 7/18

Appendix II: Lotus 18 Race Record – Chassis by Chassis

Chassis No P1		Engine:	1.5 Coventry Climax FPF 4IL (1962 F1)				
	Entrant	Date	Event	Driver	No	Grid	Result
1962	John Dalton	14 Apr	Lombank Trophy, Snetterton	Tony Shelly	15	Q12	5th – 47 laps/50
		23 Apr	Lavant Cup, Goodwood	Tony Shelly	17	Q3	3rd
		23 Apr	Glover Trophy, Goodwood	Tony Shelly	17	Q7	6th – 40 laps/42
		29 Apr	BARC 200, Aintree	Tony Shelly	19	Q13	7th – 48 laps/50
		12 May	International Trophy, Silverstone	Tony Shelly	22	Q20	Accident lap 1/52
		20 May	Gran Premio di Napoli	Tony Shelly	2	Q6	6th – 58 laps/60
		11 Jun	2000 Guineas, Mallory Park	Tony Shelly	1	Q11	8th – 72 laps/75
		1 Jul	Grand Prix de Reims	Tony Shelly	42	Q19	Engine lap 1/50
		21 Jul	**BRITISH Grand Prix**	Tony Shelly	48	Q18	Overheating lap 5/75
		5 Aug	**GERMAN Grand Prix**	Tony Shelly	29		DNQ
		1 Sep	Int. Gold Cup, Oulton Park	Tony Shelly	22	Q14	5th – 69 laps/73

Chassis No P2		Engine:	1.5 Coventry Climax FPF 4IL (1962 – 64 F1) / 2.5/2.75 Coventry Climax FPF 4IL (1966 F1)				
	Entrant	Date	Event	Driver	No	Grid	Result
1962	RHH Parnell	14 Apr	Lombank Trophy, Snetterton	Tim Parnell	14	Q9	Overheating lap 10/50
		29 Apr	BARC 200, Aintree	Tim Parnell	21	Q16	9th – 46 laps/50
		12 May	International Trophy, Silverstone	Tim Parnell	16	Q23	Oil pressure lap 5/52
		20 May	Gran Premio di Napoli	Tim Parnell	14	Q4	7th – 55 laps/60
		11 Jun	2000 Guineas, Mallory Park	John Dalton	3	Q13	Fuel starvation lap 32/75
		26 Aug	Danske Grand Prix	Gary Hocking	22	Q7	4th
	Gary Hocking	1 Sep	Int. Gold Cup, Oulton Park	Gary Hocking	23	Q11	Engine lap 62/73
1963	CR Puzey	14 Dec	Rand Grand Prix, Kyalami	Clive Puzey	15	NT	Gear selector Heat 1
1964	CR Puzey	12 Dec	Rand Grand Prix, Kyalami	Clive Puzey	15	Q15	7th – 48 laps/50
1965	CR Puzey	1 Jan	**SOUTH AFRICAN Grand Prix**	Clive Puzey	24		DNPQ
		4 Dec	Rand Grand Prix, Kyalami	Clive Puzey	17	Q11	9th – 46 laps/50
1966	Clive Puzey (Motors)	1 Jan	South African GP, East London	Clive Puzey	17	Q18	7th
		8 Jan	Cape Sth Easter Trophy, Killarney	Clive Puzey	17	N/A	5th
		5 Mar	Rand Autumn Trophy, Kyalami	Clive Puzey	5	Q6	3rd
		11 Apr	Coronation 100, Pietermaritzburg	Clive Puzey	9	N/A	Engine Heat 1
		4 May	Bulawayo 100, Kumalo	Clive Puzey	5	N/A	3rd
		28 May	SA Rep Festival Trophy, Kyalami	Clive Puzey	5	Q6	Overheating lap 19/40
		26 Jun	Natal Winter Trophy, Pietermaritzb.	Clive Puzey	5	N/A	6th
		11 Jul	Border 100, East London	Clive Puzey	5	N/A	4th
		24 Jul	Mocambique, Lourenco Marques	Clive Puzey	25	N/A	Unknown
		6 Aug	Rand Winter Trophy, Kyalami	Clive Puzey	5	Q6	Gear lever lap 14/40
		21 Aug	Fairfield Trophy, Pietermaritzburg	Clive Puzey	5	Q3	2nd
		3 Sep	Van Riebeek Trophy, Killarney	Clive Puzey	5	N/A	Fire Heat 1
		4 Dec	Rhodesian Grand Prix, Kumalo	Clive Puzey	5	Q6	3rd – 48 laps/50

www.velocebooks.com / www.veloce.co.uk
Details of all current books • New book news • Special offers • Gift vouchers • Forum

APPENDIX III
DRIVERS WHO RACED THE LOTUS 18

Fifty-nine drivers made one or more starts in a Lotus 18 over its competition life between 1960 and 1966. Of the 59, 27 (46%) were British, and, reflecting a true International flavour of drivers at the time, seven were from the USA, five each from Germany and Italy, three each from Belgium, South Africa and Sweden, two from Southern Rhodesia, and one each from Switzerland, Canada, New Zealand and France.

Stirling Moss was far and away the most successful driver of a Lotus 18. He was at the peak of his career by 1961, and rightly regarded as the man to beat; the driver against whom all others measured themselves. In 1960, he scored two Grand Prix wins and one non-Championship win, started from pole position four times, and recorded two fastest laps. In 1961, there were a further two Grand Prix wins with another five in non-Championship events, plus six starts from pole position and seven fastest laps. He continued into 1962, making three starts – two from pole position – with three fastest laps, before his enforced retirement at the wheel of the Lotus 18/21 V8 Special. He

Stirling Moss looks on as the Walker mechanics prepare his 18/21 for the 1961 British Grand Prix in a crowded Aintree paddock. (LAT Photographic)

180 | Lotus 18

Appendix III: Drivers who Raced the Lotus 18

remained the only driver to win a Grand Prix in a Lotus 18. Those four victories, plus six in non-Championship events, accounted for 50% of total Lotus 18 wins. His overall performance confirms him as the undoubted Lotus 18 'ace' of 'aces.'

Lotus 18 Race Winners by Category

	Grands Prix	Other F1	F2	Inter-continental	Total
Stirling Moss	4	6	–	–	10
Innes Ireland	–	3	2	–	5
Jim Clark	–	1	1	–	2
Maurice Trintignant	–	1	–	–	1
Tony Marsh	–	–	1	–	1
Trevor Taylor	–	–	1	–	1
Total	4	11	5	–	20

Innes Ireland made his name driving a Lotus 18, on Easter Monday 1960 at Goodwood, by beating Stirling Moss twice on the same afternoon. He quickly established himself as a leading Grand Prix driver in 1960, winning three non-Championship Formula 1 races and two in Formula 2, together with a single pole position start and four fastest laps. Five wins, although only half of Moss' score, confirmed his status as runner-up 'ace.'

Future World Champion Jim Clark began his Formula 1 and Formula 2 careers behind the wheel of Lotus 18s during 1960. He made a slightly hesitant start and initially appeared more comfortable on British circuits with which he was familiar. He won in Formula 2 at Brands Hatch in 1960, a season in which he accumulated four top six placings, two pole positions and three fastest laps. His first Formula 1 win came in the Pau Grand Prix in early 1961, this second victory aboard a Lotus 18 putting him in third place in the winners' listing.

The veteran French driver Maurice Trintignant had the distinction of scoring the final Formula 1 victory for the Lotus 18 driving the Rob Walker entry to his third career win on the demanding street circuit at Pau in early 1962. This was effectively his first drive in the car as a previous attempt in the 1961 Brussels Grand Prix ended in transmission failure during practice preventing him from making the start. Remaining wins for the 18 were accounted for by Hillclimb Champion Tony Marsh and Clark's Formula Junior team-mate Trevor Taylor. Marsh had an enviable reliability rate of 92% with his privately entry, providing him with a single Formula 2 win and six other placings in Formulae 1 and 2 over 1960-61. Taylor's single win was also scored in Formula 2 and remained his only success in seven starts with the Lotus 18, although he was a lot more successful in the Formula Junior category.

Like Jim Clark, multiple motorcycle Champion John Surtees made his Formula 1 debut in the Lotus 18. He proved competitive from the word go, but ran only a limited schedule of Grands Prix in 1960 due to his other commitments. He never actually scored a win, yet achieved an impressive second place in the 1960 British Grand Prix; then came very close to a win in the Portuguese Grand Prix, having started from pole position.

A number of other prominent Grand Prix drivers made appearances in Lotus 18s, amongst them Dan Gurney, Jo Bonnier and Graham Hill – coincidentally all members of the 1960 BRM team. Gurney instigated the purchase of an 18 by Mrs Louise Bryden-Brown (as he did the purchase of a Lotus 19 by the Arciero brothers), such was his enthusiasm for the cars. In his second of six starts, he put the Bryden-Brown 18 on pole position for the 1960 Formula 2 Kentish 100 at Brands Hatch, finished second and set fastest lap. Jo Bonnier also achieved a second place finish from his two outings in an 18, whilst Graham Hill also made two starts, finishing third on both occasions.

Lotus 18 Drivers in Grands Prix (1960-62)

	Starts	Finishes	1st	2nd	3rd	4th	5th	6th	PP	FL
Stirling Moss	11	7	4	–	–	2	–	–	4	2
Innes Ireland	8	5	–	2	1	–	–	2	–	1
Jim Clark	6	4	–	–	1	–	2	–	–	–
John Surtees	4	1	–	1	–	–	–	–	1	1
Ron Flockhart	1	1	–	–	–	–	–	1	–	–
Others	40	16	–	–	–	–	–	–	–	–
Total	70	34	4	3	2	2	2	3	5	4

Lotus 18 – Colin Chapman's U-turn

Innes Ireland in relaxed pose during the 1960 Monaco Grand Prix. (LAT Photographic)

Appendix III: Drivers who Raced the Lotus 18

Lotus 18 Drivers in non-Championship Formula 1 (1960-66)

	Starts	Finishes	1st	2nd	3rd	4th	5th	6th	PP	FL
Stirling Moss	16	11	6	2	–	1	–	–	8	9
Innes Ireland	15	9	3	–	2	–	1	1	–	1
Jim Clark	9	5	1	1	1	1	–	1	1	4
Maurice Trintignant	2	1	1	–	–	–	–	–	–	–
Henry Taylor	9	6	–	2	–	1	–	1	–	1
Clive Puzey	16	10	–	1	3	1	1	1	–	–
Ernesto Prinoth	6	2	–	1	1	–	–	–	–	–
Wolfgang Seidel	9	3	–	1	–	–	1	–	–	–
Gerry Ashmore	6	4	–	1	–	–	–	–	1	–
Jo Bonnier	2	1	–	1	–	–	–	–	–	–
Tony Marsh	5	5	–	–	2	–	–	1	–	–
Tim Parnell	17	9	–	–	1	–	3	–	–	–
Graham Hill	1	1	–	–	1	–	–	–	–	–
Masten Gregory	13	4	–	–	–	1	3	–	–	–
Ian Burgess	6	3	–	–	–	1	–	–	–	–
Gary Hocking	2	1	–	–	–	1	–	–	–	–
Alan Stacey	4	1	–	–	–	1	–	–	–	–
Tony Shelly	9	7	–	–	–	–	2	2	–	–
Jay Chamberlain	7	2	–	–	–	–	1	–	–	–
Dan Gurney	2	2	–	–	–	–	1	–	–	–
Gaetano Starrabba	5	1	–	–	–	–	1	–	–	–
Cliff Allison	3	3	–	–	–	–	1	–	–	–
John Surtees	4	1	–	–	–	–	–	1	–	–
Nino Vaccarella	2	1	–	–	–	–	–	1	–	–
Others	55	9	–	–	–	–	–	–	–	–
Total	225	102	11	10	11	8	15	9	10	15

Lotus 18 Drivers in Formula 2 (1960)

	Starts	Finishes	1st	2nd	3rd	4th	5th	6th	PP	FL
Innes Ireland	9	7	2	1	–	1	–	1	1	2
Tony Marsh	5	5	1	–	–	1	1	1	1	1
Trevor Taylor	1	1	1	–	–	–	–	–	1	1
Jim Clark	4	3	1	–	–	–	–	–	1	–
Dan Gurney	2	2	–	1	–	–	–	–	1	1
Graham Hill	1	1	–	–	1	–	–	–	–	1
Others	13	1	–	–	–	–	–	–	–	–
Total	35	20	5	2	1	2	1	2	5	6

Lotus 18 Drivers in Inter-Continental Formula (1961)

	Starts	Finishes	1st	2nd	3rd	4th	5th	6th	PP	FL
Jim Clark	3	2	–	1	–	–	1	–	–	–
Cliff Allison	2	1	–	1	–	–	–	–	–	–
Henry Taylor	2	1	–	–	–	1	–	–	–	–
Innes Ireland	4	1	–	–	–	–	–	–	1	1
Others	7	1	–	–	–	–	–	–	–	–
Total	18	6	–	2	–	1	1	–	1	1

Apart from the six drivers scoring wins driving a Lotus 18, an additional 21 drivers finished in top six positions; with a further 11 recording other placings. An unfortunate 21 drivers made one or more starts yet failed to record a single finish.

The highest number of race starts in a Lotus 18 was made by Innes Ireland at 36, a feat he achieved in eight different chassis. 22 of his starts were made in 1960, ten in 1961 and four in 1962. Stirling Moss was second to Innes on 27 starts, including seven in 1960 and 18 in 1961. Emphasising the contribution made by the private entrant in the Lotus 18 story, Tim Parnell was next up with 24 starts, spread over the period from 1960 to 1963. Jim Clark made 22 starts, Masten Gregory 16; whilst Clive Puzey made 13 starts alone in the South African Formula 1 series during 1966.

Lotus 18 – Colin Chapman's U-turn

Drivers who Raced the Lotus 18 – all Formulae 1960-1966

Driver	Country	Born	Died	Chassis driven
Abate, Carlo	Italy	10 Jul 1932		912
Allison, Cliff	Great Britain	8 Feb 1932	7 Apr 2005	915, 916
Ashmore, Gerry	Great Britain	25 Jul 1936		919
Bianchi, Lucien	Belgium	10 Nov 1934	30 Mar 1969	373, 915, 917, 918
Bonnier, Joakim	Sweden	31 Nov 1930	11 Jun 1972	914, 917
Burgess, Ian	Great Britain	6 Jul 1930	19 May 2012	902, 905, 908
Campbell-Jones, John	Great Britain	21 Jan 1930		373
Carter, Ron	Great Britain			915
Chamberlain, Jay	USA	29 Dec 1925	1 Aug 2001	908
Clark, Jim	Great Britain	4 Mar 1936	7 Apr 1968	371, 372, 373, 374,
Dalton, John	Great Britain			P2
Davis, Colin	Great Britain	29 Jul 1933	19 Dec 2012	912
Duke, Geoff	Great Britain	29 Mar 1923	1 May 2015	904
Eden, Graham	Great Britain			909
Flockhart, Ron	Great Britain	16 Jun 1923	12 Apr 1962	374
Gendebien, Olivier	Belgium	12 Jan 1924	2 Oct 1998	918
Gregory, Masten	USA	29 Feb 1932	8 Nov 1985	916, 917, 918
Gurney, Dan	USA	13 Apr 1931		903, 915
Halford, Bruce	Great Britain	18 May 1931	2 Dec 2001	374
Hall, Jim	USA	23 Jul 1935		371, 907
Hammarlund, Carl	Sweden	20 Feb 1921	15 Sep 2006	917
Hansgen, Walt	USA	28 Oct 1919	7 Apr 1966	372
Hill, Graham	Great Britain	15 Feb 1929	29 Nov 1975	374, 918
Hocking, Gary	Southern Rhodesia	30 Sep 1937	21 Dec 1962	P2
Ireland, Innes	Great Britain	12 Jun 1930	22 Oct 1993	369, 370, 371, 372, 373, 374, 912, 916
Kuhnke, Kurt	Germany	30 Apr 1910	8 Feb 1969	914
Maggs, Tony	South Africa	9 Feb 1937	4 Jun 2009	903
Mairesse, Willy	Belgium	1 Oct 1928	2 Sep 1969	909
Maring, Ernst	Germany	31 Mar 1936		373, 919
Marsh, Tony	Great Britain	20 Jul 1931	7 May 2009	909
May, Michael	Switzerland	18 Aug 1934		914
McWilliams, Vern	South Africa			911
Menzler, Helmut	South Africa			911
Moss, Stirling	Great Britain	17 Sep 1929		376, 904, 906, 918, 912, 916, 917
Nygren, Olle	Sweden	11 Nov 1929		905
'Parker' (Diel, Joachim)	Germany			914
Parnell, Tim	Great Britain	25 Jun 1932		914, 915, 917, P2
Pilette, André	Belgium	6 Oct 1918	27 Dec 1993	914, 916, 917
Piper, David	Great Britain	2 Dec 1930		919
Prinoth, Ernesto	Italy	15 Apr 1923	26 Nov 1981	913
Puzey, Clive	Southern Rhodesia	11 Jul 1941		P2
Rader, Homer	USA			371
Robinson, Philip	Great Britain	17 Jun 1941		904
Ruby, Lloyd	USA	12 Jan 1928	23 Mar 2009	907
Russell, Jock	Great Britain		22 Oct 2014	918
Ryan, Peter	Canada	10 Jun 1942	2 Jul 1962	372
Salvadori, Roy	Great Britain	12 May 1922	3 Jun 2012	904
Scarlatti, Giorgio	Italy	2 Oct 1921	26 Jul 1990	902
Seidel, Wolfgang	Germany	4 Jul 1926	1 Mar 1987	373
Seiffert, Günther	Germany	18 Oct 1937		373
Shelly, Tony	New Zealand	2 Feb 1937	4 Oct 1998	P1
Stacey, Alan	Great Britain	29 Aug 1933	19 Jun 1960	369, 370
Starabba, Prince Gaetano	Italy	3 Dec 1932		902
Surtees, John	Great Britain	11 Feb 1934		373, 374
Taylor, Henry	Great Britain	16 Dec 1932	24 Oct 2013	906, 916, 917, 918
Taylor, Michael	Great Britain	24 Apr 1934		369
Taylor, Trevor	Great Britain	26 Dec 1936	27 Sep 2010	371, 372, 374
Trintignant, Maurice	France	30 Oct 1917	12 Feb 2005	918
Vaccarella, Nino	Italy	4 Mar 1933		912
Wyllie, Adam	Great Britain	1939	1965	918

184 | Lotus 18

APPENDIX IV
ENTRANTS OF THE LOTUS 18

In addition to the factory entries made by Team Lotus, from 1960 the Lotus 18 was raced prolifically around Europe by numerous private teams and drivers. The most successful of the private teams were the RRC Walker Racing Team, entrant of Stirling Moss, and the UDT-Laystall Racing Team for whom Moss also drove on occasion. The remaining teams and private entrants ranged from well-run semi-professional outfits to gentleman drivers, pure amateurs and a number of 'hopefuls' of doubtful potential.

Team	Chassis no
Factory team	
Team Lotus	369, 370, 371, 372, 373, 374
'Professional' racing teams	
UDT-Laystall Racing Team	906, 915, 916, 917, 918
RRC Walker Racing Team	376, 906, 912, 918
Other teams/private entrants	
Team Alexis	904
G Ashmore	909, 919
Autosport Team Wolfgang Seidel	373, 914
Mrs Louise Bryden-Brown	903
Camoradi International	905, 908
John Dalton	P1
SJ Diggory	374
Ecurie Excelsior	905
Emeryson Cars	373
Equipe Nationale Belge	373, 909, 918
Jim Hall	371, 907
W Hansgen	372
J Frank Harrison	907
Gary Hocking	P2
Kurt Kuhnke	373, 914, 919

Team	Chassis no
Other teams/private entrants	
V McWilliams	911
E Maring	919
AE Marsh	909
Reg Parnell (Racing)	904
RHH Parnell	904, 915, 916, 917, 919, P2
A Pilette	916, 917
CR Puzey/Clive Puzey (Motors)	P2
A Robinson & Sons	904
Jock Russell	918
Scuderia Centro Sud	902, 905
Scuderia Colonia	373, 914
Scuderia Dolomiti	913
Scuderia Jolly Club	913
Scuderia Nord-Ouest	913
Scuderia SSS Republica di Venezia	912
Speed Sport/David Piper	919
Prince Gaetano Starrabba	902
Taylor & Crawley Ltd	369
Vandervell Products Ltd	901
J Wheeler Autosport	372
Ecurie Wolman	911

Bibliography
The following publications were consulted in the preparation of this book:

Books
Autocourse History of the Grand Prix Car 1945-65, Doug Nye, Hazleton Publishing, 1993.
A Record of Grand Prix and Voiturette Racing, Volumes 7 & 8, Paul Sheldon with Duncan Rabagliati, St Leonard's Press, 1991 & 1994.
The Grand Prix Car 1954-66, LKJ Setright, Allen & Unwin, 1968.
1½-litre Grand Prix Racing 1961-65, Mark Whitelock, Veloce Publishing, 2006.
'Coventry Climax Development,' paper to the Society of Automotive Engineers by Wally Hassan, 1960.
Grand Prix Who's Who, Steve Small, Guinness, 1994.
Racing & Sports Car Chassis Design, Mike Costin & David Phipps, Batsford, 1962.
The Road to Extinction – Decline & Fall of the Front-engined Grand Prix Car 1957-60, unpublished work by Mark Whitelock.
The Story of Lotus 1947-60, Ian H Smith, Motor Racing Publications, 1982.
Theme Lotus, Doug Nye, Motor Racing Publications, 1978.
Lotus 25 Coventry Climax, Ian Bamsey, Haynes Publishing Group, 1990.
Poetry in Motion, Tony Brooks, Motor Racing Publications, 2012.
Jim Clark, Eric Dymock, Dove, 1997.
Colin Chapman – Inside the Innovator, Karl Ludvigsen, Haynes Publishing, 2010.
Stirling Moss: My Cars, My Career, Stirling Moss with Doug Nye, Patrick Stephens, 1992.
Tony Robinson, The Biography of a Race Mechanic, Ian Wagstaff, Veloce Publishing, 2012.

Magazines
The Autocar
Autosport
Car & Driver
Classic & Sports car
Motor
Motor Racing
Motor Sport

www.velocebooks.com / www.veloce.co.uk
Details of all current books • New book news • Special offers • Gift vouchers • Forum

Also from Veloce Publishing –

LOTUS 49

THE STORY OF A LEGEND
BY MICHAEL OLIVER

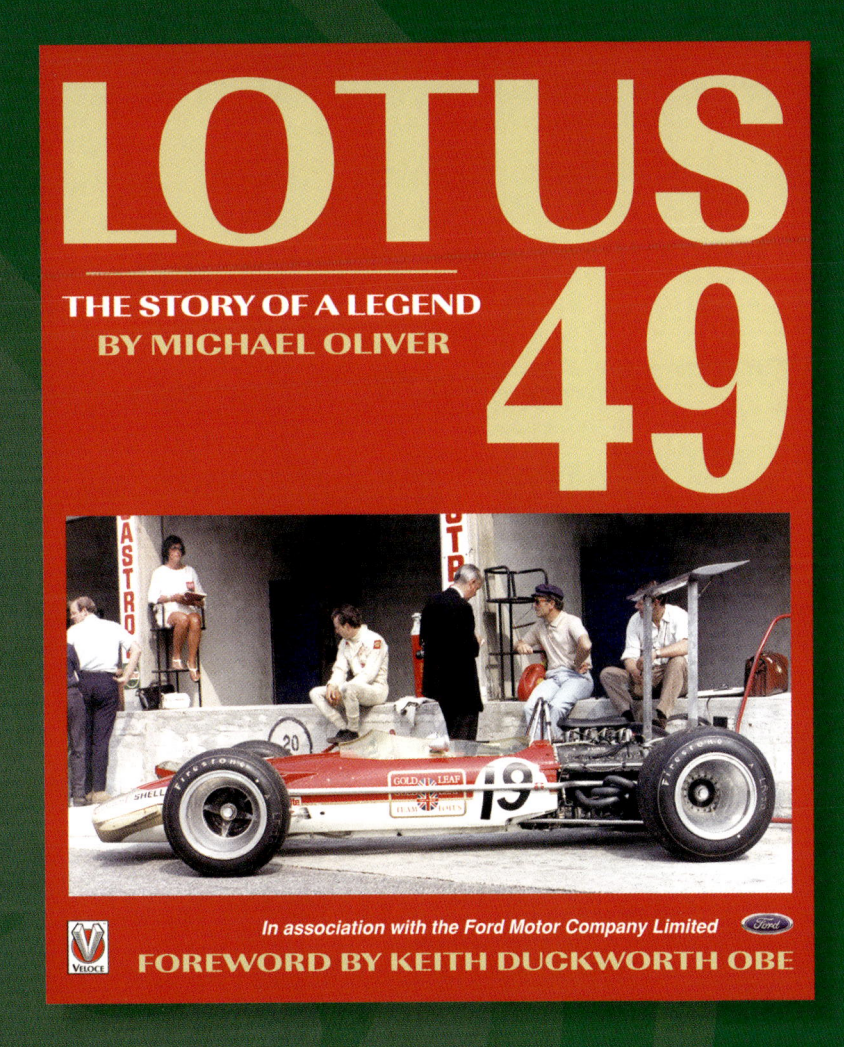

In association with the Ford Motor Company Limited

FOREWORD BY KEITH DUCKWORTH OBE

The Lotus 49 was one of the most evocative & successful Formula 1 cars of its era, & the first to use the Cosworth DFV V8 engine. Here is the definitive story from inception to the fate of the cars today. Includes a racing record & individual chassis histories. A high quality artpaper production. A highly acclaimed book.

ISBN: 978-1-904788-01-0
Hardback • 25x20.7cm • £50* UK/$£79.95* USA • 256 pages • illustrated throughout

For more info on Veloce titles, visit our website at www.veloce.co.uk • email: info@veloce.co.uk • Tel: +44(0)1305 260068
* prices subject to change, p&p extra

N. A. R. T.

A concise history of the North American Racing Team
1957 to 1983

Terry O'Neil

Luigi Chinetti's association with Ferrari, and the origins, formation and racing history of NART. An organisation inextricably linked to Luigi Chinetti Motors Inc, N.A.R.T. enjoyed success on the race tracks of the US and Europe for three decades, to rightly become a legend.

ISBN: 978-1-845847-87-6
Hardback • 24.8x24.8cm • £60* UK/$100* USA • 256 pages • 295 colour and b&w pictures

For more info on Veloce titles, visit our website at www.veloce.co.uk • email: info@veloce.co.uk • Tel: +44(0)1305 260068
* prices subject to change, p&p extra

The Argentine Temporada Motor Races

1950 to 1960
– in 220 contemporary photos

Hernan Lopez Laiseca

This beautifully illustrated book captures the entire history of the Argentine Grand Prix and the Argentina International Temporada Series, covering all the great races of the golden age of motorsport – when danger and passion defined racing.

ISBN: 978-1-845848-28-6
Hardback • 24.8x24.8cm • £35* UK/$60* USA • 144 pages • 223 b&w pictures

For more info on Veloce titles, visit our website at www.veloce.co.uk • email: info@veloce.co.uk • Tel: +44(0)1305 260068
* prices subject to change, p&p extra

1½-litre Grand Prix Racing 1961-65
– Low Power, High Tech

Mark Whitelock

This is the story of a Grand Prix formula that no British constructor wanted but which they came to almost totally dominate. It saw the career of Stirling Moss come to a premature end, and in his absence the rise to prominence of a new breed of British driver in Jim Clark, Graham Hill and John Surtees.

ISBN: 978-1-845840-16-7
Hardback • 25x25cm • £39.99* UK/$79.95* USA • 336 pages • 204 b&w pictures and line drawings

For more info on Veloce titles, visit our website at www.veloce.co.uk • email: info@veloce.co.uk • Tel: +44(0)1305 260068
* prices subject to change, p&p extra

INDEX

Abate, Carlo 130
Aintree 200 69, 72, 83, 125, 137
Alfa Romeo engine 110, 155
Allison, Cliff 9-11, 80, 82, 83, 92, 93, 117, 118
Argentine Grand Prix 11, 35, 36
Arundell, Peter 154
Ashmore, Gerry 83, 86, 97, 100, 102, 107, 123, 128, 130-132, 144
Austrian Grand Prix 141
Auto Union 15
Autosport Team Wolfgang Seidel 123, 130, 131, 138

Baghetti, Giancarlo 83, 86, 93, 95, 109, 125, 129
Bandini, Lorenzo 109, 123
Belgian Grand Prix 49-51, 92, 93
Berthon, Peter 9, 37, 39
Bianchi, Lucien 69, 93, 97, 118, 129, 130
BKL (Borgward-Kuhnke-Lotus) 138, 140, 144
Bonnier, Jo 45-47, 62, 66, 72, 79, 84, 89, 121, 123, 131, 181
Borgward engines 110, 138, 144, 155
Brabham, Jack 32, 45, 46, 48, 49, 52-62, 74, 82, 83, 100, 107, 108, 117, 119
Brands Hatch 55, 61, 72, 74, 89, 107, 118, 152, 154
Bristow, Chris 44, 51
British Grand Prix 10-12, 53-55, 97-100, 131
BRM 9, 15, 37, 40, 48, 54, 55, 83, 107, 118, 119, 121, 124, 125, 128, 137
Brooks, Tony 36, 92, 118
BRP (British Racing Partnership) 78, 157, 159
Brussels Grand Prix 68, 82, 120
Bryden-Brown, Louise 71, 72, 83, 97, 117, 181
Burgess, Ian 72, 74, 79, 80, 82, 86, 89, 93, 97, 98

Camoradi International 64, 79, 82, 98
Campbell-Jones, John 130
Carter, Ron 140, 141
Casner, Lloyd (Lucky) 64, 79, 98

Chamberlain, Jay 123, 124, 128, 130-133
Chapman, Colin 8-13, 15-17, 19, 22, 36, 64, 70, 77, 79, 80, 90, 105, 107, 128, 149, 150, 152, 160
Chapman, Stanley 10, 64
Chapman strut suspension 10, 12
Clark, Jim 16, 36, 47-51, 53-55, 59-64, 66, 69, 72-74, 78, 83, 93, 107, 110, 118-120, 123, 128, 132, 137, 153, 154, 160, 181, 183
Colotti Transmission (see also GSD) 44, 56, 160
Cooper Cars 5, 8, 10, 11, 14, 15, 17, 19, 25, 29, 34, 35-37, 40, 42, 44, 46, 47, 50-53, 55, 59-62, 64, 66, 67, 70, 72-74, 77-79, 80, 82-87, 89-93, 110, 116-119, 124, 128, 149, 150, 157
Cooper, Charles & John 30, 32, 36, 39, 79
Costin, Frank 8-10, 12
Costin, Mike 8, 10, 153
Coventry Climax engines 8, 10, 29-34, 78, 84, 105, 122, 145
Crystal Palace 70, 86, 130
CSI 43, 77

Dalton, John 121, 130, 131
Dance, Bob 78
Danish Grand Prix 73, 104, 131
Davis, Colin 130, 144
Dei, Guglielmo (Mimo) 60
Duckworth, Keith 10, 12, 153
Duke, Geoff 72, 73
Dunlop Racing Tyres 25, 43, 72, 100
Dutch Grand Prix 47-49, 70, 86-89, 128

Eden, Graham 130, 131
Equipe National Belge 93-97

Ferrari 29, 30, 36, 40, 50, 52, 55, 59, 64, 67, 68, 70, 74, 77, 83-110, 116, 121, 123, 125, 127, 129,
FIA 10, 43, 77
Flockhart, Ron 53
Ford 105E engine 152, 155
Formula 2 67-76
Francis, 'Alf' 42, 56, 84, 91, 155

French Grand Prix 12, 52, 53, 93, 94

Gendebien, Olivier 53, 93, 108, 109
German Grand Prix 12, 55, 70, 100-102, 131, 140
Ginther, Richie 84, 86, 88, 89, 93, 95, 98, 107
Goodwood Circuit 39
Goodwood Easter Monday 34, 36, 117, 123, 137
Gregory, Masten 93, 104, 107-110, 120, 124-128, 130, 155, 183
GSD transmissions 56, 83, 92, 100, 105, 121
Gurney, Dan 55-57, 71-73, 80, 83, 89, 90, 97, 98, 109, 117, 131, 157-160, 181

Halford, Bruce 118
Hall, Jim 61-64, 108
Hansgen, Walt 133
Hassan, Wally 12, 29, 30, 32
Hill, Graham 10-14, 44, 48, 54, 74, 83, 119, 121, 124, 125, 128, 130, 137, 181
Hill, Phil 51-53, 70, 84, 89, 93-95, 100-102, 107, 125
Hocking, Gary 131-134

Inter-Continental Formula 116-119
Ireland, Innes 10, 35-38, 40, 66-74, 80, 83, 86, 104, 107, 117, 120, 124-127, 130, 149, 160, 181-183
Italian Grand Prix 59, 105-107, 132, 141

Karlskoga 104, 131, 141
Kuhnke, Kurt 123, 130, 131, 138, 140, 141, 144

Lee, Leonard 29-32
Lotus cars in number order:
    Lotus Eleven 8, 10
    Lotus 12 10-11
    Lotus 16 12
    Lotus 18 – technical description 16-28
    Lotus 18 Formula Junior 152, 153
    Lotus 18/21 – technical description 90-92

Lotus 18/21 V8 Special – technical description 104-106
Lotus 19 157-160
Lotus 21 77, 89-91, 93, 98, 107, 109, 110, 150
Lotus Components 4, 14, 56, 71, 72, 78, 79
Lotus Elite 11, 15
Lotus-Ford LF engine 78, 156

Maggs, Tony 97, 98, 100, 102, 128
Mairesse, Willy 93, 121
Mallory Park 2000 Guineas 130
Maring Ernst 140, 141, 144
Marsh, Tony 72-74, 80, 82, 83, 86, 89, 93, 97, 100, 102, 107, 181
Maserati engine 60, 74
May, Michael 83, 85, 89, 93, 98
McLaren, Bruce 36, 51, 54, 79, 118, 124, 125
McWilliams, Vern 134
Mediterranean Grand Prix 131, 141, 144
Menzler, Helmut 110, 134, 155
Modena Grand Prix 74, 104
Monaco Grand Prix 43-47, 83-86, 129
Monte Carlo circuit 86
Moss, Stirling 11, 35, 45-67, 72, 74, 77-110, 118, 120-125, 131, 149, 155, 157, 158, 180, 183
Mundy, Harry 10, 29, 30, 42, 59

Naples Grand Prix 86, 129
Naylor, Brian 60
Nürburgring 102
Nygren, Olle 131

Oulton Park Gold Cup 60, 61, 68, 107, 131, 141

'Parker,' (Diel, Joachim) 144
Parkes, Mike 118
Parnell, Reg (Racing) 66, 72, 118
Parnell, Tim 73, 74, 79, 82, 86, 89, 97, 104, 107, 118, 121, 122, 128-131, 133, 137-140, 183
Pau circuit 123
Pau Grand Prix 79, 122, 123, 137
Pilette, André 137, 140, 141
Piper, David 128, 130

Porsche 67-70, 72, 74, 77, 79, 83, 84, 93, 97, 98, 107, 109, 110, 121, 123, 128, 131, 137, 155
Portuguese Grand Prix 55-59
Preis von Wien 74, 82
Prinoth, Ernesto 82, 83, 107, 109, 132, 137, 141, 142
Puzey, Clive 142, 144-147, 183

'Queerbox' 12, 14, 20, 27, 47, 56, 57, 82, 83, 157

Rader, Homer 133
Reims Grand Prix 130
Riverside Raceway 61, 62
Robinson, Phillip 131, 137, 140
Robinson, Tony 90, 91
Rodriguez, Ricardo 107, 123
Rome Grand Prix 138
Ruby, Lloyd 108, 109, 160
Russell, Jock 137, 144
Ryan, Peter 108, 109

Salvadori, Roy 10, 66, 86
Scarlatti, Giorgio 104
Scuderia Centro Sud 60, 72-74, 104
Scuderia Colonia 79, 83, 89, 97
Scuderia Dolomiti 82, 107, 109, 132
Scuderia Jolly Club 132, 137, 142
Scuderia SSS Republica di Venezia 120, 122, 130, 131
Seidel, Wolfgang 79, 82, 83, 89, 93, 97, 98, 102, 107
Seiffert, Günther 123, 124, 130, 131
Shelly, Tony 121, 124, 125, 128-132
Silverstone International Trophy 34, 39, 40, 117, 125, 137
Snetterton 59, 79, 117, 121, 137, 144
Solitude Grand Prix 70, 98, 130, 140, 144
South African racing 110-112, 133, 134, 142, 150, 155, 156,
Stacey, Alan 10, 36, 40, 42, 45-48, 50, 51, 69, 70, 152, 154

Starrabba, Prince Gaetano 104, 107, 109, 129, 137, 138, 141
Surtees, John 40, 42, 45-47, 54-62, 66, 68, 73, 80, 83, 90, 93, 124, 125, 130, 153, 181
Syracuse Grand Prix 68, 83, 137

Taylor, Henry 78, 79, 86, 89, 92, 93, 97, 98, 104, 107, 118
Taylor, Michael 40, 49, 52
Taylor, Trevor 70, 79, 86, 89, 92, 107, 154, 181
Taylor & Crawley 40, 49
Team Lotus 8, 9, 11, 14, 34, 36, 40, 43, 44, 47-51, 53-57, 59, 61, 62, 64, 66-69, 71-74, 77, 79, 83, 86, 90-95, 104, 107-110, 117-119, 149-155
Terry, Len 18
Trintignant, Maurice 122-124, 128, 151, 181
Trips, Wolfgang von 53, 67, 70, 84, 89, 93, 95, 98, 101, 105, 107

UDT-Laystall Racing Team 79, 80, 82-86, 90, 92, 110, 116, 117, 120, 155, 158, 159
United States Grand Prix 19, 61-64, 107

Vaccarella, Nino 120-123, 128, 130, 131
Vandervell, Tony 9, 40, 59, 118
Vanwall, 9, 36, 40, 59, 60, 118
Vyver, Syd van der 110, 154, 155

Walker, Rob (Racing Team) 11, 30, 34, 39, 40, 42-45, 47, 56, 61, 62, 64, 66, 68, 69, 74, 77, 78, 82, 83, 91, 102-105, 107-110, 118, 120-124, 128-130, 133, 134, 137, 144, 150, 151
Williams & Pritchard 25, 60, 91
Wyllie, Adam 137

Yeoman Credit Racing Team 44, 51, 53, 66, 80, 86, 90, 93, 155

Zeltweg, Flugplatzrennen 74, 107
ZF Transmissions 10, 27